FOR MIGHT AND RIGHT

A VOLUME IN THE SERIES

Culture in Politics in the Cold War and Beyond

EDITED BY

Edwin A. Martini and Scott Laderman

FOR MIGHT AND RIGHT

Cold War Defense Spending and
the Remaking of **American Democracy**

MICHAEL BRENES

University of Massachusetts Press
Amherst and Boston

Copyright © 2020 by University of Massachusetts Press
All rights reserved
Printed in the United States of America

ISBN 978-1-62534-522-6 (paper); 521-9 (hardcover)

Designed by Jen Jackowitz
Set in Minion Pro and Raleway
Printed and bound by Books International, Inc.

Cover design by Frank Gutbrod
Cover photo by Wendy Hallmark, *Night falls at Puget Sound
Naval Shipyard and Intermediate Maintenance Facility, Bremerton,
Washington, as work continues on USS* Ohio *(SSGN 726).* Ohio *is one
of four Trident submarines undergoing conversion to a new class of
guided missile submarines.* March 15, 2004.—United States Navy.

Library of Congress Cataloging-in-Publication Data
Names: Brenes, Michael, author.
Title: For might and right : Cold War defense spending and the remaking of
American democracy / Michael Brenes.
Description: Amherst : University of Massachusetts Press, 2020. | Series:
Culture and politics in the Cold War and beyond | Includes
bibliographical references and index. |
Identifiers: LCCN 2020019280 | ISBN 9781625345219 (hardcover) | ISBN
9781625345226 (paperback) | ISBN 9781613767719 (ebook) | ISBN
9781613767726 (ebook)
Subjects: LCSH: United States—Politics and government—1945–1989. | United
States—Economic conditions—1945– | United States—Armed
Forces—Appropriations and expenditures. | Defense contracts—United
States—History—20th century. | Militarism—United
States—History—20th century. | Political participation—United
States—History—20th century. | Political culture—United
States—History—20th century. | Cold War—Influence.
Classification: LCC E743 .B733 2020 | DDC 306.2093209/04—dc23
LC record available at https://lccn.loc.gov/2020019280

British Library Cataloguing-in-Publication Data
A catalog record for this book is available from the British Library.

Portions of chapter two first appeared in a different form as "Disarming the Devil,
The Conservative Campaign against a Nuclear Détente in the 1960s," in *The Right
Side of the Sixties: Rethinking Conservativism's Decade of Transformation,* ed. Laura
Jane Gifford and Daniel K. Williams (New York: Palgrave MacMillan, 2012), 181–
200. Portions of chapter four first appeared in a different form as "Making For-
eign Policy at the Grassroots: Cold War Politics and the 1976 Republican Primary,"
Journal of Policy History 27, no. 1 (2015): 93–117. Reproduced with permission. Por-
tions of chapter five first appeared in a different form as "Peace through Austerity:
The Reagan Defense Buildup in the 'Age of Inequality,'" in *The Cold War at Home
and Abroad: Domestic Politics and U.S. Foreign Policy since 1945,* ed. Andrew L.
Johns and Mitchell B. Lerner (Lexington: University of Kentucky Press, 2018).

TO MICHELLE AND NATHAN

CONTENTS

ACKNOWLEDGMENTS

This book tells a story of United States history, but its existence as a material product is a story in and of itself. A story that saw birth, death, struggle, joy, love, friendship, and many rewards and pitfalls along the way. I hope these acknowledgments—which I confess, I find to be the most interesting and revealing part of any book—express part of that story: a near ten-year journey to see this book come to life. I accumulated many debts along the way; it is a pleasure to finally thank those individuals who made this book possible—and better.

The intellectual origins of this project began when I was an undergraduate history major and sheepishly knocked on the door of an unknown professor my junior year. That professor was Jonathan Rosenberg, who soon became a consummate mentor and advisor. Jon invested time in me in a way no teacher had—and in ways I never expected a person would—often spending more than an hour in his office talking to me about history and the historical profession. Whatever convinced him to spend those hours of time with me I don't know, but I am truly thankful. In those conversations he encouraged me to read and keep reading. Jon also taught me the historians' craft: how to think historically, and how to write like a historian (and in general, how to write). It is safe to say I would not be a historian without Jon. I continued to rely on his advice after graduate school, requesting a phone call to chat about a job, the book, or life as an academic with a young family. He has always consented to those requests and been willing to recreate those office hours over the phone (and when we can afford time, in person). I am acutely aware that a few published lines will not be enough to express how much his mentorship, and now friendship, mean to me.

My admission into the City University of New York Graduate Center as a PhD candidate eventually led me to Robert David "KC" Johnson, my dissertation advisor. KC's dedication to history, his deep faith in the historical project and the need to keep it alive, is obvious to anyone who spends an iota of their time with him. KC is a master of his craft; his encyclopedic knowledge of congressional history is a thing to behold, and I relied on it more than once. KC and I agreed on the significance of high politics and diplomacy, on the importance of the "state" in American history, but we also disagreed on many things. But in those disagreements, he was always supportive, kind, and generous.

Other professors at CUNY helped shape my intellectual development. Among them Josh Freeman, David Nasaw, Thomas Kessner, James Oakes, Andrew Robertson, and Helena Rosenblatt, but none more so than Judith Stein, to whom I regret I cannot pass along a copy of this book. Professor Stein—none of us dared called her "Judith"— was a dedicated teacher and intellectual. I will never forget her class on Political Economy after 1973, which, for me, sparked an interest in political economy as a field of study. I regularly miss her public intellect, and I cherish the time I spent in her classrooms.

Kim Phillips-Fein read chapters of the book when it was a dissertation and took time out of her busy schedule to meet with me and discuss the project. She also graciously agreed to serve on my dissertation committee and has written countless letters of recommendation on my behalf. Other colleagues, including Brent Cebul and Seth Offenbach, read portions of the book as a dissertation and offered useful comments. Conversations with Sam Rosenfeld helped sharpen my thinking as well. Mark Wilson read an early version of the book manuscript and provided constructive feedback at various stages of the writing process. Tim Keogh's research on the defense industry on Long Island proved invaluable to my thinking about the local politics of military spending. Tim also read chapters from the manuscript and confirmed that I was on to something with my analysis of the Cold War economy. The multiple citations to his dissertation do not convey the totality of what his work has done to shape my own.

Thanks also to those who commented on this project when presented at various conferences: Andrew Preston, Jason Friedman, Kevin Kruse, David Farber, Mitch Lerner, Julian Zelizer, Jennifer Mittelstadt, and Katherine Epstein. Chris Dietrich let me present portions of chapter five to the Twentieth Century Politics and Society seminar at Columbia University, and I thank him for his support over the years. Participants of the 2015 SHAFR Summer Institute held in Columbus, Ohio—particularly Amanda Demmer, Chris Foss, Henry Maar, Simon Miles, Dan Hummel, and Lauren Turek—offered useful comments as well. My appreciation goes to the hosts of the institute, Andy Johns and Mitch Lerner, for including me in the proceedings. Mitch continued to be supportive of this project long after I left Columbus and has championed the book in numerous ways. Andy: I look forward to exchanging more notes on Hubert Humphrey.

Every decent historian knows that archivists are essential to their craft. Archivists at the Bentley Historical Library; the Hagley Museum and Library; the Hoover Institution on War, Peace, and Revolution; the Library of Congress; the Richard Nixon Presidential Library; Special Collections at the University of Washington; the Jimmy Carter Presidential Library; the Ronald Reagan Presidential Library; and the Harry S. Truman Library deserve special mention. Jeremy Schmidt, then at the Ford Library, guided me to essential documents on defense spending in the 1970s and sent me links to digitized documents from the library's website. Several individuals also granted me access to restricted archival collections. Christopher Buckley granted me access to his father's papers at Yale, while the family members of Paul H. Nitze gave me permission to use his papers at the Library of Congress. William Rusher also approved my request to view his papers before he passed away.

Research funding for this project was provided from numerous sources. My gratitude goes to the Harry S. Truman Presidential Library Institute, the Gerald R. Ford Presidential Foundation, the

Bentley Historical Library, the John Anson Kittredge Foundation, and the City University of New York for financing my research trips to various parts of the country.

After teaching part-time at Hunter College (and other colleges and universities in the New York City area) for many years, I came to Yale University in 2017 to take a position as an archivist at Manuscripts and Archives, a position I held for over two years. My thanks to Chris Weideman and Mary Caldera who made this transition possible, and to the friends made along the way, particularly Bill Landis, Stephen Naron, and Camila Tessler. As an archivist, I often felt like an interloper, but Chris, Mary, and the entire staff at Manuscripts and Archives assured me I was welcome—I was part of their professional community. I can't thank them enough for that.

It is a great honor to work for (and with) Beverly Gage in the Brady-Johnson Program in Grand Strategy. Bev is a model scholar, teacher, and public intellectual, and I have learned a great deal from her in the short time we have worked together. Thanks also to Liz Vastakis and Kaitlyn Wetzel, who made the transition to Grand Strategy a smooth one, and who regularly help me navigate the logistics of the program. I look forward to seeing what the future of Grand Strategy brings.

This book was considered for publication by another academic press and editor for many years. That experience taught me a great deal—about how lopsided, arcane, and outdated the peer-review process can be; about the difficulties of revising a book as an adjunct and new father; about the struggle to get the book done, along with the desire to get it "right." The comments I received from peer reviewers prior to working with UMass improved the book a great deal (and I thank those anonymous reviewers), but I am eternally grateful that this project found an editorial home with Matt Becker, who is the epitome of what an academic editor should be: patient, responsive, encouraging, kind, and firm on deadlines. My thanks to him and the entire team at University of Massachusetts Press, including Rachael DeShano and Courtney Andree, for ushering this book to publication. If books can have homes, then there is no better location for this one than UMass Press. Thanks also to Ed Martini and Scott Laderman who saw enough potential in this book to include it in their edited series on the Culture and Politics of the Cold War and Beyond.

Final thanks go to my close friends and family. Peter-Christian Aigner and Tim Keogh remain close friends from graduate school—and occasional coauthors—and our regular text message chain on the state of American politics, foreign policy, and academia keeps me grounded, and from falling into despair. Kevin Lee opened his spare bedroom to me when I came to do research in Washington, D.C., many years ago. More than Kevin's willingness to provide accommodations, I treasure our long-standing friendship. Julie and David Tasker gave me more than just shelter for my two research trips to the Hagley Library in Wilmington, Delaware: they also gave me transportation, delicious meals, great wine, good conversation, and wonderful hospitality. My brother- and sister-in-law, Sean and Kathleen Murray, were always encouraging, and Sean provided a springboard for some of my ideas before I knew I was going to write a book about them. My nephew Connor's enthusiasm for playing soccer, and for playing it with me, provided a welcome distraction from research and writing. I could not have asked for more generous, warm, and caring in-laws than Paul and Karen Wereszynski. They provided child care, company, and good advice at just the right times. Karen Parsons regularly told me how proud she was, which is all a son needs to hear from his mom.

Finally, there is my wife Michelle and my son Nathan, to whom this book is dedicated. I have tried to shield Nate from the writing process as much as possible, and I have mostly succeeded. When he was born, nap time was writing time; day care hours were research opportunities; school days were utilized for household chores, errands—and writing. Only in the past few months, when I told him that my first book is getting published, did he seem to realize why his dad needs to occasionally spend some time on his laptop. He now picks up books around our home and says, "Did you write this, Daddy?" Up until now, I have politely said, "No, not that one." But no book offers as greater a sense of fulfillment than does his presence in our lives. The joy of everything I have ever known, let alone the publication of a book, pales in comparison to his smile and laugh.

And then there is Michelle: my companion on research trips, my fiercest champion, and the best critic anyone could ask for. She encouraged me not to give up when the job market got tough, or when I had lost confidence in this project—when I never thought I would see this book get published. Her honesty, kindness, and humor are unmatched; her caring, giving spirit unrivaled. She has given me love, a family, and a lifetime to be grateful for. She is, in the truest sense, my partner. Thank you, Michelle. On to the next one.

FOR MIGHT AND RIGHT

INTRODUCTION

Theresa Bruno was a thirty-year employee of defense contractor Textron Lycoming, based in Stratford, Connecticut, when the federal government cancelled the company's contract for the M-1 tank. With the collapse of communism abroad and pressure to reduce the federal deficit at home, in 1990 President George H. W. Bush considered the M-1 tank program outdated.

Bruno worked to inspect M-1 tanks before they left the plant, and she worried the cancellation of the M-1 would jeopardize her job. "We work and strive to give [the federal government] a good product," she said, and she had trouble understanding "why they have to eliminate it." Robert Koetsch, a security guard at the plant, believed the end of the M-1 tank program was representative of "a plan to get our defenses down, get our guard down. If they shut this place down, and something happens in two or three years, it's going to take a while to start up again." A recent retiree of Textron Lycoming, John Morrison, concluded the cuts must mean "the generals have enough tanks to play with for a while." But Robert Miere, who made parts for M-1 engines, dismissed this logic. The Cold War was over, but the world remained unstable—it was no time for the federal government to sever its responsibility to defense workers. "Just because the Berlin Wall went down doesn't mean there's no threat. There are still other countries," he said.[1]

Home to Sikorsky Aircraft and the Stratford Army-Engine Plant (until 1998, when it was closed) as well as Textron Lycoming, Stratford depended on defense contracts, and the Cold War that provided them for decades. The state of Connecticut received $4.9 billion from the Department of Defense—the eighth highest total in the country and third in per capita spending—even though it was twenty-eighth in overall population. The defense business was concentrated in southern and western Connecticut. Sikorsky Aircraft in Stratford was the largest defense contractor in the western part of the state, while General Dynamics Eastern Boat Company in Groton, which made submarines for the U.S. Navy, was located on the southeastern coast. Like Textron, General Dynamics began to lay off workers following the reduction of tensions between the United States and the Soviet Union. By 1991, General Dynamics eliminated over 25 percent of its workforce. Such cuts were necessary, executives claimed, to keep the company afloat in a time of peace. (Executives at General Dynamics received bonuses after making the cuts, since the layoffs increased the price of the company's stock.[2])

The economic situation for General Dynamics in Groton was so dire in 1991 that the company threatened to close its doors if it did not receive a new defense contract for the Seawolf submarine— which General Dynamics had built since 1983. The elected official fighting hardest to keep General Dynamics solvent was Democrat and Connecticut senator Christopher Dodd. Among the class of "Watergate babies" elected to Congress in 1974, Dodd was a liberal on most issues: he championed the interests of organized labor and the expansion of the social safety net and was pro-choice. Dodd's liberal credentials earned him a 93 percent rating from the Committee on Political Education of the American Federation of Labor-Congress of Industrial Organizations (AFL-CIO), but a 9 percent approval rating from conservative groups like the American Conservative Union and the Chamber of Commerce.[3] On foreign policy and national defense, Dodd opposed the Reagan defense buildup in the 1980s, strongly criticized the administration's Central American policies, and voted against additional funding for the missile defense program entitled Strategic Defense Initiative (SDI).

But on the Seawolf submarine and its importance to American foreign policy, Dodd was a defense hawk. Dodd argued the Seawolf program was not only vital to the economy of southeastern Connecticut but that it also protected the interests of national security because "stealth marine technology is critical to the country." Lobbying for the Seawolf contract alongside Dodd was his Connecticut colleague in the House, Democrat Sam Gejdenson. Both sought to cut defense spending during the Reagan years—which led the *New York Times* to comment on the "paradox" of Dodd and Gejdenson's quest to secure additional defense contracts for General Dynamics. "When the cold war was alive, Mr. Dodd and Mr. Gejdenson made careers of fighting the Reagan administration's military buildup. Now they are warning that the country had better not cut military spending too sharply, even when peace is at hand." In attracting support for the Seawolf, Dodd accumulated unlikely allies, maneuvering a coalition of Democrats and Republicans in the Northeast to obtain more federal funds for the Seawolf along the way, earning the nickname "the wolf."[4]

Thanks to Dodd and Gejdenson, General Dynamics won its contract for the Seawolf in 1992. When Dodd and Gejdenson visited Groton after news broke of the contract, both men were greeted with cheers, the union leadership telling workers, "Say hello to Chris and Sam. They're the guys keeping us afloat. We would have lost our jobs without them." Sue Mack, a weight estimator at the Groton plant, said that Dodd had "given us a sigh of relief," and she and her fellow defense workers are "going to be loyal to these legislators." On the other side of the aisle, Republican senator John McCain was quick to call Dodd a hypocrite. McCain opposed the Seawolf program but favored increased military spending and wished that Democrats like Dodd would "at some point develop an equal passion for the overall defense of our nation and weapons systems that are not made in their state."[5]

The example of the Seawolf submarine (and its relationship to local, national, and international events) demonstrates how diverse interests supported the political economy of American defense—ones that collectively transformed American politics in the United States after

World War II. Cold War military spending created a coalition whose major goal was to keep the military-industrial complex thriving, and this coalition—which consisted of defense workers, community boosters, executives of military contractors, labor union leaders and rank-and-file workers, current and retired members of the military, political activists, and local, state, and national politicians—became joined in their efforts to ensure America's global fight against communism served their respective interests and ends.[6]

This book examines the history of this "Cold War coalition." What follows is ultimately a national story: a story of how Cold War defense spending remade participatory politics and American democracy. *For Might and Right* shows how the Cold War gave rise to a new political economy; how this new political economy transformed Americans' politics and political choices; and how these choices created strange bedfellows (ones that crossed the political aisle) in ways that made American citizens increasingly look to military spending, rather than to social welfare programs, to alleviate unemployment and economic turmoil. Cold War defense spending, I argue, transformed the nature of social democracy in the United States, altering American politics and creating a unique coalition of individuals vested in the "military-industrial complex" for personal and political gain.

Key to this history of American politics (and foreign policy) is the distribution of defense spending across the United States—the ebb and flow of defense spending throughout the Cold War. Large-scale defense appropriations provided the basis for American power abroad, but Cold War military spending also gave rise to a "warfare state" at home, one that functioned as a social welfare state for many Americans. U.S. national security policy in the twentieth century underwrote personal and financial security for many Americans, particularly veterans and defense workers. As historian James Sparrow has argued, the warfare state also satisfied the demands and expectations among Americans after World War II that the federal government protect its citizens from threats at home and abroad—and provide personal security.[7]

And as Cold War military spending financed both domestic welfare and national security, it transformed Americans' connections to U.S. military power. Since the era of the New Deal, defense spending bankrolled weapons building, but also health care benefits to veterans, housing subsidies and education grants for military families, and companies that invested in scientific research and development. Defense spending supported public works projects in the 1930s, the construction of airports and highway systems during World War II, and research centers in American universities in the 1950s and '60s. As a result, defense spending transformed industry and the labor market across the United States—from the Rust Belt, through the Sunbelt, and up and down much of the West Coast. Jobs in infrastructure, manufacturing, clerical work, and research and development followed, as did a host of businesses (both large and small) that catered to the consumerist needs of defense workers. Defense spending therefore created local economies where the proverbial coffee shop, pharmacy, or department store was just as reliant upon military spending as the workers in the plants.[8]

The Cold War thus created a large group of Americans who sought to capitalize on the financial incentives offered by a large defense budget. These Americans made up an important constituency within the Cold War coalition. Defense spending animated job prospects for Americans across suburban towns (Bethpage, New York on Long Island, or Newton, Massachusetts) and large cities like Detroit, Seattle, St. Louis, San Antonio, and Washington, D.C., and gave Americans a heightened sense of the role the federal government played in their lives, as federal decisions affected the next defense contract for their town, city, county, or district. As financial "captives" of the military-industrial complex, the livelihoods of those employed by—or who invested in—defense spending also inspired their political preferences and choices. When hard times inevitably fell upon defense workers and executives—and communities who depended on the military—they were reminded of how national security affected their lives in profound ways. Cuts to the defense budget entailed economic anxiety and uncertainty, which they sought to avoid at all costs.

The looming fear of defense cuts—and the inevitable job losses that followed—therefore mobilized members of the Cold War coalition to lobby elected officials to increase defense spending after 1945. As was clear from the comments made by Dodd and Connecticut defense workers, employees of the Cold War military-industrial complex possessed significant leverage over members of Congress. When General Dynamics employee Sue Mack said she and her colleagues were "going to be loyal" to Dodd and Gejdenson, she encapsulated how the national security state rested on democratic approval (or acceptance) from ordinary Americans. Defense capitalism survived by the electoral process, by the fact that defense offered jobs and financial security for many Americans who did not want to give them up and who promised to reward politicians that produced— and protected—those jobs. Politicians from both major parties were beholden to these pressures, which only increased in the Cold War as defense spending declined as a percentage of GDP. And once large donors and organizations—not just workers—lobbied for defense spending on behalf of their constituents, those pressures mounted. In addition to corporate lobbying by defense contractors, the defense industry had powerful allies within labor, including in the International Association of Machinists—represented by the AFL-CIO—as well as groups friendly to defense business, among them the National Association of Manufacturers and Chamber of Commerce. Republicans and Democrats in Congress, fearing the electoral repercussions, often caved to their collective demands for more defense contracts— making them, too, part of the Cold War coalition.[9]

But defense spending influenced, rather than determined, the politics of the Cold War coalition—whose political behavior was riddled with contradictions, rather than consistencies—throughout the United States. Individuals within the defense industry in states like Indiana and Washington defended the military-industrial complex but opposed its role in perpetuating the Vietnam War; others in New York and South Carolina argued for the federal government to mandate better wages and benefits in the defense workforce but wanted to reduce federal benefits provided to other Americans; residents of states like Colorado and California wanted more defense contracts to build intercontinental ballistic missiles (ICBMs) but encouraged policy makers not to deploy them to resolve international crises; in places like Wyoming and North Dakota, residents vowed to defeat communism with military superiority but protested when the government built missile silos and fallout shelters in their towns and neighborhoods. And some defense workers in states like Massachusetts wanted to do away with their defense jobs altogether—and replace them with peacetime work.[10]

These political positions can be classified as neither "left" nor "right," "liberal" nor "conservative." Such cognitive dissonance within the Cold War coalition had stark implications for electoral politics in the United States. Few defense workers in the Northeast and Northwest were wedded to conservative causes—even fewer still were the ideological foot soldiers for Barry Goldwater's 1964 presidential campaign or right-wing organizations like the John Birch Society.[11] While the converse might be true in areas such as Southern California, states in the Northeast, particularly New York, Massachusetts, and Connecticut, received a significant number of individual defense contracts, even more than the Pacific region of the country after 1966, but were not hotbeds of conservative activism.[12]

The impact of Cold War defense spending on American politics therefore goes far beyond dollars and cents—and beyond the parochial concerns faced by members of the Cold War coalition. Indeed, the Cold War created a marriage of convenience between those who materially benefited from defense spending and groups of national political actors who backed the defense economy for ideological reasons. These national figures—like local defense workers and employers too—did not fall into simple partisan categories. The first of these groups consisted of national security elites, including policy mak- Group 1 ers and diplomats. Many of these elites were foreign policy intellectuals whose anticommunism formed the basis of their support for increased defense spending. This list includes Cold War liberals and such neoconservatives as Jeanne Kirkpatrick, Dorothy Fosdick, Paul Nitze, Paul Wolfowitz, Edward Teller, and Richard Perle, many of whom had policy positions in the federal government during the Cold War and were unencumbered by the pressures of elected office. The Cold War coalition also included right-wing intellectuals and activists such as *National Review* editor William F. Buckley Jr. and the antifeminist activist Phyllis Schlafly. As an advocacy group, right-wing intellectuals and activists had little influence on policy making in Washington, D.C., but policy makers and presidents (such as Richard Nixon) placated them to appease their political base. However, Cold Warriors on the Right and Left played an important role in financing institutions, events, and elections that kept the political economy of the Cold War afloat. They attracted participants for anticommunist "Cold War seminars," attended rallies on behalf of right-wing figures like General Edwin Walker and Jerry Falwell, and supported Ronald Reagan in his runs for the presidency in 1976 and 1980. This activism made an indelible impact on Cold War politics.

Economic interests among the Cold War coalition therefore interacted with—and at times, translated to—ideological motivations among its members. Parochial politics mattered for their ability to assemble diverse constituents behind the military-industrial complex; to enlist allies who operated outside the orbit of economic self-interest; and to produce ideological justifications and rationales (anticommunism and national security, among others) for increased defense spending. Economic anxieties within the Cold War coalition often manifested as anticommunist ideologies—and right-wing activists (such as William Buckley) and politicians (such as Barry Goldwater and Ronald Reagan) often mobilized economic concerns to the benefit of their ideological interests. Indeed, elite policy makers, politicians, and business officials often depended on the parochial concerns within the Cold War coalition to defend, justify, and promulgate their ideological agendas that furthered the expansion of American military power. The interaction between economics and anticommunist ideology generated a feedback loop within the coalition, making it hard to pin down where parochial politics ended and ideological concerns began. The two relied on each other.

Members of the Cold War coalition thus collaborated in their use of makeshift, haphazard, and unofficial means, ones that invariably produced unintended ends for American politics. For whatever reason they came to support increased defense spending (personal, financial, ideological, or strategic), the various components of the Cold War coalition reinforced each other in their universal goal of continued defense spending and the growth of the military state. The collaboration among national policy makers, activists, intellectuals, and defense employers and workers was tenuous on issues outside of defense spending—considering the disagreements between union leaders and conservative activists—but was unified to increase American military might.

Moreover, members of the Cold War coalition did not always view themselves as allies, nor did they always question, or even recognize, their interrelationship. Anticommunist activists did not deliberately conceive of defense workers or labor leaders as political allies, while financial dependents of the Cold War did not always think about or question their relationship to anticommunism and American grand strategy—nor did they necessarily feel committed to it. Since its members lacked, or resisted, knowledge of a formal alliance, one that even included their political adversaries, the Cold War coalition rarely succumbed to partisan rifts, allowing the coalition to be dynamic in its influence throughout the postwar period.

In this way, the Cold War coalition had much in common with the New Deal coalition. For instance, historian Ira Katznelson has noted that the New Deal united individuals who had little in common with one another besides their commitment to a specific version of democracy, one that often excluded African Americans. There is no doubt that white members of the New Deal coalition (mostly white southerners) sought to deny African Americans the opportunity to benefit from New Deal programs.[13] But as racist as many New Deal policies were, African Americans received jobs under the Works

Progress Administration and Civilian Conservation Corps, were appointed to positions in the Roosevelt administration, and voted in large numbers for the Democratic Party after 1936—and ultimately used the New Deal coalition as a vehicle to challenge white supremacy after 1945. The New Deal coalition included white working-class Americans in both the agricultural South and the industrial North; prosegregationist white southerners, as well as anti–Jim Crow activists; white and black women who profited from New Deal work programs; and employers who worked to disenfranchise women in the workplace. Such was the contradictory nature of New Deal liberalism. What tied these disparate groups together in a coalition behind the Democratic Party was the fact that the New Deal offered material subsidies and benefits to each of these groups—even on unequal terms—which manifested in electoral support for New Deal Democrats. The efficacy of the New Deal coalition lay in its ability to provide social democracy (albeit briefly and unevenly) for Americans across racial, gender, partisan, and sectional divides.[14]

In its makeup, the Cold War coalition also transcended class, race, and gender schisms, and many supporters of the New Deal— particularly white, working-class Americans—were a part of that coalition. A key argument of this book is that the Cold War allowed new coalitions to emerge from the New Deal order, ones that rejected rigid binaries of "liberal" and "conservative."[15] The history of the Cold War coalition is not simply a story of "the rise of the Right," or its corollary, the "decline of liberalism."[16] Liberalism thrived in the Cold War and in a familiar form relative to the New Deal. Franklin Delano Roosevelt's New Deal established the foundations of America's modern social welfare state but also used federal power to expand American military power abroad. In doing so, New Deal Democrats relied on private companies to produce and reproduce the domestic sources of American imperialism and in the process remake the United States itself. New Deal programs marshaled defense spending—and militaristic rhetoric—to modernize the economy, provide jobs, and defeat existential threats to U.S. national security. New Deal liberalism therefore laid the groundwork for the Cold War national security state and created a precedent for the federal government to provide social protections to Americans in times of need.[17]

And just like the New Deal coalition, the class, racial, and gendered boundaries of the Cold War coalition defined its limitations and successes. The political economy of the Cold War had always distributed its resources asymmetrically across the country—and it is true that the defense industry primarily benefited the highly educated, affluent, and upwardly mobile.[18] But defense companies employed working-class Americans too. In the early 1980s, 58 percent of the labor force in defense consisted of blue-collar workers.[19] Janitors, cafeteria workers, security guards, and assorted unskilled industrial workers were yoked to defense capitalism as well. There were also the working-class Americans who provided lunches to the workers, pumped gas into their cars after they left the factory, mowed their lawns in the summer, and fixed their pipes when they froze in the winter. This work was ancillary to the Cold War economy, but working-class Americans who lived within communities where defense contractors were the major employer realized they were dependent upon defense capitalism. Many of these working-class Americans were the biggest victims of defense cuts, particularly the black working class. Black Americans were barred from many defense jobs after World War II, despite campaigns by the NAACP and CORE in the 1960s to force defense companies to hire more blacks. Racial discrimination in the defense workforce led to the ghettoization of black neighborhoods in New York and Los Angeles, creating rings of housing segregation and inequality amidst affluence.[20]

The story of the Cold War coalition is partly one of how wealth was expropriated from working-class to wealthy Americans, and how American democracy was transformed in the process. As historian Mark Wilson has suggested, the story of the political economy of American defense spending after 1945 (at least in terms of GDP) is one of its decline, rather than its ascendance, its privatization rather than consolidation.[21] Defense spending fell dramatically as a percentage of GDP after the Korean War (when it was 15 percent) and never reached its wartime numbers. As defense jobs—particularly in manufacturing—disappeared after 1945, the wealthiest and whitest members of the Cold War coalition benefited to the detriment of racial minorities and working-class Americans, resulting in greater rewards for the economic elite.

Inequality within the Cold War coalition was compounded by the politics of defense contracting—a politics that produced a zero-sum game. Federal standards that determined which company—in which area of the country—received defense contracts were regimented in their practices, but capricious in their results. Those communities that won individual contracts celebrated the job growth and economic development bestowed on them, while the losers faced plant closures and job layoffs with little hope of federal aid. And following World War II, many areas in the Northeast and Midwest began to lose out to this contracting regime, which meant more losses in defense manufacturing and unskilled defense jobs that disproportionately affected the working class and workers of color.

But while inequality proved to be the largest source of tension among members of the Cold War coalition, it was also a perverse source of unity. The complexity of the Cold War coalition was amplified by the fact that its members knew they did not equally benefit from Cold War defense spending, but they still fought for those benefits. For instance, working-class Americans had the most to lose from defense cuts. Because the Cold War prioritized development of advanced technology, unskilled or semiskilled jobs were the first ones lost to layoffs. While working-class defense workers received less material support from the Cold War economy after 1945, they nonetheless remained vocal champions of the Cold War to serve their interests and needs. Indeed, they often worked alongside their upper-class counterparts to increase defense jobs. Despite the schisms between the white and black working class, unskilled and skilled (and highly paid) defense workers, these class and racial divides temporarily melted away as the coalition fought for a common goal: to keep their jobs. In fact, when class inequality mounted in the 1950s and 1960s, and as industrial centers in the Midwest and Northeast saw defense jobs disappear (and allocated to suburbs in the South and West), the strength of the coalition only grew.

Economic distress—and economic inequality—was a persistent concern within the Cold War coalition but became a greater problem in the 1970s. The 1970s proved to be a "pivotal decade" for the Cold War. The economic crisis of the 1970s questioned the promise made by liberals to middle and working-class Americans that the federal state could save the world from communism and deliver economic growth and international stability, giving way to the resurgence of the free market as a panacea to global and domestic problems.

As the New Deal state eroded in the 1970s, increased defense spending also seemed attractive to resolve international conflicts and stimulate economic growth at home. When economic recession threatened communities dependent upon the military in the 1970s, local politicians turned to the Department of Defense for help in lowering unemployment, raising tax revenue, and eliminating local and state budgetary deficits. Even in the 1980s, the defense economy served as a proxy for economic development in areas affected by high unemployment. And in a growing period of austerity, officials in local, state, and national office sought defense contracts to relieve localities that were victims of cuts to social programs, even while promoting such cuts. Elite members of the Cold War coalition prospered the most in the context. American democracy benefited those who economically thrived in a militarized economy, but even more so in the 1970s and 1980s, as austerity led to the erosion of social programs that offered protections and security to the most precarious members of the Cold War coalition.

The 1970s gave birth to a reemergence of free-market capitalism alongside the remilitarization of American foreign policy. The fall of South Vietnam to communism in 1975, the Soviet invasion of Afghanistan in 1979, and the subsequent collapse of superpower détente between the United States and the Soviet Union weakened the legitimacy of those who supported the reduction in American defense budgets. As the country questioned America's role at home and abroad in the 1970s, efforts to increase the defense budget were used to justify cuts to social programs, limit government regulations on business, and reduce federal expenditures unrelated to defense spending. Discussions of higher defense spending therefore served as rhetorical weapons used to make policy arguments about the need to scale back social programs to spend more on defense and national security—while using the military state as a substitute for social programs. The decline of the social welfare state (combined with job losses in defense for unskilled workers) heightened bellicose rhetoric toward the Soviet Union within the Cold War coalition, reinvigorating Cold War anticommunism in the service of economic austerity—and vice versa.[22]

The Cold War coalition, and a political economy supported by massive defense spending, was also a product of the American party system. Political bipartisanship supported a national security state to confront the threat of communism at the outset of the Cold War, with Democrats being the largest proponents of the national security state until the 1960s. Indeed, the enlargement of the national defense budget occurred under the stewardship of liberal Democrats like Henry Jackson, Hubert Humphrey, Stuart Symington, and John F. Kennedy, who believed the federal government could also be a force of justice for disenfranchised racial minorities and the poor. From the New Deal to the Great Society, the Cold War was a "Democratic" war, the national security state having been conceptualized, proposed, and implemented by New Deal and Cold War liberals and being an outgrowth of New Deal policies. The defense industry seemed to offer a panacea to Democrats concerned about the challenges the United States faced in both the international and domestic arenas. For Democrats, the Cold War state thwarted communist aggression, created jobs, and kept American prosperity moving forward, which Democrats argued was not only important for the economy but to blunt Soviet critiques of the capitalist West.[23]

The anti–Cold War Left—those individuals who rejected a warfare state codified by anticommunism—was largely relegated from the Democratic Party until the Vietnam War. The presidential candidacy of former vice president Henry Wallace in 1948 represented the first major political challenge to a permanent war economy. Wallace condemned massive defense spending in the name of anticommunism and feared American interventionism would lead to global instability. After Wallace's defeat, remnants of the Cold War Left appeared in the antinuclear and civil rights movements of the 1950s, only to resurface in party politics during the late 1960s. When the war in Vietnam proved that military power could not defeat a well-disciplined communist insurgency, Democrats in Congress began to adopt antimilitarist positions, calling for foreign policy retrenchment and cuts in defense spending in the 1970s. By 1972, South Dakota Democrat and presidential candidate George McGovern called for an $30 billion cut to the defense budget, a substantial departure from previous Democratic candidates.

But Democrats often had to sacrifice their antimilitarism to the interests of their constituents—and to the structure of the national security state. Individuals who supported the Cold War (for economic or ideological reasons or both) would not tolerate rhetoric and policies that eliminated defense jobs without immediate replacements. Antimilitarist Democrats did not have a convincing solution to this dilemma, nor did they have good answers to the problems created by a warfare state. Most Democrats opposed to a large defense budget favored the conversion of defense jobs to nondefense work, but this position never gained traction among other members of the Cold War coalition, particularly after the American economy declined in the 1970s. When threatened by deindustrialization and federal spending cuts, defense jobs became more valuable and important to the communities who depended on them. With occupational options restrained for American defense workers during the later years of the Cold War, the possibilities for a significant drawdown on military spending drifted further from view.

Right-wing Republicans—and Americans who self-identified as "conservative"—faced a similar problem. Republican support for large defense budgets meant that their faith in the unfettered private market was often superseded by their political and ideological desire to militarize American foreign policy through defense increases, leading to a nuclear arms race and a markedly expansive military footprint. Throughout much of the postwar era, conservatives favored—or participated in—the allocation of federal spending to the Cold War economy in large numbers. Republicans appropriated funds for the expansion of military bases, the installation of ICBM silos, and experimental missile defense programs—from the anti-ballistic missile program to the SDI. Right-wing conservatives (and Democrats) argued that these programs were necessary to defeat communism and to keep America's economy strong. The willingness of the Republican Right to use the national security state to achieve its political objectives therefore limited its ability to reduce the overall size of the federal government, a long-standing, stated goal of Republicans.

The history of the Cold War coalition thus illustrates how the anti-government, antistatist tendencies among the Right are misleading. In fact, many members of the Right supported military Keynesianism during the Cold War. While they claimed to oppose the defense economy as a means of job creation or increasing consumers' purchasing power (as Cold War liberals did), the Right understood that defense spending could be a stimulant for economic growth, a solution for high unemployment, and an aid in efforts to modernize and improve infrastructure in states and localities—which in turn created more jobs and growth. Few members of the Right recognized or admitted to deliberately promoting military Keynesianism, since it would belie their stated claims about the proper role of the federal state. But as the Right participated in the building of the national security state, it relied on the Cold War as an engine of job creation and economic development, which enhanced its power. As Republicans increasingly came to power in the postwar period, the Right became willing and active architects of a federal state that contradicted its traditional suspicion of big government.

By embracing the structure of the national security state as an alternative and replacement for social welfare programs, right-wing members of the Cold War coalition also relied on the New Deal state to gain access to the halls of power and policy making. With Republicans at the helm, government entities, particularly the State Department and the Department of Defense, steered federal funds to right-leaning groups that favored a hard-line approach to U.S. foreign policy; and organizations such as the American Security Council, the National Security Information Center, the Committee on the Present Danger, and the Coalition on Peace through Strength worked alongside congressmen, presidential cabinet appointees, military officers, and defense company executives to form ideological and economic partnerships. These organizations—individually and collectively—argued that the United States needed to increase its military spending to defeat the Soviet Union and its satellite states. Their actions guaranteed the profitability and perpetuity of defense companies during the Cold War, particularly after the 1970s when the military establishment came under attack in response to the quagmire of the Vietnam War. The deep-rooted and interdependent connections among right-leaning special interest groups, political action committees, federal money, and employees and benefactors of the Cold War state pressured, if not compelled, policy makers to adopt measures that enlarged American military power. By the 1970s, economic precarity provided cover for the Right to campaign for further defense increases and military interventionism that regularly gained the attention of elected officials (both Democrats and Republicans) and others responsible for carrying out U.S. national security interests.[24]

As it did to their counterparts on the Left, a permanent Cold War economy proved disastrous to Cold War critics on the Right. Anti-internationalists like Robert A. Taft and Kenneth Wherry worried that the United States' entry into a global Cold War would lead to a garrison state at home, which would absorb the nation's financial resources. Right-wing activists like Dan Smoot, John T. Flynn, and Gerald L. K. Smith of the Christian Nationalist Crusade questioned the premises that justified Cold War defense spending. In vehemently racist and anti-Semitic terms, Smith and Flynn offered a right-wing nationalist foreign policy, arguing that federal expenditures on large-scale foreign aid programs (such as the Truman Doctrine or Marshall Plan, for example), defense bureaucracies, and a standing military defied the constitutional limits of American foreign policy. These anti–Cold War, right-wing factions persisted beyond the 1950s, but largely outside or at the fringes of the Republican Party until the early twenty-first century. The libertarian wing of the antiwar movement in the 1960s, evangelicals' support for the nuclear freeze movement, and the handful of Republicans who favored a reduction to the defense budget following the Cold War reflected the long legacy of the pro-Taft wing within the Republican Party. Once opponents of the Cold War were marginalized, fissures among the American Right on national defense policy were therefore not over whether the federal state should be enlarged to fight international communism but to what dimensions, and for what purposes.

Some clarification is necessary regarding the terms used to describe the political actors in this book, particularly national figures within the Cold War coalition. As implied above, the bipolar paradigms of left/right, liberal/conservative, Democrat/Republican are inadequate to accurately characterize many members of the Cold War coalition.[25] Since the terms "liberal" and "conservative" are insufficient when discussing the backers of Cold War national defense policy, I have modified them to account for their inadequacies. In denoting a liberal or Democratic proponent of the Cold War, I use the term "Cold War liberal" or "Cold War Democrat." This term is applied to figures such as Senators Hubert Humphrey and Henry Jackson, who were liberal minded on social issues, including civil rights and labor rights, but adamant that the United States must answer Soviet communism with military and nuclear superiority. The popularity of Cold War liberals was confined to a specific historical context—from 1945 to the mid-1960s. Cold War liberalism fell out of favor by the late 1960s and early 1970s as the class of "New Democrats" or "Watergate babies" came into office after 1972. I have termed these latter individuals "antimilitarist" or "antimilitarist Democrats." Like the term "Cold War liberal," I use the term "antimilitarist" within a specific period and context. I define an antimilitarist as an individual opposed to massive defense increases following the Vietnam War. This term was also used in the

late 1960s to denote New Left activists and policy makers who sought
a reduction in the defense budget. I have used the term for these reasons, rather than apply an original one that would be anachronistic.[26]
I also distinguish between the terms "Democrat" and "liberal." Democrats did not have to be liberal, while liberals were not necessarily
Democrats. The linguistic shuffling between the terms "Cold War liberal" and "antimilitarist Democrat" overcomes the vagueness of the
term "liberal."

The terms "conservative" or "conservatism" also need to be qualified, considering their multiple meanings and applications. For
decades, historians have struggled to unite the various strains of conservative thought to explain how a conservative "movement" congealed after 1945. Most have acknowledged the theory of "fusionism"
promulgated by journalist Frank Meyer and historian George H.
Nash. Fusionism posits that after 1945, anticommunism among the
Right made allowances for the involvement of the state in matters of
national security, even while conservatives continued to uphold free
market and antistatist principles. Moreover, conservatives prioritized
the private market over the public sector but accepted that the federal
government best handled national security policy. The prewar and
postwar Right shared the belief that the state had a responsibility to
ensure the security of the American people against external threats.
The differences between the Old Right and the New Right were over
the degree to which the state could intervene in Americans' lives to
defeat the threat of communism.

In applying the term "conservative" to certain groups and subjects
in these pages, I have rejected the idea of a conservative "movement"
and the notion of "fusionism." In terms of the Cold War coalition,
there was no conservative "movement"—for a movement would
imply unity. Many individuals on the Right were willing to use the
power of the state to confront economic and social issues, rather than
market forces, if state power was deemed necessary for the purposes
of national defense. Few of the conservatives in this project were antigovernment purists. Modern conservatives, with the exception of a
few libertarians, sought to reduce the proportions and influence of

the state on Americans' lives but fell victim to the tensions between their anticommunism and antistatism, or better yet, relied on these tensions to further their political agendas. While members of the Right maintained coherence between antistatism and their support for an expansive military—both philosophically and intellectually—when it came to national defense policy, anticommunism (and parochial politics) often took precedence over antistatism. The limits of antistatism as the basis of their political agenda prevented the postwar Right from achieving their ultimate objective during the Cold War: ending the New Deal state.

conservatives

The conservatives in this project were not "traditionalists" who wanted to conserve or preserve institutions. Through state intervention, the modern Right sought to promote policy changes that would reverse the gains made by the New Deal and Great Society during the twentieth century, but they also aimed to institute new political and cultural norms using state power. I consider this analysis when I use the term "conservative." In a specific sense, many modern conservatives proposed policies that would lead to an even larger military than what much of the public envisioned after World War II. While Cold War Democrats expanded the size of the military and national defense regime to an unparalleled scope, had conservatives taken control of both houses of Congress and the presidency during the Cold War, the national security state's power and reach would have been broader. Many of the individuals I label as conservative also self-described as "conservative," further preventing the use of improper labels to a person or group of people.

My decision to discuss the Cold War coalition beyond binary and partisan frameworks also aims to capture the political contradictions and hypocrisies expressed by Americans—to show that voting against one's interests is often in the interest of many Americans, and to demonstrate that democratic politics emerged from a variety of interests, no matter if those interests worked toward the long-term disadvantage of their proponents. In the process, this book explores how Americans understand the purpose of the federal state and how they seek to hold the state accountable—whether they be Democrats or Republicans, liberals or conservatives—when it does not deliver on its expected responsibilities to the public. It places Cold War foreign policy and the national security state at the center of analysis, since national security interests often defined who "deserved" federal benefits and who did not: they delineated the obligations the state held toward its citizens.[27]

Moreover, the concept of national security unified disparate interests under a common cause and proved durable in its ability to accommodate Americans' contradictions between anti-welfarist positions and support for an institution and a network—the American military or military-industrial complex—that was a significant generator of welfare and social protections for Americans. For these reasons, the Cold War national security state proved adept at coopting Americans' long-standing support for social democratic policies since the New Deal. During the Cold War, Americans were often asked to choose between continued prosperity through exorbitant military spending or the (re)allocation of military funds for domestic welfare. This was a false choice that emanated from the politics of massive defense spending. The manifestation of the national security state as the basis for social democracy during the Cold War inhibited the creation of broad-based political coalitions that could champion social democratic politics, while providing opponents of the New Deal state (and proponents of austerity) a political cudgel—one that they wielded effectively and helped pull voters to right-wing policies.

Finally, while the Cold War ended in 1991, its legacy continues to remake American politics. Democrats and Republicans (albeit to much different degrees) are reluctant to trim the national defense budget, and there remains bipartisan support for massive defense spending. At the same time, the public responds favorably to anti-government rhetoric, even while 96 percent of Americans receive aid or subsidies from the federal government—many of which are provided under the auspices of "defense"—and continue to support plans for universal health care and a job guarantee. Some of the answers to this seeming paradox are found in the history of the Cold War coalition. Indeed, Americans continue to enjoy the fiscal benefits of the

Cold War defense economy—and view them, in ideological terms, as earned (necessary, even) rather than given—because of the absence of social democracy in the United States. How the political economy of Cold War defense spending shaped American democracy during and after the Cold War is the story told in the following pages.

CHAPTER ONE

Where the Global Meets the Parochial

Few defense employees in the 1950s foresaw the fate that befell the industry in the 1990s. In 1949, President John Jay Hopkins said that Electric Boat was "in the strongest financial position in its history," as the Connecticut defense contractor reported "the largest backlog of unfilled orders" from government business—both domestic and international—and expected a "level of production high in contrast to that experienced by the company prior to the year 1941." Three years later, in April 1952, Hopkins's predictions came true: the company's procurement backlog more than tripled, and the company had record profits—$3,872,203 in 1951 dollars. Hopkins also envisioned future gains from Cold War technology as the company was poised to bring an influx of jobs to southwestern Connecticut from "applications of atomic energy and nuclear fission." Sure enough, three months later, the secretary of the navy, Dan Kimball, announced that the hull for an atomic power submarine would be built by Electric Boat because the defense contractor had "the design talent and nearly all the facilities necessary to begin work on the carrier immediately."[1]

Kimball was not alone in this assessment. Individuals across the country, not just in Connecticut, thought the defense economy would be a reliable source of jobs throughout the 1950s. Indeed, on October 9, 1951, in the depths of the Korean War, the head of the United Auto Workers (UAW), Walter Reuther, wrote to President Harry S. Truman urging him to ensure federal assistance to workers affected by the transition to a wartime economy because there were plenty of jobs to be created from war. In December 1950, Truman launched the Office of Defense Mobilization (ODM) to handle the war at home by allocating defense contracts to businesses, hiring manpower, and streamlining production of necessary equipment. Reuther claimed that the rapid shift to defense urged by ODM had left civilian workers unemployed. Reuther, a man of the political Left who cut his teeth in socialist circles in the 1930s before helping found the Americans for Democratic Action (ADA) in the 1940s, wrote that the "working people of America are prepared to make whatever sacrifices are necessary to defend freedom against the threat of communist tyranny." But their sacrifice demanded remuneration, as "defense work must be integrated in civilian plants to assure that the unused productive capacity" is utilized to resolve postwar unemployment.[2]

Republicans too wanted the federal government to spend more funds on national defense to put Americans to work. Another figure from Michigan and the Midwest, Republican representative Gerald Ford, sought defense funds for his constituents in the months before the Korean War broke out. Ford urged the National Security Resources Board (NSRB)—the predecessor to the ODM—to declare Grand Haven, Michigan (located in his congressional district), "a critical area" in need of defense contracts in order to help "the labor market conditions" in the city. Like Reuther, Ford wanted the federal government to provide full employment through the defense economy—as it had done during World War II.[3]

When the Cold War confronted "everyday life" in the late 1940s and early 1950s, it reconfigured the public's relationship to the federal state. Americans' lives at home were irrevocably affected by the United States' global assault on communism during these decades.[4] As the comments by individuals as diverse as John Jay Hopkins, Walter Reuther and Gerald Ford make clear, the public consistently sought access to the financial and social benefits provided by the Cold War. Americans regularly turned to the Cold War state for jobs and financial security when economic recession threatened their interests. In the absence of a broader social safety net, Cold War defense spending delivered federal benefits without the stigma of social welfare. Defense spending during the Cold War provided stable employment and economic prosperity to many Americans, for military Keynesianism to deliver Americans from unemployment.[5]

The precedent for military spending as a means of social welfare—to further economic interests, not just the interests of national security—emerged during the New Deal. In addition to delivering unemployment insurance, social security benefits, strengthened labor laws, and price controls on commodities, Franklin D. Roosevelt's New Deal relied on national security spending to put unemployed Americans to work. During FDR's first two years in office, the Public Works Administration (PWA) funneled federal defense funds into shipbuilding outside industrial centers in the Midwest and Northeast, furthering the fortunes of companies like Electric Boat—which increased their payrolls by five hundred workers from 1934 to 1935. As early as 1934, FDR's close advisor, Harold Ickes, remarked that the "Navy has more Public Works money tied up than anyone else." From 1933 to 1935, the army and navy were allotted 45 percent of federal funds from PWA projects combined. "There isn't enough money in the United States Treasury to satisfy the Navy," Ickes would later comment. By July 1940, another New Deal agency, the Works Progress Administration (WPA), had spent over $500 million on defense projects that had broader nondefense outcomes. Even before American entry into World War II, road construction for "defense" constituted 36 percent of the WPA's employment figures on highways and various roads, even though these programs were "not always visible to the public as defense work per se."[6] The WPA also worked directly on defense projects during the war. The WPA remade seventeen civilian airports in Florida for the purposes of accommodating the military, and between 1935 and 1943, the WPA built 480 airports and retooled 470 others for reasons of national security.[7] As historian Jason Scott Smith has argued, the New Deal was ultimately a massive public works program designed to stimulate employment while building American infrastructure. Much of the funds for public works were justified under the umbrella of "defense," even if they went toward programs geared more toward social welfare, such as housing and hospitals for military personnel. Indeed, the New Deal was an expansive "public works policy," where the "big winner in such a policy was national defense."[8]

World War II enhanced the role of the defense industry as an agent of economic progress, as military spending brought near full employment to Americans by 1945. During the first few months of the war, military expenditures grew from $1.8 billion to $6.3 billion, with the federal government spending $304 billion on defense over the course of the war. Whereas unemployment hovered near 17 percent in 1937, by 1939 it dropped to less than 10 percent. And by the end of the war, unemployment would be less than 5 percent, with defense spending growing to 46 percent of gross domestic product. This was accomplished almost entirely through wartime production. Agencies such as the Defense Plant Corporation (DPC) and the War Production Board were dedicated to ensuring necessary manpower was available for a wartime economy. Out of the $15 billion allocated to private investment by the federal government since 1945, the DPC was responsible for "nearly two-thirds."[9] And because the war brought jobs, rising wages, and recovery from the Great Depression, the war years also fetishized military Keynesianism among the war's architects (many of them Democrats), making defense spending the default for the liberals who left the Roosevelt administration, according to historian James Sparrow, still yearning for the "dream of full employment . . . well into the postwar years."[10]

Once World War II ended, global economic forces made the military economy permanent. Indeed, the Cold War policy of containment encouraged the production and free exchange of goods to prevent the spread of communism to America's trading partners, along with an expansive military. As President Harry Truman acknowledged in a speech on American economic policy to the American Legion in 1949, "World prosperity is necessary to our own prosperity in the United States." For the United States to achieve economic growth, it also must be spread to the world.[11] Indeed, throughout the Cold War, U.S. economic policy sought to keep European and

Japanese markets open to American commodities, and vice versa. A Pax Americana boosted the economic fortunes of America's allies, as the defense economy fueled growth abroad to preserve the security of the North Atlantic Treaty Organization (NATO). Japanese steel was used in American weapons during the Korean War, while American requests for one thousand trucks a month during the war became "Toyota's salvation."[12] As countries profited from the products made by the Cold War, the defense economy became a structure and cultural symbol of American capitalism—in both a domestic and international context—which contributed to the growth of the national security state.

Policy makers' thoughts on America's proper role in the world also ensured the expansion of the warfare state into the Cold War. In the immediate months following the surrender of the Japanese in the fall of 1945, the Truman administration—and members of Congress—extracted several lessons from the war's experience. One of the enduring lessons of the war was that the United States must prevent the recurrence of a surprise attack like Pearl Harbor. American leaders vowed to never again let U.S. security be jeopardized by a foreign attack. As the United States prepared to confront the threat of the Soviet Union (and more broadly, communism), the metaphor of Pearl Harbor became even more profound. Concerns that the Soviet Union would be the next Third Reich also generated an anticommunist ideology at home, one that reinforced a political economy premised on American militarism and shaped global affairs and the coming of a great power conflict between the United States and the Soviet Union.[13]

Members of the Cold War coalition sought to take advantage of these global changes in parochial terms. Wanting to keep the "American Dream" alive in their districts and states, local and national politicians subsidized the defense industry to serve their respective political agendas. Facing these parochial demands, Republicans and Democrats—across the political spectrum—rewrote the tax code to allow defense companies tax write-offs and lower marginal tax rates during the Cold War. Cheap land grants were given to the Pentagon by southern Democrats to establish air and naval bases, military hospitals, and other federal defense facilities in the South, citing the desire for more high-skilled jobs and industrial progress in the region. After the 1950s, concerns of a nuclear attack from the Soviets and access to federal funds convinced Cold War Democrats to finance the construction of missile silos in the South Dakota plains, leading the Air Force and Army Corps of Engineers to coerce farmers into selling their land to the federal government for the sake of nuclear deterrence.[14]

As elected officials fortified the military-industrial complex during the early Cold War, they increasingly relied on anticommunism to justify their support for military Keynesianism, for jobs provided by the defense industry. Anticommunism thus drastically shaped the Cold War coalition on a local and national level. Whereas the New Deal and World War II provided the basis for the warfare state, the Cold War made the military-industrial complex permanent. In areas where the defense economy dominated, Democrats and Republicans relied on Cold War ideology to keep federal defense spending flowing to their districts and states; defense and military workers then employed Cold War rhetoric to urge politicians to keep defense contractors alive in their communities. Business figures and military officials with connections to U.S. foreign and national security policy, as well as political activists and organizations, joined the fray, seeking more defense funds to further their ideological agendas. It was this strange mixture of economics and ideology—of individuals that transcended partisan lines—that formed a Cold War coalition sizeable enough to ensure continued government spending on defense.

But the Cold War coalition would not achieve its goals on equal terms. Coalition members located in the Northeast and Midwest saw their jobs relocated to the Sunbelt South, which became a major site for investment in aerospace and innovative Cold War technology. As a looming conflict with the Soviet Union demanded a massive military buildup of unprecedented proportions, inequality increased among areas where military spending contributed to the personal fortunes of workers. The inequality experienced because of this phenomenon allowed the defense economy to shape electoral politics in interesting ways—which shaped the ideological and economic positions of members in the Cold War coalition. The early years of the Cold War thus mobilized a diverse array of individuals behind the military-industrial complex, even as many of these individuals experienced fewer gains from defense spending.

* * *

Democrats' and Republicans' decision to grow the warfare state to contain the Soviet Union made both major parties into vehicles of anticommunism—and proponents of the military-industrial complex—after 1945. Indeed, Americans' overwhelming reliance on the national security state was not determined after World War II but was a product of Cold War politics. President Truman initially wanted defense *reductions* during his early years in office, not defense increases. The onset of peacetime demanded a reorganization of budgetary priorities for the president. The defense budget was important, but not as significant as expanding domestic programs for middle-class and working-class Americans. From 1946 to 1949, Truman struggled to consolidate his "Fair Deal" for Americans, which would have broadened the New Deal through a program of national health insurance, new social security benefits, and civil rights reforms. Truman also wanted to prevent rising inflation rates, and like Roosevelt, embraced the need for a balanced budget. Reducing defense spending would go a long way toward achieving these goals, Truman felt.

But Truman's opponents in Congress stymied his domestic agenda and halted his Fair Deal. While Truman confronted some anti–Fair Dealers from his own party—such as fiscal traditionalists like Maryland senator Millard Tydings—attacks on Truman's domestic program were more prominent on the Republican Right.[15] When Republicans gained a majority in both houses of Congress following the 1946 midterm elections, they quickly targeted Truman's Fair Deal programs. A Republican congressional majority shut down national health insurance and the more social democratic aspects of the Fair Deal that enfranchised labor unions and the working class, including full employment.[16] A Republican majority made the passage of Taft-Hartley in 1947 possible (over Truman's veto), a bill that gutted unions by allowing right-to-work laws in states and abolishing the closed shop. As Americans contemplated the threat of a communist monolith abroad, Republicans used the moment to portray unions and left-wing constituencies as communist inspired. Republicans like Joseph Ball of Minnesota claimed that the political activism of the Congress of Industrial Organizations (CIO) comprised "a combination of many left-wing elements together with the Communists and their fellow travelers" and these leftists were affiliated with the Truman administration.[17]

This political culture of anticommunism gave Republicans power and political advantage unseen since the 1920s. For much of the New Deal period and World War II, Republicans were an embattled party. After the 1936 elections, there were eighteen Republicans in the Senate. By 1943, that number grew to thirty, but Democrats had a two-thirds majority over the GOP. The early years of the Cold War, however, provided opportunities for Republicans to make the party popular again in the name of fighting communism. Republicans argued that the emerging threat of the Soviet Union—and the possible spread of communism to Eastern Europe—undermined the United States' status and strength as a superpower after the war. American power was perpetually precarious and relied upon an attentive democracy, said Republicans. For example, Republican congressman from Michigan John B. Trevor spoke for many Republicans when he said that because Americans were not sufficiently mindful of the communist threat, "apathy and timidity are stifling patriotic action, so—Communism marches on!"[18]

Republicans thus felt it was their duty to educate the public on just how palpable and urgent the threat of communism was to the American way of life—while using institutions of federal power to silence political opponents. During the Red and Lavender Scares, Republican anticommunists broadened the national security bureaucracy of the federal government to pursue suspected enemies of the state without much concrete evidence. Working with the Federal Bureau of

Investigation, the State Department, and the Department of Defense, Republicans passed or supported laws that required loyalty oaths for federal employees, denied security clearances for suspected communists working in defense plants, and withdrew the passports of Cold War dissidents and civil rights activists like the African American singer Paul Robeson. And then there were Republicans like the senator from Wisconsin, Joseph McCarthy, who infamously exploited a long history of anticommunism in the United States to acquire electoral popularity. Beginning in 1950, McCarthy used his post as chairman of the Senate Investigating Committee to ferret alleged communists out of government, claiming that he had a list of documented communists employed by the State Department, one that soon grew to encompass other federal employees. Indeed, McCarthy's name became synonymous with the Red Scare because of his skill in labeling all members of the Left as communists, and then singling out specific ones as traitors worthy of congressional scrutiny—a strategy that denuded the Left of its more radical and social democratic elements during the Cold War.[19]

But McCarthy was only one of many Republicans who promulgated anticommunist rhetoric for self-serving reasons. Republicans like Kenneth Wherry of Nebraska accused homosexuals in the State Department of being Soviet spies, forcing hundreds of gay federal employees to resign or be fired, many of whom had come to Washington, D.C., during the New Deal era. What historian David K. Johnson has called the "Lavender Scare" saw a deliberate and strategic campaign to demonize homosexuals as "deviants," "sex offenders," and "sex perverts" easily manipulated by communists. The New Deal brought homosexual spies to Washington, D.C., Republicans argued—implying that the New Deal was the means used by communists to bring down the American republic. Wherry's own 1950 investigation equated homosexuality with communism—and therefore, disloyalty—to purge intellectuals and gay professionals from the federal government to undermine the New Deal state. Wherry's right-wing supporters admitted as much, saying "fairies and fair dealers" brought licentiousness and criminality to the nation's capital, and the "whole nest of appeasers, left-wingers, welfare-staters, do good-ers and queer intellectuals" needed to go.[20] As the historian Ellen Schrecker has commented, "The Cold War and the GOP's campaign against the Truman administration's alleged softness on Communism had transformed dissident into disloyalty," in an ultimate effort to kill New Deal reforms.[21]

As they became the vigilant watchdogs of domestic communism, Republicans rebuilt their shattered coalition to resounding success in the years after World War II. The 1946 midterm elections pro-vided evidence of a correlation between anticommunism and elec-toral victories. Republicans pilloried labor strikes, price controls, and reconversion in 1946 as examples of liberalism run amok and equated the Soviet Union—and totalitarianism overall—with New Dealism. Republicans' skill in conflating antistatism with anticommunism in 1946 pushed fifty-five House Democrats out of Congress, some of them New Dealers like Representative Jerry Voorhis from California (defeated by Richard Nixon) and Emily Taft Douglas from Illinois, one of only eleven women in the House of Representatives during the Seventy-Ninth Congress.[22]

The 1946 midterm elections made Republicans the party of red-baiting throughout the Cold War, giving them the ability to weaken New Deal liberalism in the postwar period in ways they could not during the 1930s and World War II. But Republicans' anticommu-nist positions also compelled their reliance upon the institutions of the New Deal to enhance their power. Far from repudiating the New Deal state, Republicans embraced its legacy to further their anti–New Deal agenda. As we shall see more in later chapters, Republicans (and conservatives) turned to institutions strengthened by Franklin Roosevelt's New Deal (the expansion of the executive branch, the cre-ation of a national security bureaucracy designed to further Ameri-can hegemony, and a national defense industry that put Americans to work in times of economic hardship) to weaken New Deal lib-eralism. Republicans therefore relied on the creation, and eventual expansion, of the warfare state during World War II to displace the New Deal programs that provided social benefits and employment to

Americans through increased defense spending. As Illinois Republican Everett Dirksen argued, "With so many crises in faraway places, emphasis will have to be on guns" during the Cold War. Dirksen and other Republicans thus searched for "ways the domestic budget and so-called welfare items can be trimmed in view of the delicate international situation." This statement encapsulated the Republican ethos during the Cold War.[23]

Democrats and liberals tried to counter the Republican Party's strategy to reverse and dismantle the New Deal with red-baiting tactics by claiming they were the genuine party of anticommunists—a party that actively purged communists. Minnesota Democrat Hubert Humphrey, for instance, rose to national distinction having pushed socialists and communists from the Democratic Farmer-Labor (DFL) Party in Minnesota in 1943. Humphrey believed that if communists remained in the DFL, Republicans could label all Democrats as "radicals or Communists." Pro-Soviet leftists in the DFL like Elmer Benson, Humphrey argued, were albatrosses around the necks of liberals working toward an expanded welfare state. Alongside his close advisers, Orville Freeman and Art Naftalin, Humphrey sent anticommunist Democrats into Minnesota precincts and district caucuses in 1947, stacking the deck against the more radical DFL members in preparation for the Senate race the following year. As Minneapolis mayor in 1947, and soon candidate for the United States Senate, Humphrey argued that "progressives [should] clean their own ranks instead of giving the Republicans and the reactionaries" more opportunities "to stab at us in every campaign, on every occasion." Once in Congress, Humphrey even went so far as to try to ban the Communist Party in 1954, a move that generated significant backlash from his own party and anticommunist liberals like the historian Arthur Schlesinger Jr.[24]

Humphrey's anticommunism did not make him less of a liberal on workers' rights and civil rights, however. When elected to the Senate in 1948, Humphrey represented the left liberals of the party, promoting social democratic policies such as full employment, the repeal of Taft-Hartley, a permanent Fair Employment Practices Committee to bar racial discrimination in the workplace, and an equal rights amendment to the Constitution to end gender discrimination. Humphrey believed that none of these goals could be accomplished if the left wing of the Democratic Party allowed room for communists. Allowing radicals (socialists, communists) to remain within the Democratic Party would only give comfort to Republican red-baiters. Humphrey concluded that if Democrats were committed to social justice—as many of them were in the years following World War II—it was essential to be an anticommunist.

Humphrey personified what Schlesinger termed the "vital center" of postwar American liberalism. In his book with the same title (*The Vital Center*) published in 1949, Schlesinger argued that liberal Democrats sought to use the federal state to "produce a wide amount of basic satisfaction and preserve a substantial degree of individual freedom."[25] In Schlesinger's view, New Deal liberals were the balanced alternative to two polar extremes: totalitarian communism and right-wing fanaticism. But the "vital center" thesis backed liberals into a corner. Postwar liberals had to distance themselves from more left-wing allies to explain why liberals were not communists. Any deviation from the "center" (however loosely defined) required qualification. Such a position entailed constant monitoring of liberals' political ranks and allies. To mobilize against socialist and communist infiltration of American liberalism, Schlesinger, Humphrey, and other Cold War liberals created and championed groups like ADA, who had a mission to ward off radical elements in the party. The ADA and the larger response to Republican red-baiting turned New Deal liberals into Cold War liberals, as the concerns over a communist monolith overshadowed (and prevented) the expansion of a larger welfare state. The ADA liberals emerged from the New Deal and World War II committed to working-class unionism and civil rights just as much as an international anticommunist foreign policy, but the reconciliation of the two proved problematic throughout the postwar period.

Much has been made about how (or whether) anticommunist liberals killed leftist politics within the Democratic Party after 1945. While it now seems clear that Cold War liberalism did not keep the spirit of New Deal reforms alive, it was a rational—albeit problematic— response to what prescient liberals knew would be a political issue for them.[26] While anticommunism proved unable to do much for Democrats in terms of strengthening labor unions or creating universal health care, it allowed them to funnel federal funds to localities and individuals, to further job creation and economic growth in the private sector under the ulterior motives of national security.[27] Such policies provided federal protections and benefits to Americans through military Keynesianism but also made them active supporters of Cold War state building to provide economic and political rights to more Americans. In other words, Cold War liberalism furthered military Keynesianism. Moreover, by employing anticommunism to fight for rights-based protections for African Americans and women in the 1950s and 1960s, Democrats gave Republicans a choice: support the state's growth to neutralize Soviet communism and protect the tenets *dilemma* of American democracy (and civil freedoms), or criticize growing appropriations in federal spending on American foreign policy and risk appearing contradictory in their rhetoric and policies toward communism.[28]

In 1947, the Truman administration's anticommunist rhetoric earned bipartisan support for his internationalist policies. Anticommunism compelled congressional Republicans to support the Truman Doctrine, a $400 million program that allotted federal aid to Greece *How much* and Turkey to protect both countries from communist insurgen- *of U.S.* cies, as Truman warned Congress that "terrorist activities . . . led by *debt today* communists" against the Greek state compelled the United States to *attributable* "ensure the peaceful development of nations" threated by commu- *to fighting* nism.[29] The Truman Doctrine divided Republicans, but many voted *communism* for it, citing anticommunism as the main reason for their decision. Truman then asked Republicans to help to rebuild Europe in 1948 through the European Recovery Program (ERP), commonly known as the Marshall Plan. Truman argued that billions of dollars in grants to Europe would prevent communist governments from exploiting the economic and political disarray sweeping across the continent after the fall of the Third Reich. The Marshall Plan faced stiffer Republican opposition than the Truman Doctrine, but it still passed by a vote of 69–17 in the Senate, and 329–74 in the House. Republican Kenneth Wherry tried to lead a bloc of midwestern Republicans against the Marshall Plan, but it was a pitiful minority—even noninterventionists and fiscal conservatives like Republican Robert Taft voted for the Marshall Plan. NATO was created in 1949, and the Southeast Asia Treaty Organization followed—both spearheaded by Truman and Democrats in Congress.

As Cold War liberals cloaked their politics in anticommunism, Republican opposition to Truman's foreign policy became a problem for the GOP. In addition to attacking domestic spending, Republicans also bristled at Truman's foreign policy as financially unsound for its size and misguided for its internationalist commitment to Europe and the fate of the free world. Questioning the viability and necessity of an internationalist foreign policy exposed Republican congressional elites to critiques that they too were "soft" on communism—at least in their willingness to use state power to deal with the Soviet threat. This predicament contributed to a disconnect between policy and principle among the Right that it struggled to reconcile in the months after World War II. Communism needed to be vanquished, Republicans said, but defense monies were better spent on projects other than what Truman asked for from Congress. Aid to Europe through the Marshall Plan subsidized socialist countries with taxpayer dollars, compounding federal deficits and leading to increased inflation. Republican representative from South Dakota Karl Mundt accused Truman of abetting the "pansy-like attitude of our State Department" toward the threat of communism. Mundt argued that the Marshall Plan reflected the administration's "self-contradictory policy" toward the Soviet Union, as the ERP permitted exports to the USSR, even though it was designed to stop the spread of communism.[30] Georgia Democratic representative Carl Vinson commented on his Republican colleagues shortly after they expressed their opposition to the Truman Doctrine, "They don't like Russia, they don't like Communism, but they don't want to do anything to stop it."[31]

Normative thinking on the relationship between communism and fascism among the Right exacerbated this dilemma. For instance, in his manifesto on the free market, *The Road to Serfdom* (1944), Austrian economist F. A. Hayek implied that there was no difference between communism and fascism, as there existed "a relative ease with which a young communist could be converted into a Nazi or vice versa."[32] Soviet exile Ayn Rand spent her life and career arguing that American civilization—its system of free enterprise and individualism— were under constant threat by communists who were no different from fascists.[33] The fascist/communist analogy employed by Rand and Hayek lent credibility to Truman's policies that expanded the size of the federal government for reasons of national defense. If communism was identical to National Socialism in form, purpose, and content, then logic led members of the Right to the conclusion that the U.S. government was justified in obstructing the international spread of Soviet communism with the same means it did to thwart fascist Germany. Within this intellectual framework, antistatism on national defense issues increasingly had less weight. Trapped within this paradigm of how to fight the Cold War, the Right found it harder to be both antistatist and anticommunist—in terms of supporting military spending. Rejecting the federal state meant capitulating to communism; rejecting a foreign policy to fight communism led to the same outcome.

Given the connections between anticommunism and their electoral power, Republicans in the 1940s and early 1950s within Washington, D.C., were not as antistatist as they claimed to be. As evidenced by Republicans' behavior during the Red and Lavender Scares, elements of the Right welcomed the expansion of the national defense bureaucracy, believing the Cold War had great potential for coalition building. The primary debate among the Republican Right during the early Cold War, therefore, was not whether to increase or decrease the size of the Cold War state, but how the state would function in a postwar context. To maintain power, the Right worked within the Cold War state to secure influence among the American people and positions of power in the federal government. In propounding anticommunist discourse and policies, Republican antistatism was a means toward statist ends.

In the early Cold War, the differences between many Democrats and Republicans were in the technical details of where, how, and to what extent the money for defense was spent, not over whether the United States should have a large defense budget. While debates and differences would continue between the Left and the Right over the Cold War, members of both parties agreed that a defense economy (in some fashion) was needed to defeat America's foreign foes. As we shall see, hawkish Republicans—a relatively new breed of Republicans—helped build the national security state by aligning themselves with Cold War Democrats, many of them southern Democrats who kept the racial hierarchies of the South intact. Southern Democrats widely backed Truman's measures on Cold War spending, so much so that political scientist Ira Katznelson has argued that among "all the blocs in Congress that backed the Truman administration's international polices, southern Democrats were the most steadfast."[34]

And while some Republicans were against a large defense budget, few wanted a return to a prewar military. Many Republicans thought an expansive air force could replace a standing army and a permanent military footing. Indeed, Republican critics of Cold War containment (like Ohio Republican senator Robert Taft) wanted restraints on defense expenditures, but not on the national security state in its entirety. Congressional Republicans wanted a defense budget that was smaller and redesigned to accommodate their worldview on how to defeat communism. Rather than a muscular army and marines, congressional conservatives worked to reallocate defense funds to a stronger navy and air force—which would be more cost efficient. While Taft complained that the defense budget figures requested from the Truman administration were too high, he also said that more funds were needed to modernize the air force. According to historian Michael J. Hogan, Taft stated that because "the United States could not match the Red Army man for man, he thought it was better to counter Soviet strength on the ground with American strength in the air, particularly in air-atomic power."[35] While Taft was opposed to the militarization of American democracy, he was among the individuals responsible for America's overreliance on air power following World War II. When the Soviet Union tested its first atomic bomb in 1949, it proved to Taft "above everything else the necessity of building up an all-powerful Air Force."[36]

Taft distrusted the relative *size* of a large military budget, not a large military budget as an actuality. True, Taft was the leading Republican in Congress who feared America's financial downfall would be from high defense budgets and a bloated military, but Taft (and Republicans like Wherry and John Bricker from Ohio) did not oppose a national security state; they opposed a garrison state.[37] Taft believed that the constitutional purpose of the federal state was to protect the country from immediate external threats—Republicans opposed the New Deal and social programs on these grounds as well. Taft shared with his fellow Republicans a limited role for the state on economic matters, and the belief that the threat of communism warranted the expansion of the state for the purposes of national security. Where Taft disagreed with his Republican colleagues was when they argued for exorbitant military power without limits. To Taft, communism was a threat that must be fought, but building a leviathan to fight it placed limitations and restrictions on Americans that the Founders feared, sacrificing well-preserved civil liberties in the process. Taft was not opposed to exorbitant defense spending on its own terms, but he resisted it when it was accompanied by price controls, inflation, and government influence in the market—which were anathema to the America he envisioned. Taft's biggest critique of the defense budget was that it posed the question of "whether we can maintain a reasonably free system and the value of our dollar, or whether we are to be weakened by inflation and choked by government controls which tend to become more arbitrary and unreasonable." Taft's goal was therefore not to eliminate America's large military, but to put a cap on defense spending to balance the budget and decrease taxes.[38]

In the first months of the Cold War, Taft and other congressional members of the Republican Party remained divided about the amount of federal dollars spent on defense but still worked with

Democrats to pass defense budgets even larger than requested by Truman. Appropriations for modernizing aircraft met the approval of Democrats and Republicans alike. Missouri representative Clarence Cannon, often a fiscally prudent Democrat on military spending, complained that since World War II (when the United States spent 41 percent of its GDP on national defense), "every branch of our armed forces has deteriorated until our military might is but the shadow of its war peak strength." More air power was needed to confront the Soviets, but the United States also "must be provided at all times with the latest military, air, and naval equipment fully abreast of the latest research findings." Kenneth Wherry, a supposed isolationist on American foreign policy, said there must be "a strong air force capable of defending the national security of the United States of America, and that if cuts in expenditures are to be made they should be made in some other place, either in the other branches of the military or on the economic front."[39]

But even while a bipartisan consensus on the need for massive defense spending emerged in Congress as the 1940s neared their end, outside Capitol Hill, a handful of Cold War critics on the Left and Right sought to impede the growth of the defense economy. These individuals saw growing defense budgets as a break with America's past, one that threatened to supplant the American republic with a military autocracy. Influenced by a nationalist, and at times, anti-imperialist political tradition in the United States, these individuals warned that the United States was becoming an interventionist power in the years after World War II—which would erode the institutions of American democracy at home. A foreign policy without limits, these left-wing and right-wing critics said, made Americans more willing to find comfort in massive military power to protect the United States from external threats.

Cold War critics on the Right were often remnants of the America First movement, and many were from the Midwest, where a nationalist strain in American foreign policy dominated the region. In the years between the Civil War and World War II, noninterventionist Republicans combined a Jeffersonian suspicion of foreign alliances with a Hamiltonian desire for a strong, free market economy. They also invoked George Washington's Farewell Address and his caveat that the United States should be cautious of engaging in alliances with other powers. Foreign entanglements that made U.S. foreign policy beholden to the dictates of its allies were to be avoided. Non-interventionists also criticized America's incursions into Cuba and the Philippines to secure the business interests of American corporations and take up the "white-man's burden." Right-wing nationalists were also opposed to a standing army. They were convinced that the militarization of the American economy would bankrupt the United States. Prolonged conflicts drained revenues from the state, creating vast deficits that imperiled America's economic might.[40] Finally, foreign policy nationalists were suspicious of governing institutions that centralized power, from the Federal Reserve to the League of Nations. As one conservative Senator misleadingly said about the League, "We are 'Americans' and no international Banking syndicate can terrify or bulldoze us!"[41]

In the 1920s, noninterventionist Republicans in Washington continued to call for a more restrained global footprint. The human destruction created by World War I, and the failure of the United States to join the League of Nations, spurred a demand for international peace among global powers. Republicans (and progressive Democrats) in the 1920s embraced these events. Noninterventionist Republicans shared the concerns of midwestern progressives over militarism creeping into the body politic. These Republicans were at the forefront of attacks on the "merchants of death," those companies that profited from trading with the central and entente powers during World War I and that were accused of perpetuating the war for financial gain. Individuals such as author Felix Morley, who would go on to contribute to the magazine *Human Events*, found themselves in company with liberal Republicans like North Dakota senator Gerald Nye, who laid the blame for the war at the feet of greedy business interests.

By the 1930s and '40s, nationalists on the Right merged hostility with New Deal economics and an interventionist foreign policy, believing they were symptomatic of the mistaken efforts by Democrats and their Republican sympathizers to use government power to regulate the outcomes of global and domestic affairs. A constituent of Michigan congressman Clare Hoffman, Mrs. Ja Reindel, wondered why certain Republicans are "not in favor of [the] draft" and universal military training but continue to "advocate using labor to build ships, planes, bombs, etc." Another Michigan resident, Mrs. Grant Ballantine, in discussing her distaste for foreign aid to Greece under the Truman Doctrine, said that Republicans were more bedfellows than enemies to Democrats. She claimed to speak for "all true Republicans [who] are sick and tired of 15 years of FDR ism." Despite most of the Republicans in Congress after 1946, the leading members of the GOP are "just [Republican] in name only. That's why we get no real change from New Deal ism. Our hopes are blasted."[42] George Sefcik told his congressional representative that he was tired of the United States "spending Billions of dollars in building up Europe and defending them from communism. You are taking from our people money they don't have to spend in Europe."[43] L. E. Osmer from Grand Rapids, Michigan, felt likewise, wondering why "the American taxpayer" had to shell out hard-earned money for a nation like "Turkey, a country who didn't help us out in our hour of need during world war II." Osmer argued that the United States was "good and big and generous but we are not good enough to bail out the rest of the world and, if countries like France want Communism and countries like England want Socialism, there isn't a thing that you or anyone else in Washington can do about it."[44] Chicago resident and banker Ralph M. Shaw said that as "a strong, unwavering Republican and . . . patriotic American citizen" he was appalled at the foreign aid to Greece and Turkey under the Truman Doctrine. Shaw said that the "best way to protect America is to discharge the unnecessary feeders at the public crib in Washington and elsewhere; decrease the taxes; pass much needed remedial labor legislation," and allow the United States to "then make ourselves so strong from a naval, military, and atomic point of view that no nation would dare attack us."[45]

Colloquial criticism of an interventionist, anticommunist foreign policy among the Right contrasted with the consensus in Congress among Republicans like Michigan senator Arthur Vandenberg, the congressional architect of Truman's Cold War, that America must save the world with its military power. Vandenberg—who played an important part in shaping a supposedly bipartisan foreign policy during the Cold War—had flirted with internationalism since the 1920s but did not commit himself to an internationalist foreign policy until after World War II. Indeed, Vandenberg offered a careful analysis of his internationalism beginning in the 1920s. Vandenberg recognized the value of international alliances in the postwar world but still lauded American exceptionalism and the importance of nation-states. Whereas the "wrong kind of 'internationalism' is an effort to submerge 'nationalisms' beneath a political super-sovereignty which futilely attempts to rely upon international force instead of international conscience," the "right kind of 'internationalism'" is a mutually respected "justice" between sovereign "nationalities." Vandenberg also favored a World Court and alliances with countries that "do not have to become world vassals in order to deal justly with each other and to be scrupulous in their engagements." Distorting the lessons of American imperialism in Latin America, internationalism could not encompass the "Far Eastern brown races" as they would not be welcomed "into our own unrestricted citizenship." But Vandenberg repudiated restraint in the postwar environment. "Actual national isolation is a ridiculous anomaly in this day when pioneering genius has put the veritable wings of the morning upon world communication and world contacts. There is no such thing as isolation."[46]

When Vandenberg became chairman of the Senate Foreign Relations Committee in 1947 (the first Republican to become chairman in nearly fifteen years), he worked with Truman to solidify an internationalist foreign policy predicated upon American primacy. Citing the horrors unleashed by World War II, Vandenberg officially renounced isolationism in a Senate speech in 1945 and quickly collaborated with Truman on the Truman Doctrine and the Marshall

Plan—much to the chagrin of some of his colleagues.[47] For crossing the aisle on foreign policy matters, Vandenberg soon received letters of criticism from his Republican right-wing constituents upset at his willingness to work with Democrats on international affairs. One critic of Vandenberg complained that because of his collaboration with Democrats on foreign policy issues, the Senator had "gone over to the New Deal body and soul." Jones Luther Risk thought Greece and Turkey were a distraction from more seminal issues. Risk wrote, "[I] cannot see why we should go in unless there is as some say a chance for Russia to take over Turkey or at least make it a communist country." Instead of singling out Turkey, "why not close in on Russia before they are able to put up any fight." Local newspapers in Michigan also lashed out at Vandenberg. Malcolm Bingay of the *Detroit Free Press* criticized the Marshall Plan as "an international W.P.A." unproven to defeat communism. He also called it a program that will surely waste "17 billions [*sic*] to fight a tottering economic system," to which Vandenberg countered with a scathing letter that defended the Marshall Plan as "a program geared toward self-help," not government handouts with impunity.[48]

Feeling that their voices went unheard in Congress, midwestern noninterventionists searched for allies among foreign policy populists. The more infamous foreign policy nationalists such as the members of the America First Party (AFP) also attacked the New Deal as communistic—but combined that message with an argument for foreign policy retrenchment to preserve nationalist policies for white Americans at home. Created by right-wing activist and Minister Gerald L. K. Smith in 1943, the AFP was an outgrowth of the America First Committee, the organizational home for foreign policy nationalists during World War II. Now that the war was over, the AFP demanded deterrence against foreign threats through expansion of the national security state. The AFP said that the United States "must remain a strong nation. We must defend our outposts. We must maintain a great Navy and a strong Army." Military strength could be assured through increased expenditures for military salaries, and "not be done by peacetime conscription. It should be done by making the pay of the soldier, the sailor, and the marines so attractive in peacetime that men whose temperaments lean toward the military will actually seek the opportunity to serve with our armed forces." Rather than loans financed by government debt, military personnel "must be paid with Constitutional money, guaranteed and underwritten by the productive capacity of our nation." The AFP therefore called for a redistribution of federal resources away from foreign aid and toward veterans' benefits. "If we cancel the Lend Lease debts of foreign nations to ourselves, it will mean a donation to foreigners of about $2,000 per American family." Instead of the forgiveness of foreign debt, "each mustered-out veteran should get 1,000 cash."[49]

The Christian Nationalist Crusade, also founded by Smith, blended evangelical Christianity, anti-Semitism, racism (particularly racist screeds over miscegenation), xenophobia, "internationalists," bankers, and elites into a nationalist worldview on foreign policy. Through his news bulletin, the *Nationalist News Service*, Smith promoted an anti-internationalist message to his followers, many of whom were from midwestern states including Missouri, Indiana, Ohio, and Nebraska, as well as Southern California—which had many transplants from the Midwest. Subscribers to the *Nationalist News Service* flocked to Smith because of his vehement anticommunism and his call to enlarge the fight against the Soviet Union after World War II. Smith thought Stalin was an expansionist despot who cared little for national sovereignty and sought to run rampant over Asia. What would eventually be termed the "domino theory" was sure to be a reality if the United States did not stop communist aggression, Smith warned. Concerned about the threat of communism in China, Smith wrote that when "Stalin takes China he will take Japan, the Philippines, and cross the Bering Strait into Alaska. He, or whoever his successor may be, in cooperation with the Communist Party in America will threaten the very future existence of our Christian nation." The defeat of communism could only be realized by an "America First" foreign policy that disregarded the concerns of the international community in favor of American nationalism. The United Nations could not be trusted to lead the world in the defeat of communism.

Moreover, many of the United Nations' members were countries of color that Smith believed could not govern themselves, let alone determine the fate of the free world.[50]

But right-wing nationalist groups like the Allied Patriotic Society (APS) and the Christian Nationalist Crusade had difficulty selling American nationalism to a large bloc of Americans after 1945. The policy platforms of the AFP demonstrated the growth (and limits) of right-wing noninterventionism after World War II. After the bombing of Pearl Harbor, the APS wanted to take back its earlier opposition to American entry into the war. The APS now expressed its "regrets on unpreparedness" as its members had "surprise and disgust for failure at Pearl Harbor and a <u>strong</u> feeling that we have <u>not</u> yet had <u>all</u> the Truth." The war was necessary, and needed to be won by the allied powers, but this required more government monies for America's military. Instead of continued social programs, APS members wanted federal dollars for defense. In one meeting, it was noted that there were "many complaints on reckless spending for the idle instead of on <u>work</u> for <u>defense</u>." The APS assumed that the federal government's spending on domestic programs had cost the United States dearly in the early months of the war. This presumption underlay their priorities for defense over all other federal responsibilities.[51]

While there was a strong nationalist ethos among the Right, Iowan and former vice president Henry Wallace personified an anti-imperialist tradition on the Left. Postwar progressives identified with Wallace, who offered early criticism of what he called America's "Get tough with Russia" policy. To Wallace, the Cold War drained resources from important domestic programs and led to an ominous standoff between the United States and the Soviet Union. In an article written for the *New Republic* in 1946, Wallace presciently discussed the coming arms race between the superpowers. If the United States continued its military buildup, Wallace argued, the results would be devastating in an age of atomic weapons. American belligerence toward the Soviet Union will mean the "Russians will redouble their efforts to manufacture bombs, and they also may decide to expand their 'security zone' in a serious way." To prevent nuclear Armageddon, U.S.

policy makers needed to empathize with the Soviets and engage them in diplomacy.[52]

As the nominee for the Progressive Party during the 1948 presidential campaign, Wallace amassed more than a few followers for his assessment of the Cold War. Running to the left of Truman, Wallace offered an alternative to massive military spending in the name of anticommunism. His foreign policy consisted of a "one world" program premised not simply on coexistence, but also on cooperation with the Soviet Union on issues such as nuclear energy and trade— his foreign policy offering a vision of free trade combined with redistributive justice and government-backed economy security. As a prominent supporter of the UN, Wallace felt the organization could solidify justice abroad through collective diplomacy: the UN could unite the particularistic demands of countries in a singular body. This is while Wallace also embraced racial justice in the United States, calling for an end to Jim Crow segregation and restrictions to black voting, as well as a working-class agenda that freed American labor from a militarized economy.[53]

Much of Wallace's support came from Popular Front communists, the socialist-leaning American Labor Party, radical members of labor unions, white southern progressives, and farm groups in the Midwest. Several rank-and-file workers also backed Wallace, causing rifts between pro-Wallace union members and the national leadership that endorsed Truman from unions such as the Electrical Workers Union, the Fur and Leather Workers Union, and the Farm Equipment Workers. In his speeches on foreign policy, Wallace pulled few punches in attacking the moneyed interests that he believed had much to gain from the Cold War. Wallace applied the attack on "merchants of death" in the 1920s to the context of the Cold War, arguing that the "Wall Street war group" that profited personally and financially from the Cold War ran the Truman administration.[54] The Cold War was a "crisis" created from "willful men with private interests [who] are dictating our foreign policy. Their interest is profits, not people."[55]

Wallace kept close associations with communists and radicals throughout his campaign, which ultimately doomed his presidential run. Wallace's ties to the radical Left deterred endorsements from mainstream labor organizations (such as the CIO) and Democratic officials. The American Federation of Labor (AFL) called Wallace a "front, spokesman, and apologist" for communism, while Walter Reuther readied his membership to take "on Wallace and his Joe Stalin associates."[56] Red baited by Truman, his supporters, and Republicans for his associations and connections with communists at home and abroad, Wallace was painted as a patsy for the Soviet Union. Anticommunism tainted Wallace's insurgence against the Cold War, preventing his third-party candidacy from gaining momentum outside of radical circles. Wallace ended up with a little over one million votes, in fourth place behind Strom Thurmond's States Rights Party.

But Wallace's holistic plan for a postwar foreign policy, one that rejected anticommunism and prioritized equality at home and abroad, resonated within left-wing circles beyond his campaign—and lifetime. As the historian Michael Kazin has argued, Wallace was "the last, best opportunity to reverse" the Cold War Red Scare prior to the 1950s; he personified the potential for an enduring alternative to anticommunism as the basis for postwar liberalism.[57] Wallace's ambitious anti–Cold War agenda rejected the conflation of a welfare and warfare state, positioned economic and racial justice as the priority for American decision-making, and offered an internationalist foreign policy premised on cooperation, rather than competition through containment. This political program inspired future generations of leftists. As we shall see in later chapters, Wallace's vision would later be taken up by left-wing activists looking to roll back relentless military spending, pursue a policy of restraint with the Soviet Union, and denuclearize and demilitarize American foreign policy in the 1960s and '70s.

Moreover, Wallace's campaign offered an expansive vision for coalition building beyond the structures of the Cold War national security state. His "Gideon's Army" of leftist activists, socialists, and communists were denigrated in their time, but their composition as a set of political actors demonstrated the types of coalitions that could have been built outside a framework of Cold War anticommunism.

True, Wallace's coalition might have been too tenuous—it lacked the electoral potency to pull off even a modest win at the ballot box—but in its small scale it nevertheless represented an archetype of what was possible but never realized due to the dominance and durability of the Cold War (its politics and economics) over Americans' lives.

* * *

Wallace could be bombastic and unspecific in his criticisms of American foreign policy—"the Wall Street gang in Washington," for instance—but he was correct in stating that the Cold War spawned assorted financial dependents. Just as support for Cold War foreign policy united Democrats and Republicans, the political economy of defense spending united groups of people normally at odds with one another and offered remuneration to an array of actors. Military officials, business executives, local politicians, labor leaders, and unemployed factory workers realized the defense economy's resources could serve their respective ends.[58]

The United States' entry into the Korean War in September 1950, following the invasion of South Korea by North Korean forces, amplified collaborations between such individuals, spurring the growth of the Cold War coalition into the latter half of the 1950s. The Korean War solidified the permanence of the Cold War conflict (and anticommunism), as it demonstrated that communism represented an existential threat to the world and needed to be defeated. Moreover, the Korean War unleashed a patriotic fervor that further constrained and suppressed previous critics of the Cold War (like Henry Wallace)—one that enhanced Republican support for the warfare state and pressed Democrats to defend their anticommunist credentials. The war also provided the political means for the public to envision the warfare state as a welfare state in perpetuity—the war created the political imagination needed for members of the Cold War coalition to *expect* the perpetuation of the warfare state, rather than merely *anticipate* its continued support.

The outbreak of war in North Korea also lent momentum to voices promoting military Keynesianism following the collapse of Truman's

Fair Deal agenda and the rising threat of communism. Hawkish voices in the Pentagon (such as Secretary of the Navy John Sullivan, who argued for a "program of publicity" that could "prepare the American people for war") were clamoring for defense increases in the months leading up to the war; but Truman held steadfast against Sullivan and others in Washington "who would like to go back to a war footing." Korea changed the nature of the foreign policy discussion; it proved that a defense buildup was necessary—and therefore imminent. The 1950 publication of NSC-68, which called for unprecedented military spending to meet the threat of communism, seemed to be another innocuous policy document in the months before the war. But the arguments of its authors (Secretary of State Dean Acheson and the head of the Policy Planning Staff, Paul Nitze) were legitimized by the North's invasion of the South.[59]

As defense spending climbed to near 15 percent of GDP to meet the demand for war mobilization, the Korean War provided the impetus for the 1950 Defense Production Act (DPA)—which allowed the federal government to mobilize the economy for war through regulation of the private market and takeover of industrial production.[60] Despite grumblings among fiscal conservatives that the DPA represented a Fair Deal in disguise—given that portions "of the DPA were nearly identical to passages of Fair Deal planning bills that had failed to pass in 1949," according to historian Tim Barker—a broad consensus of Democrats and Republicans were in favor of the act.[61] The bill passed the Senate by a vote of 85–3 and the House by a vote of 383–12. The "yea" votes for the DPA included the bloc of Senate Republicans normally critical of massive defense budgets, including Taft and Wherry—even though the DPA gave powers to the government to intervene in the economy in ways unseen since World War II. Under the act, the government could control prices, build defense plants, regulate credit, and streamline resources and products for manufacturing, all of which meant a possible "nationalization of the economy."[62] While the pressure to appear to be patriotic supporters of the war was a factor in supporting the bill, Republicans also saw the potential benefit defense production had for their constituents.

The Illinois Democrat and Senate majority leader Scott Lucas felt that lawmakers were "proposing amendments, trying to protect some particular commodity" within the legislation, to which Republican John Williams of Delaware responded that if such amendments had "been enforced during the last war, we would have saved the Government or the farmers of the Del-Mar Peninsula, along more than $10,0000,000." Williams was just making sure that the DPA was going "to protect the farmer" under his jurisdiction.[63]

The DPA remilitarized the American economy to levels unseen since World War II. In a report also issued by the NSRB, the agency stated that one of the primary goals of the DPA of 1950 was an "expansion of the economy as a desirable characteristic of the mobilization effort." A memorandum to Stuart Symington from the NSRB implied that a thriving defense economy could create opportunities for growth in the economy. Symington understood the administration's opinion to be "that current and contemplated national security programs will be of such magnitude as to require a measure of control upon the economy, but not of such magnitude as to prevent, concurrent with defense production, an expansion of the over-all economy." But in the rush to place its citizens and economy on a wartime footing, Symington wrote that the United States "cannot lose sight, however, of the vital importance of maintaining the economy of this country on a stable and secure basis. If in allotting help to others [through humanitarian aid] we create weakness in our own economy, then all our aims and objectives will be lost; and such an occurrence here will act as a negative catalytic agent throughout the free world." The United States must be cautious as "defense spending increases monetary purchasing power, while at the same time it fails to increase the amount of goods available for sale to the public." While the NSRB called for a "more Spartan existence," it continued to encourage economic growth through militarization.[64]

Alongside the DPA, additional federal mandates such Defense Manpower No. 1 and Defense Manpower No. 4—whose goal was "to bring defense work to the worker"—brought requests for defense contracts from multiple sources. Along with Representatives Nixon and Knowland, the AFL worked to use the military-industrial complex to aid economically depressed areas. The AFL specifically hoped Defense Manpower No. 4 could resuscitate the textile industry in New England after companies moved to the South in search of cheaper land.[65] Business executives also wondered how they could receive defense contracts from the war effort. Corporate representatives from Merck & Co., for instance, asked Truman officials if there was anything "relative to the application of Defense Manpower Policy No. 4 to the drug and pharmaceutical industry."[66]

The Korean War, like the New Deal and World War II, offered economic stimulus through growth liberalism—or military Keynesianism. Like Franklin Roosevelt in the 1930s, Harry Truman used national defense as a means toward full employment. In 1952, Truman urged the Council of Economic Advisors (CEA) to view defense production within the framework of other public works projects that provided federal relief and employment to Americans. Suggestions were made to the CEA to put forward a "work program" that would create "'Development and Welfare Programs' in the areas of natural resources (water, land) transportation infrastructure, health (hospitals, medical research centers), education (new schools, scholarships, teaching training) social security and welfare ("possible extensions of coverage to additional persons"), and finally, atomic energy, housing, veterans programs ("housing credit, welfare, and transfer payments"). The CEA commented that these types of "programs . . . are equally essential for defense and for nondefense purposes" as the organization should not operate with the presumption "that simply because budget categories separate defense from other expenditures, we are therefore barred from other approaches which recognize that most so-called nondefense development programs are vital to long-range security. A particular power dam, training program, public health item, or highway may, for example, be more necessary for defense than a particular military expenditure."[67]

The Korean War thus continued the precedent set by the New Deal and World War II for the warfare state to function as a welfare state. Even as the Truman administration deliberately distributed defense contracts to aid industries and workers, it was careful to avoid the claim that they intentionally marginalized the private sector through a government-directed economy. Defense spending, Truman officials assured the public, aligned with the needs of private business, not overrode them. Administration officials claimed that the Korean War revived the private-public alliances the government established during World War II without eroding the power of corporate capitalism.[68]

CEA head Leon Keyserling, a proponent of full employment through national security spending, was forced to refute charges in the months following the Korean War that he believed the defense economy was needed to keep the economy growing and employment levels high. He told the now Senator Stuart Symington he did not think that "a tapering off of defense spending would necessarily bring hard times." Keyserling went on to say that "on grounds of national security I favor an increase rather than a decrease in defense spending, but I do not do this on the ground that a decrease would be inconsistent with a healthy economy. I believe that we can have a healthy economy either with a decrease or an increase in defense spending, and that the level of such spending should be decided on grounds of national security and world conditions." Keyserling said he had "the profound conviction as a Democrat that there is high political desirability in reformulating and popularizing a very different approach to the relationship between Federal spending and economic prosperity from that traditionally voiced by or at least attributed to the New Deal and the Fair Deal." Keyserling still self-identified as a New Deal Democrat "who does not deviate in the slightest from the objectives and general philosophy of the New Deal and the Fair Deal," but he thought the Cold War was a new era in which liberals "should learn from experience and adjust to the present and the future instead of living in the past."[69]

Keyserling's conclusions rested on a presumption that defense work during the Korean War was a temporary means of employment and economic stimulus—but the Americans who sought such work from the Truman administration did not view it as impermanent.

They saw it as a source of reliable income to support themselves and their families for the near future. The defeat of the Fair Deal—and its implications for an expanded social safety net for unemployed, aged, and infirm workers in the United States—combined with the urgency of war, made Americans turn to the national security state as a source of employment. Keyserling's reservations about the defense economy aside, the public welcomed the employment opportunities the war created. As pleas from the unemployed poured into the White House, rising defense production during the Korean War became an easy but temporary means of adding Americans to payrolls. Wartime employment automatically dismissed previous concerns over the size of the federal budget, providing employment to a total of four million Americans during the Korean War—facilitated by an increase in defense spending by 300 percent. Cold War military spending came with expectations that the federal government would provide help to unemployed or underworked Americans during wartime.

The sudden injection of federal dollars into the economy to fight the war provided an additional stimulus to the postwar recovery, one that revivified Americans' positive feelings toward the defense economy during the war years—and brought fresh memories of prosperous times rushing back. Coming only five years after World War II, the remilitarization of the economy to fight the Korean War offered hope for continued prosperity for Americans sent to the unemployment lines by demobilization. For instance, Republic Aviation, with its twenty-two thousand workers, became the largest employer on Long Island, and "the workhorse of Korea," in the words of the local press; and 40 percent of residents in Levittown, the quintessential blue-collar American suburb, found work in defense. Reading Long Island newspapers during the Korean War, one would think there was perpetual prosperity in defense, that endless economic growth was inevitable.[70]

But the wartime defense buildup during the Korean War disguised long-term trends in the American defense economy, ones that were detrimental to industrial areas in the Midwest and Northeast and led to greater inequality within the Cold War economy. As Ann Markusen has demonstrated, "The 1950s were years of massive buildup of missile and space systems, catapulting the Air Force to a prominence it never subsequently lost." The hegemony of the Air Force after 1950—"solidly a western service," according to Markusen—led to the precipitous decline of heavy machinery produced during World War II (ships, tanks, and automotive vehicles, made by blue-collar labor in midwestern states). This meant that states like Michigan, the home state of both Walter Reuther and Gerald Ford, received shrinking portions of the defense pie, as contracts for Cold War weapons increasingly went to the Sunbelt South. States like Texas increased their share of defense contracts by 10 percent, while California became the largest recipient of prime defense contracts with 21 total percent. After 1952, Sunbelt states like California, Texas, and Georgia saw their number of prime contracts by the Department of Defense nearly double by the 1980s, while Mid-Atlantic and east-north-central states saw their contracts cut in more than half.[71] This is while Ohio, Michigan, Illinois, and Indiana all saw their numbers drop to the point that none of these states could be found in the list of top ten recipients of defense contracts. Indeed, defense contracts to midwestern companies declined by nearly 75 percent from 1951 to 1984.[72]

However, when demobilization and deindustrialization crept into the industrial landscape of midwestern cities like Detroit during the 1950s due to capital flight, automation, and job losses—and as auto plants in the Midwest began to lay off workers—workers still turned to the war economy for relief—and wages. John Sonnenberg from Michigan wrote to his congressman Clare Hoffman in 1954 for help in "alleviating the critical unemployment here" as a Kaiser Motors plant in Detroit where he worked was scheduled to close within the following few months. Sonnenberg was sure that "there MUST be a Defense contract which needs to be filled by experienced, capable men and, with your sympathetic understanding of our problem and what it means to the moral [sic] of Michigan, we are sure you will do whatever is necessary to correct this condition." William Zizzi also risked losing his job after over twenty years of employment with Packard Motor Car Co. located in Michigan. Zizzi's company was responsible for building a variety of products for the government during wartime including motors for PT boats and a jet motor for Rolls Royce. Zizzi and his fellow "workers are proud of our past performance" and it was for this reason that he also requested Hoffman "to do all in your power to see to it that our Gov't executives provide us with some kind of defense work until such time that we can get back on our feet in the auto industry. We pray that you face up to this enormous task."[73]

Workers like Zizzi and Sonnenberg adopted the ethos of New Deal and wartime job creation through national security spending, but they were not alone. Other residents of states in the Midwest proved just as desperate for defense jobs given the declining manufacturing sector and the absence of wartime work. Edward Wren was one of these Americans who looked to the defense industry for work, having been turned away from many other jobs. Wren was a victim of ageism; he was consistently passed over for jobs by younger workers. But in 1950, Wren argued the federal government should provide him one, as it had done for other Americans in the recent past. Wren said he "never dreamed that such a cockeyed era would arrive in this country when our government would approve a pension plan that would compel industry to discriminate against men over forty years of age in securing a job, and this unquestionably effects [sic] the white collar [worker] more than the skilled laborer. Billions of dollars have been given and are still being given to help Europeans—billions to subsidize farmers, industries, etc., in fact just recently one hundred and twenty five [sic] million dollars" was provided to Argentina "who did everything in their power to help Germany during the last war. Not the slightest effort however is being made to assist in any way the downtrodden white collar man in securing a job and that's what he wants and nothing more." Wren asked what "this forgotten man" will do to earn an income before he can qualify for a pension.[74] Another out-of-work American, Denver M. Christy from Jasonville, Indiana, sought work at the Crane Naval Ammunition Depot in Crane, Indiana, during the Korean War. Christy was unable to work in the past, having been diagnosed with arthritis for twenty-four years, and had "a stiff hip which bars him from occupational insurance." But even though Christy now felt "perfectly healthy and has had no pain," he still could not find work. The Crane Naval plant was his last hope since he did "not want relief."[75]

Defense workers on the East Coast, a region concentrated in defense manufacturing and heavy aircraft production, faced similar problems. J. Willard Washington from Baltimore made similar comments to his midwestern counterparts. Washington was upset over the large number of unemployed workers in Baltimore, which he said was close to sixty-five thousand residents. To resolve this crisis in local unemployment, Truman should "halt extravagant spending abroad and bring back the C.C.C. [Civilian Conservation Corps]" on a wartime footing. John C. Wolf from Pennsylvania felt the federal government discriminated against his state in awarding shipbuilding and other defense contracts. According to him, New York State and areas on the West Coast were awarded more work by the federal government. Wolf wrote to President Truman to express his thoughts "in the interest of my fellow shipyard worker's [sic] and in the interest of National Security." Wolf then complained that several workers at Sun Shipbuilding Yard in Chester, Pennsylvania, had been laid off in recent months, some with "16 to 18 year's [sic] of Service." This was even though the "shipyard worker's [sic] were a great as-set [sic]to the Nation and to the World in World War 1 and 2." Wolf concluded his letter by pleading with Truman to, "Please investigate as to why we don't get Defense work or Ships to Build."[76]

Workers in the Pacific Northwest also pleaded with their representatives to bring more defense jobs into the area. During the Korean War, defense jobs continued to be an attractive alternative to employment in other industries. One resident of Bellingham, Washington, and another from Lynden, wrote to Congressman Henry Jackson for his help in acquiring a job working in defense in 1951. They wanted to work at "Boeing's in Seattle as guards" to escape the hardships of farming wheat and corn without receiving enough compensation to support their families. "We have family enough to handle the two farms," Jackson's constituents noted, "but the two farms cannot support us all."[77] Jackson promptly wrote to a Boeing executive on their behalf, saying he "would appreciate your giving them every proper consideration." Workers in the Pacific Northwest also echoed John C. Wolf's sentiments that defense contracting was a zero-sum game—that a few communities were benefiting from defense contracts while much of the country suffered. One shipyard worker reported rumors that "five [defense contracts] have been awarded to a shipyard in Bath, Maine; five to Sturgeon Bay in the Great Lakes; [and] five to Ingalls Shipbuilding in the Gulf area," all totaling approximately $700 million dollars. He was at an utter "loss to understand why the Pacific coast has been completely disregarded and particularly the Seattle area" for these defense contracts, as the region has the "facilities and manpower to do this work."[78]

Defense cuts in the Northeast and Midwest, and the shift to missile defense systems and military technology, primarily affected unskilled, blue-collar workers, particularly workers of color. As mobilization for the Korean War transferred defense production to the South at the expense of the Midwest and Northeast, it led to job layoffs for working-class African Americans—but higher salaries for predominantly middle- and upper-class whites. With companies like Grumman (based on Long Island), where 88 percent of the black workforce was in blue-collar occupations, the loss of defense jobs from the Mid-Atlantic and Midwest was disastrous. In Detroit, after defense contracts exited the region, blacks faced a 15.9 percent unemployment rate, compared with 5.8 percent for whites.[79] Those companies that did hire blacks looked to fill occupations in management and professional, skilled jobs—which primarily went to whites. Between 1953 and 1954, DuPont (based in Wilmington, Delaware) made a concerted effort to hire more black workers at a nuclear plant in South Carolina, including three black chemists, eight lab technicians, and a few clerical positions; but only five hundred black employees were represented in a workforce totaling eight thousand. Most blacks remained in unskilled jobs in the defense industry, but those jobs dwindled in number as manufacturing positions were replaced by mechanization or were outsourced to subcontractors.[80] The decline of blue-collar defense jobs left African Americans with few available occupations besides low-wage work after the 1950s. Indeed, facing widespread employment discrimination, which barred blacks' reentry into the defense workforce after World War II, black defense workers were often forced take low-wage jobs in greater numbers after defense jobs went to the South—or disappeared altogether. For instance, after a massive layoff within the Long Island defense workforce in 1957, both black and white working-class workers increasingly took jobs in retail and construction or as cab drivers—jobs that paid 10 percent less annually, and barely paid the bills. After fleeing farming and service jobs in the 1940s that, in the words of one defense worker, "paid practically nothing," the newly unemployed had no recourse put to return to such jobs.[81]

As Democratic and Republican members of Congress from the Northeast and Midwest watched the epicenter of the defense economy shift from the Rust Belt to the Sunbelt, they acted to protect their constituents from job losses. In 1951, Matthew J. Connelly of Pennsylvania wrote to Representative Daniel Flood about the "acute unemployment" in the Wilkes-Barre-Hazelton area, part of Flood's district. Flood prudently replied to Connelly, telling him, "I want you to know that the people and the leaders of the community are doing their share to alleviate the situation and are not simply sitting back and crying for Federal help. Every possible effort is being made locally to do our bit to help solve this problem, but as you are aware, it is of such a nature and magnitude that it is physically impossible for the solution to be brought about by local effort alone." In a statement on the House floor, Flood decried the inadequacy of the federal government's efforts to resolve chronic unemployment through wartime spending for his constituents. "War plants, installations, and war contracts of all descriptions are being channeled into congested, seriously congested, defense areas where there is a need for manpower, but in my area there is not work," Flood said. "This is a deplorable economic waste. The most valuable asset of the Nation is its manpower, and here I cite you a case of where vital and essential and badly needed workers stand idle, yet eager for work and to participate in the defense effort."[82]

Flood was not alone among northeastern congressional representatives who panicked over the decline of military employment in
their districts. Rapid declines in military spending led to increased
unemployment in localities and districts dominated by defense
contractors—which led members of Congress to lose their seats in
an election year. Republicans (and Democrats) who represented
Long Island, New York, for instance, knew this well. In the Second
District, Democrats did not have an extended presence in New York
until after Vietnam and Watergate. But this was not the case in the
neighboring First District. Democrats and moderate Republicans, or
"Rockefeller Republicans" (a term coined to distinguish voters who
favored New York governor Nelson Rockefeller), governed the First
District of New York—home of defense contractors Grumman and
Republic. In 1950, New Deal Democrat Ernest Greenwood won the
district by beating out Republican incumbent W. Kingsland Macy by
135 votes. After his ouster two years later, for much of the 1950s, the
First District was represented by Stuyvesant Wainwright, a moderate Republican demonized as a "New Deal Republican" by his right-
wing opponents. When Wainwright lost in 1960 to Democrat Otis
Pike, Pike went on to represent the First District until 1978, when
prominent House Democrats lost their seats—Pike, however, retired.
What each representative had in common—either Democrat or
Republican—was their strong support for defense spending when
it furthered the interests of their constituents. Democrat Otis Pike
was such a dedicated backer of Grumman that he frequently tussled
with the Department of Defense when it cut contracts to Grumman
to build more airplanes during the 1960s. The continuity between
Republican and Democratic officials in terms of their support for
defense industries in their districts indicates that ideology and interests coincided in ways that did not categorically fit into a bipolar paradigm of American politics. In fact, the history of electoral politics
during the Cold War demonstrates how the threat of defense cuts
intensified a political consensus that the military-industrial complex
was essential to the survival of America's economic, not just national
security, interests.[83]

The public's commitment to the defense economy for employment therefore obligated politicians (whether Democrat or Republican) to finance the military-industrial complex as a jobs program, or face electoral defeat. In local and state elections throughout Ohio and Pennsylvania, Republicans continued to dominate House districts, despite the demilitarization of the Midwest: an indication that the Republican Party made peace with the national security state while still critiquing the New Deal state. Republicans in Ohio kept their seats in the 1950s in most districts, including the First, Second, and Third Districts (which included Columbus). Democrats like Flood, however, lost their jobs in 1952 partly due to the declining defense work, while other Democratic representatives in Pennsylvania, like William Barrett of the First District (which comprised south Philadelphia) held their seats into the 1970s.

Men like Washington senator Henry Jackson stayed in office having learned these lessons early. Jackson earned the reputation of being the "senator from Boeing" during the 1950s, but he did so at a time when Republicans held every House district in Washington from 1952 to 1960. Given his minority status in a predominantly Republican state, Jackson's commitment to the national security state provides evidence of his political savviness, not just an ideological commitment to anticommunism. Jackson was surely a Cold War liberal, but he was also a politician who sought to ensure his constituents were pleased with his performance on economic issues for Washingtonians, preventing his ouster from the Senate—as his Republican colleagues noted.[84]

Jackson's counterpart in the South was the Democratic representative Mendell Rivers (aka "Rivers Delivers"). The Korean War established Rivers as the personification of the South's postwar dependency on the military for economic gain—and how a parochial desire for increased defense spending aligned with Cold War anticommunism. A dedicated segregationist and anticommunist, Rivers came out in support of a "fighting force in readiness" a month after North Korea invaded South Korea and openly wished Truman would "threaten North Korea with an atomic bomb." As a shrewd, productive politician—and a member of the House Armed Services Committee—Rivers put his anticommunism into legislative actions for his constituents after 1950. With defense funds increasingly pouring into the Sunbelt, Rivers saw the potential gains for his political seat and his constituents, creating several military bases and providing comfortable investment opportunities for Lockheed Martin and McDonnell Douglas. With defense spending employing one out of every ten workers by the 1960s, Rivers made sure South Carolina shared in the benefits. By some estimations, Rivers brought enough defense funds into his state to employ one-third of its residents. Even as the Sunbelt South experienced an economic boost from increased defense contracts (from 7 to 15 percent) after the Korean War, its residents still lobbied for more defense funds, wedding southern voters to the Cold War coalition.[85]

Rivers also exemplified how the diversion of federal resources away from the Northeast and Midwest and into the South, Southwest, and West Coast shaped the Republican Party, as power in the GOP swung away from noninterventionist midwesterners to southern Republicans—many of whom were Democrats before the 1960s. Republicans had no local political operation of significance to speak of in the South prior to the 1960s, but the GOP made inroads into presidential politics—where national defense issues were addressed in greater volume—during the 1952 election. Indeed, Eisenhower picked up votes in the Black Belt in 1952, and as historian Kari Fredrickson has noted, in states like Georgia, South Carolina, and Mississippi, "there was a strong correlation between counties that supported the Dixiecrats and those that endorsed Eisenhower." Eisenhower also won Florida, Tennessee, Texas, and Virginia, states that had been Democratic strongholds since the Civil War.[86]

The nationalization of the Cold War defense economy during the Korean War eroded the solid Democratic South—and laid the groundwork for the political realignment to come in the 1960s. A 1952 advertisement from the North Carolina Citizens for Eisenhower summed up the new relationship between the South and the Cold War defense industry—and how the electoral realignment of the

South mobilized voters into the Cold War coalition. The political ad asked voters in the state to "Help the South Rise above Political Tyranny" by repudiating the Democratic Party, since it was now controlled by "Northern City Bosses, Crooked Politicians and Radical College Professors." The group warned defense workers in the South that if Democrat Adlai Stevenson was elected to the presidency in 1952, it would mean significant losses in employment to the region, since Stevenson supposedly favored giving more defense contracts to the North to divert jobs and employment from the South, allowing the government to "take bread out of your child's mouth and send it to the North." With bold headlines such as "Negro Bosses in the Mill if Stevenson Elected" and "White Workers Beware of Democrat F.E.P.C. Plants," the Republican organization circulated pamphlets that used racism to scare southern whites into thinking blacks would take over their defense jobs. Once African Americans experienced economic gains from the war economy (giving them social and economic upward mobility through skilled jobs), southern whites mounted resistance against efforts to integrate defense work to ensure that the financial gains of federal employment went to whites. Southern whites increasingly thought the Republican Party would safeguard their racial and economic interests, as it would protect defense jobs for whites and "allow each state to work out its own solution to the Negro question." As southerners benefited more from defense contracts, they became more protective of their defense jobs and thus more willing to support racist policies to keep blacks out of the defense workforce.[87] This was while investment in Cold War technology allowed Jim Crow employment policies to invade federal contracting in the South.[88]

And as the Sunbelt defense economy prospered alongside the decline of the industrial Midwest, dependents of the defense economy (in both regions) grew further committed to the national security state. Seeing little option than to continue requesting more federal defense dollars, the industrial North and the Sunbelt South demanded—indeed, expected—federal assistance from defense spending. Requests from members of the Cold War coalition to

create jobs and resolve economic problems through military spending coincided with the expansion and contraction of the defense
industry across diverse areas of the country. By 1957, the *New York
Times* wrote that the "motor City can no longer claim to be the arsenal of democracy," as a rapid "shift in emphasis in defense production since the Korean war has robbed Detroit and Michigan of the
proud title." California now led the country in defense contracts, the
site of "aircraft, guided missiles and electronic products, rather than
military trucks and wheeled vehicles—Michigan's specialty." While
Detroit was battered by the defense cutbacks, Los Angeles saw "no
real distress" from post-Korea demobilization. Labor leaders in the
UAW predicted the transfer of defense jobs to the Sunbelt would
cause "serious trouble" for Detroit workers and urged elected officials
to end layoffs in the defense industry. The UAW warned that it was
"not the time to retrench" American military production but to "cast
off the coat of complacency and act with greater vigor and decision."
The Soviet Union presented an existential threat to the United States,
the UAW stated, and cutting back on Cold War defense spending was
therefore "socially irresponsible and economically questionable."[89]

* * *

The remaking of American democracy during the early Cold War—
the broad public acceptance of military Keynesianism, along with the
dominance of anticommunism by both political parties—weakened
support for anti-interventionism and antimilitarism within the body
politic. The confluence of these historical forces deterred a broader
social democratic politics in the United States—the constant fight
for jobs in the absence of a peacetime employment economy, coupled with the totalizing, ideological threat of communism, derailed
and discouraged a politics beyond the warfare state. The codification
of the defense economy as an engine of employment, as the basis
for federal job growth, thus coincided with the marginalization of
anti-interventionism in the political system, making the Cold War
an entity that Americans at the local and national level would be
beholden to for the next fifty years.

Due to the dominance of prodefense, internationalist voices in the Republican Party by the Korean War, dedicated noninterventionists within the Right like Robert Taft and Kenneth Wherry acquiesced, and at times embraced, the notion that the Cold War state was a structural necessity to defeat communism. Right-wing activist Phyllis Schlafly, who held isolationist tendencies prior to Korea, felt that the war was a conflict worth fighting, but that it should have been done through a congressional declaration of war, rather than a decision reached by the UN Security Council. Schlafly saw the Korean War as empirical proof of communism's march to predominance: the war proved the persistent threat of global communism. As her biographer Donald T. Critchlow has noted, Schlafly justified increases to the defense budget not only to roll back communism in Korea, but also because a "strong defense was necessary to prevent war with the Soviet Union, the main enemy that faced the nation."[90] This is while the Old Right isolationist Frank Chodorov, who ran the libertarian journal the *Freeman*, argued that the U.S. government should reallocate spending on social welfare programs to add another $2 billion in defense spending for the war in Korea and place one million Americans "on the public payroll . . . [to] be put on the military assembly line."[91]

Indeed, the Korean War proved problematic for Taft, the most famous midwestern Republican "isolationist." Taft felt the pressure of an interventionist public during his remaining years in the Senate. Taft's gravitation toward militarism was apparent during the 1952 campaign, when he began to make statements like "I feel that Russia is far more of a threat to the security of the United States than Hitler in Germany ever was." Taft also criticized Truman for his unwillingness to assist nationalist leader of China, Chiang Kai-Shek. "I only insist that we apply to Asia the same basic policy which we apply to Europe," Taft stated. Taft accused Truman of leaving Korea unprotected from communist aggression, as the president evacuated "all troops from Korea and announced that they would not undertake to defend Korea by the use of American soldiers." This left Korea exposed to "complete domination of Korea by the Russian Communists" which now poses "a threat to the security of Japan." Truman therefore "failed to arm the South Koreans with modern weapons" to defend themselves.[92] Taft made these comments after Cold War Democrats, seeking to depose Taft of his Senate seat in 1950, claimed, "Taft votes the Communist line on foreign policy matters. Yes sir, every time Congress was asked to shell out money to fight Communism, Taft was against it. You can take his votes against the Marshall Plan, the arms assistance program—and it fits exactly what the *Daily Worker* approves."[93] One confidant of Truman, Robert Holiday, said that Taft vacillated on national defense issues in 1952 for "when Harry ordered the troops into Korea, he and MacArthur agreed that it was the greatest thing that had been done in 100 years for peace, and now they want to jump Harry for it."[94]

Considering the hard-line stance taken by Taft as a presidential candidate, it is a misnomer to label him a strict isolationist by the early 1950s. Opponents of an internationalist foreign policy like Taft did not target the fight against communism in its concept, but in its design. By this time, Taft had moved away from his earlier skepticism of the Cold War. On the campaign trail, Taft was not wholly against an interventionist foreign policy and a large defense budget to support that foreign policy, but he was opposed to the scope of such a strategy.[95] Taft proved reluctant to repudiate the national security state after Korea, telling a favorable audience in Dayton, Ohio, in 1950 that "because of the Administration's strong Communist sympathies, which apparently existed in the Administration before and about the time of the Yalta Conference, we have placed Russia in a commanding position in Europe from which they threaten the security of Western Europe, and a commanding position in China from which they threaten the security of the Far East." The only way to deal with these circumstances is "to build up armed forces sufficient to make it absolutely certain that Russia cannot gain a position from which they might threaten the security of the United States."[96] Indeed, when one considers Taft's policy in Asia during the Korean War, Taft was more interventionist than Cold War Democrats. Taft now accepted elements of the domino theory, collective security, nuclear deterrence, and the policy of containment. Taft said in an article in 1952 that his major concern was that few policy makers "have worked out a comprehensive plan for the application of this strategy [of containment], or any coordinated use of the many policies necessary to carry it out." The Truman administration must pay attention to the fiscal constraints to "our economic and manpower capacity, and . . . we must be selective and restrained in determining the extent to which we can carry out our basic strategy."[97]

But while Taft liked to criticize Democrats for lacking a coherent and well-constructed foreign policy strategy, he suffered from the same flaw. Republicans like Taft wanted a restrained defense budget yet at the same time sought to extirpate communism from the globe; they requested tax cuts for defense corporations but wanted further appropriations for military projects and America's global empire. The Korean War made men like Taft into cheerleaders for increased defense spending, unable to reconcile a fiscal conservatism with an ideology premised on the extirpation of global communism.

When Taft died in 1953 (and as other noninterventionists died or left Congress in the 1950s), conservative critics of the military-industrial complex remained in small corners of right-wing magazines and think tanks promoting a nationalist foreign policy—one often combined with racist and xenophobic overtones. Ex–New Dealer and *Human Events* contributor John T. Flynn argued that the United States has no need to fight enemies abroad when the threat to democracy is first and foremost at home. "Of course America must be prepared to resist assaults on us by a foreign power," Flynn said, but Americans "must never forget that there is an infinitely more dangerous enemy within our gates than Russia": the threat from "Communists, socialists, various editions of collectivists, One Worlders, plus a variety of economic and sectional groups interested for political or business reasons in measures that will break down and finally destroy our free society." Flynn argued that "Russia as an enemy has become almost a necessity to our government. It is the bugaboo used to frighten our people into fantastic spending of taxes and borrowed money."[98]

Texas libertarian and right-wing provocateur Dan Smoot echoed Flynn's criticisms of the federal government's efforts to justify increased defense spending, stating that "practically every major spending program of the federal government has been sold to the public with the argument that the program was necessary as a part of our struggle against communism." Americans were "quite willing to make sacrifices to fight communism," but Smoot said that the sacrifice also meant higher rates of taxation, which he was unwilling to accept. "Americans are also almost unanimous in their belief that they are enduring a crushing burden of taxation," Smoot wrote, but when they protest against higher tax rates, "they are reminded that their money is being used to maintain our national defenses against communism." This made Americans reluctant to speak out against foreign policy, creating a reverse McCarthyism since it "puts an ugly stigma on anyone who is against the President's [defense] program."[99]

But Flynn and Smoot were a dying breed among the Right. Given the significant structural transformations that occurred in the party system in the immediate postwar years, including changes to U.S. grand strategy toward the Soviet Union and the rise of an American economy whose prosperity hinged and thrived on building weapons the country supposedly needed to defeat communism, the noninterventionist Right could not exist as a formidable presence in American politics. Their eagerness to fight the Cold War through the national security state brought Republicans closer to military Keynesianism and made the GOP amenable to defense appropriations that disregarded deficits—particularly if defense spending benefited constituents of the party. In 1952, when William F. Buckley told the Right they must "accept Big Government for the duration" of the Cold War to vanquish the threat of communism, they already had.[100] With noninterventionists at the wayside, the Right looked to resolve the Cold War through levels of military spending that rivaled their previous suspicions about a militarized state. The militarization—combined with the southernization—of the Republican Party would remake its outlook toward foreign policy and its relationship to domestic politics for the next forty years.

Critics of American foreign policy on the Left faced their own dilemma in the early Cold War. During the 1940s, the anti-imperialist

tradition within leftist politics battled for the soul of American foreign policy (and democracy), only to lose out to Cold War anticommunism. The defeat of the Henry Wallace campaign in 1948, and the
failure of the anti–Cold War Left to attract a greater following—or
to weather years of red-baiting—meant that the Democratic Party
became increasingly monolithic on national defense policy, as Democrats consistently outvoted Republicans on military appropriations
up to the late 1950s. Left-wing opponents of the Cold War were there-
after concentrated in social movements outside the party system. The
antinuclear movement of the 1950s and 1960s—and groups such as
the National Committee for a Sane Nuclear Policy (SANE), formed
in 1957—were the offspring of the Wallace wing of the Democratic
Party, pressuring it to adopt policies that reduced American reliance
on military power up to the Vietnam War—which revealed the folly
and weaknesses of Cold War containment.

The partisan reordering of American politics ultimately provided
the legitimacy needed to keep the warfare state intact in the postwar
period. Once both parties spurned the social democratic elements
of Franklin Delano Roosevelt's New Deal, the national security state
became the biggest federal apparatus, responsible for delivering full
employment, economic growth, and regional development to Americans. Anticommunism, internationalism, and militarism set the foundations for American foreign policy after 1945 and reinforced Americans' material commitments to the Cold War economy. The origins of
the Cold War coalition thus lay in the bipartisan support for Cold War
anticommunism—albeit on partisan terms—as Republicans and Democrats abandoned fiscal restraint on matters of national security and
welcomed job creation and social welfare through defense spending.
When policy makers embraced Keynesianism without considering, in
the words of economist Joan Robinson, "what employment should be
for," they elevated the military-industrial complex as "a prophylactic
against stagnation," and thus, "Keynes' pleasant daydream was turned
into a nightmare of terror."[101] As a result, Cold War critics—those who
rejected the warfare state as a substitute for social democracy, or who
were ideologically opposed to a garrison state—were pushed out of

the party system. The marginalization of dissenting voices toward the military-industrial complex deprived Americans of an alternative to a warfare state, or to envisioning a federal state that provided social benefits in the absence of a militarized society.

The remaking of political culture in the years after World War II also coincided with Americans' growing financial attachment to the defense economy—and wedded the parochial elements of the Cold War coalition to an anticommunist foreign policy. With fresh memories of near full employment in their minds from World War II, and in the absence of alternatives, workers fought efforts to cut defense jobs that had offered them social mobility and economic security—and courted political elites who promised them that jobs would always be there, that they would redress unemployment in the name of national security. Defense workers were not necessarily jingoistic or militaristic (even though some were), but because the military-industrial complex had been their sole employer for many years—and rewarded them with stable, good-paying work when no better employment options awaited—they appropriated bellicose rhetoric and Manichean, hawkish ideologies to lend credibility to their cause.

Cold War anticommunism therefore served economic ends in this context, and those ends gave currency to an absolutist worldview promulgated by political elites that perceived the military budget as the only means to salvage the livelihoods of Americans across the country—and democratic peoples around the world. For without defense contracts, joblessness became the default, poverty the imagined endpoint—and Soviet domination the consequence. And once the "military-industrial complex took charge" after 1945, it was the interminable source of perceived financial stability for these workers—even though, as many Americans discovered during the Korean War, it could (and would) not be in perpetuity—and the substance of their politics, of their faith in Cold War anticommunism.[102]

The formation of a Cold War coalition thus emerged from a symbiotic and self-perpetuating interaction between economics and ideology that became the basis for a new politics: a politics of grievance—of anger toward the state and its failure to provide jobs and economic protections, its unwillingness to adhere to the postwar social compact—but at the same time, a faith that the state needed to be massive, strong, and vociferous in its fight against communism. Moreover, antagonism toward immediate defense cuts provided the basis for parochial politics within the Cold War coalition—which were increasingly determined by the trajectory of the defense economy. And the Cold War coalition's commitment and connections to the national security state only intensified after the Korean War, as new coalition members collaborated with preexisting ones based upon their shared economic, political, and ideological investments in the Cold War.

CHAPTER TWO

The National Politics of International Stability

In December 1963, Secretary of Defense Robert McNamara announced significant cuts to U.S. defense spending, a decision that led to the closing of military bases, elimination of defense programs, and increasing numbers of unemployed defense workers. Since McNamara's statement occurred in the aftermath of the Cuban Missile Crisis, the signing of the Limited Test Ban Treaty (LTBT), and the rise of an antinuclear movement, reporters asked McNamara whether his position reflected his "plans on disarmament." He and President Lyndon Johnson had no designs for a large-scale reduction of U.S. military forces, McNamara responded, as the defense cuts were "purely related to obtaining the maximum defense at the lowest possible cost, and had no relationship whatsoever to changing the strength of our defense forces." The Johnson administration sought to revamp and streamline the American military to restore efficiency to the defense budget, and nothing more. Nevertheless, advocates of smaller defense budgets like George McGovern, the Democratic senator from South Dakota elected in 1962, welcomed McNamara's announcement, having announced proposals for defense conversion only months earlier.[1]

Policy makers had chipped away at the size of the defense budget since World War II, but the strategic context of the Cold War in 1963 made drastic downsizing in defense possible. Indeed, McNamara's policy was ten years in the making. Since taking office in 1953, President Dwight Eisenhower argued that exorbitant defense spending was strategically unnecessary (and financially imprudent). Eisenhower made a series of speeches in the 1950s advocating a serious reduction in military forces and nuclear weapons relative to the years of World War II and the Korean War. But by the mid-1960s, following the Cuban Missile Crisis, public support for defense reductions dominated opinion polls, and criticism of nuclear weapons permeated the national conversation on American foreign policy. McNamara's justifications for significant cuts to the defense budget, while lacking the antimilitarist fervor of the Left, were unprecedented, and welcomed by many Americans as a rational response to the new era in the Cold War.

But changes to U.S. defense policies in the 1960s spurred a backlash by diverse constituents of the Cold War coalition. Some of the more hawkish members of the coalition felt any potential defense cuts jeopardized national security and represented a long-term plan to gut American's military and nuclear arsenals. These members of the coalition felt post-Korea budget cuts ignored the reality of the Cold War. Declarations from the executive branch on the need for trimmed defense budgets and reductions in nuclear weapons heightened fears within the Cold War coalition that American economic and political stability was in the balance. Cold Warriors—particularly members of the American military, hawkish Democrats, and movement conservatives—believed the Soviet Union and global communism were still the primary threats to the United States and that military superiority was the only means to prevent a communist attack.

Reduced defense spending (as a portion of GDP) during the Eisenhower, Kennedy, and Johnson administrations also destabilized Americans' material circumstances, even while it contributed to international stability—despite the continuation of the arms race and the development of thermonuclear weapons. Those employed by, or who benefited from, the business of the Cold War approached the stirrings of détente and stability (and the defense cuts that came with that stability) in the 1960s with a range of feelings, from reluctant acceptance to outright hostility. They did so while leadership within labor unions like the AFL-CIO and sectors of American business—particularly defense industry executives in the Sunbelt—aligned to prevent defense cuts after the Korean War for economic reasons.

And while the Cold War coalition's collective cries against defense cuts were not new, they now occurred alongside racial progress made by the civil rights movement in 1950s and 1960s—and the federal government's response to that progress. As the new era for American defense policy coincided with an increase in federal dollars toward enfranchising African Americans (and the funding of Lyndon Johnson's Great Society), following decades of racial injustice, critics argued that the federal government misused taxpayer dollars, that these social programs held little relevance to fighting communism. Southern Democrats and anti–New Deal Republicans, who used military spending as an instrument to weaken New Deal liberalism in the early Cold War, increasingly relied on racialized rhetoric to argue that Great Society programs imperiled American security and deprived Americans of the defense jobs—and the military—they needed. Post-Korea defense cuts therefore gave reactionary elements in the Cold War coalition the rhetorical ammunition they needed to build an antistatist, antigovernment politics that would dominate American political culture after the 1960s.

Those anxious about the impact growing defense cuts had on their lives in the 1960s continued to find new and powerful local, state, and national figures willing to back the national security state for a variety of reasons. Interdependency among national security, economic, and political interests among the Cold War coalition congealed in hawkish sentiments that reinforced the democratic underpinnings of the national security state. Collaboration among ideological Cold Warriors and economic beneficiaries of the national security state took shape in new public venues, including "Cold War seminars" (or national security seminars). Created and led by anticommunist activists and politicians to generate support for U.S. foreign policy among "ordinary" Americans, organizers of Cold War seminars relied on anticommunism (or Cold War liberalism) to sell the national security state to the broader public. Financed by subtle connections between the Department of Defense (DOD), the United States military, local politicians, and private corporations, attendees of Cold War seminars embraced the position that it took not only a strong military to defeat communism but also communities of ordinary citizens willing to preserve the American "way of life."[2]

Cold War seminars created opportunities for the Cold War coalition to engage in political activism, while the flaws in the defense economy allowed that activism to resonate with those employed by it. New post–Korean War procurement policies threatened the fiscal solvency of the defense industry, but they did not significantly alter the Cold War political economy. Indeed, defense spending increased under the Eisenhower and Kennedy administrations, but it did so at a slower pace relative to previous years. (Defense spending declined as a percentage of GDP by nearly one percentage point, from 9.4 to 8.5 percent between 1961 and 1964.) Instead of relying on conventional weaponry that demanded large-scale manufacturing, Eisenhower and Kennedy aimed to subsidize innovative—yet still expensive— weapons programs that maximized destruction while minimizing costs. After 1953, the DOD desired the allocation of more federal funds for high-tech weapons programs over traditional ordnance— jobs predominantly occupied by working-class whites and defense workers of color. For while he liked McNamara's proposals, senators like George McGovern had more drastic plans in place to assist unemployed defense workers with defense conversion—and to ameliorate structural changes to the Cold War economy. However, an overarching, systemic policy for defense conversion never materialized. America's war in Vietnam derailed defense conversion, and military contractors continued to lay off workers without having to restructure their labor force (the economic prospects for working-class defense workers—both white and black—worsened in the 1960s, with black Americans suffering more). Even as the Lyndon Johnson administration sought to end poverty and increase black employment, defense workers of color were abandoned to the mercies of the market, as domestic reforms did not tackle the structural weaknesses in the American economy. A broader economic overhaul of defense employment left black Americans—and the white working class—clinging (at times, reluctantly) to the Cold War coalition, holding out hope that the defense work that once paid them well and provided a good standard of living would be restored.

As constituents of the Cold War coalition grew increasingly anxious about the future of their job security and America's Cold War mission to fight communism, they sometimes felt compelled to back candidates who promised increased defense spending without limits. Politicians like Republican presidential candidate Barry Goldwater, for instance, excelled at uniting disparate parts of the Cold War coalition. During his 1964 presidential campaign, Goldwater frequently linked the "decline" of America's defense policy to domestic reforms on civil rights and poverty, and courted Americans employed by defense industries in the process. While Goldwater mostly made gains in the Deep South—losing badly in other areas of the country—he was the first presidential candidate to build a national political constituency from the Cold War coalition, to create political momentum behind the interconnection among national security economics, anticommunism, racial politics, and class inequities. Goldwater's failed candidacy would also provide lessons for future Republican candidates—particularly Ronald Reagan in 1976 (not 1980)—on the saliency of national defense in American politics and would propel the Cold War coalition forward into the second half of the 1960s. These political figures relied on economic anxieties within the Cold War coalition to reinforce their antistatist agendas. And in the hands of such politicians, financial insecurities were manipulated, and transformed, into an agenda that worked against those who were dependent on the military-industrial complex.

* * *

Once he took office in 1953, President Dwight Eisenhower took gradual steps to draw back the wartime economy during the Korean War. Eisenhower was never comfortable with runaway defense budgets and steadily reduced them beginning around 1955.[3] Defense spending was at a postwar record high 15 percent of GDP when Eisenhower took office. By the time he left the presidency that number was down near 10 percent.

During his first term, Eisenhower rebuked the militarization of American foreign policy and the ways it distracted the United States from domestic problems—while failing to reduce hostilities with the Soviet Union. Eisenhower's "Chance for Peace" speech in April 1953, followed by his "Atoms for Peace" speech in December of that year, expressed his antagonism toward an ever-rising defense budget. In both speeches, Eisenhower critiqued America's willingness to place the militarization of the Cold War over other domestic priorities. The president said that, "every gun that is made, every warship launched, every rocket fired signifies, in the final sense, a theft from those who hunger and are not fed, those who are cold and are not clothed."[4] Eisenhower reinforced his distaste for massive defense budgets with his "New Look" policy, which prioritized nuclear deterrence to protect America's national security interests, not a conventional military arsenal. Rather than a relentless military buildup across the armed services, the New Look advocated for a strategic reliance upon the destructive power of thermonuclear weapons to deter Soviet aggression. Eisenhower ultimately thought the New Look would preserve national security while decreasing defense expenditures. Defense spending therefore dropped considerably below the levels seen during the Korean War, never to reach 15 percent of GDP again.[5]

Eisenhower's cuts in defense spending rippled across the Cold War economy. The National Association of Manufacturers (NAM) noted how the drop in the defense budget had constrained the opportunities for growth among defense contractors. While "total defense spending appears to have leveled off at a fairly high plateau," there remained "specific industries" that had been hurt by the "extent of emphasis, and funds provided for aircraft, nuclear weapons, guided missiles, and related special items," to the point that it had "brought about a significant increase in competition for certain defense contracts." Even then, there was little guarantee that the contracts would

[handwritten margin note: I agree with above but the militarization brought jobs here]

be profitable, considering the vast competition and the possibility that even the "least impact of unanticipated costs may well throw a modest profit into a loss."[6]

Even as defense spending increased during the second half of the 1950s, it failed to fuel economic growth across all parts of the country, highlighting the limits of military Keynesianism. Industrial areas in the Midwest and Northeast continued saw net job losses in defense, as California and states in the South continued to take up a larger share of prime defense contracts. Articles appeared in Long Island newspapers in the mid-1950s that decried reductions in the defense workforce, particularly at the island's two major contractors: Grumman and Republic. By 1957, the top five defense contractors on Long Island announced massive job cuts, including Grumman, who cut five hundred workers in that year. Unemployment in defense caused political unrest in these areas. On Long Island, twelve thousand machinists rallied to oppose defense cuts enacted in the 1950s, asking local and national politicians to bring the defense budget back to Korean War levels. Staring at unemployment, the Long Island Conference of Machinists threatened a strike to force Congress to raise the debt ceiling to approve "further appropriations for defense needs" and for Eisenhower to "repair the damage already done to the national preparedness program and the well-being of the American people."[7] While the machinists scored concessions from employers, by the end of 1957, 2,200 defense workers had lost their jobs. The *Bayport News* reassured Long Islanders that the cuts "are not due to any contract cancellations," but Grumman and Republic continued to lose contracts to defense companies in the South and West, particularly in California.[8]

But defense spending did decrease during Eisenhower's presidency, and defense cuts destabilized the industrial workforce and hurt some defense contractors, but the Cold War economy remained profitable in many parts of the country. Suburban areas in Southern California grew to be the prime centers for producing weapons, and Los Angeles became the "aerospace capital of the world" in the 1950s. Defense firms such as Boeing, Convair, Lockheed, and Northrop all saw production and profits skyrocket. Much of these gains were due to the Air Force's demand for greater production of intercontinental ballistic missiles (ICBMs), long-range missiles capable of carrying multiple nuclear warheads to targets, the cornerstone of Eisenhower's New Look. The increase in the number of ICBMs intensified the relationship among the military, industry, and the growth of the postwar suburbs, as Americans flocked to California from the South and Midwest in search of high-paying, technically specialized jobs in defense plants—causing further economic decline in the Rust Belt.[9]

Eisenhower's defense policies thus show that while the president rejected a garrison state—like Republicans (such as Robert Taft) before him—he did not reject the Cold War economy. Eisenhower hoped to trim America's reliance on defense spending through production of ICBMs rather than heavy weaponry, but the missile program still made "the country tied to defense spending." The New Look had a corollary, "massive retaliation," that gave full reign to bureaucracies in the national security state to pursue a range of tactics (psychological warfare, CIA-backed covert action) to stamp out global communism. The administration's rationale for massive retaliation—the Soviet Union remained an all-encompassing, totalizing threat to humanity and the United States must be "able to respond vigorously at places and with means of its own choosing"—kept Cold War anticommunism hegemonic in American politics, even as Eisenhower tinkered with the defense budget in terms of conventional weapons. The consequences meant that Eisenhower's critiques of the military-industrial complex were mostly empty rhetoric, since the discourse never aligned with the material reality and failed to appeal to the public—and the Cold War coalition. As we shall see, Eisenhower's defense policies angered those who lost their jobs due to defense cuts, who pointed to the administration's dire warnings of the Soviet threat as a reason to keep their jobs, and ignited new and more strident appeals to Cold War anticommunism that upheld the political utility of the military-industrial complex in the minds of members of the Cold War coalition.[10]

Few events better reflected the weaknesses and the contradictions of Eisenhower's defense policies than the response to the Soviet launch of the unmanned *Sputnik* satellite into the Earth's atmosphere in 1957. *Sputnik* derailed deeper reductions to defense during the Eisenhower years, as the event unnerved Americans, who up until this point, believed that the United States led the world in technological developments. *Sputnik* encouraged policy makers and the public to take further steps to increase defense expenditures for innovative projects that would outpace the gains the Soviets had made in space exploration. It also revived the demand for more military spending, as the threat of Soviet Union appeared (once again) urgent.[11]

Cold Warriors, upset at Eisenhower's cutbacks on defense, felt validated by *Sputnik* and lambasted the public's inattentiveness to Cold War foreign policy—which they argued created events like *Sputnik*. Hawkish figures in the Cold War coalition felt the public needed to be edified on the dangers of communism after *Sputnik* and pointed to the 1958 National Defense Education Act (NDEA) as an opportunity to educate Americans in public forums financed by the federal government en masse. While the NDEA would soon incentivize future American students to pursue degrees in science and mathematics through low-interest loans (in an effort to outcompete the Soviets in brainpower), national security officials felt that the future was too far off, that the federal government had a duty—an obligation—to raise awareness of the existential threat posed by communism in the months and years ahead.

This belief had us do a lot of crazy things

To this end, members of the National Security Council (NSC) wrote a memorandum that instructed military officials to launch federal efforts to educate the public about the evils of communism and the benefits of American democracy and capitalism wherever, and whenever, possible. The NSC directive suggested that high-ranking military officers communicate the message that each American was a one-person army in the fight against communism. James S. Russell, vice chief of naval operations, referred to the 1958 NSC document when he sent a memo to all personnel under his command requesting "ideas which the Navy could use in its day-by-day operations to further U.S. cold war efforts." Russell was afraid that "since the cold war is the responsibility of all, it may, in fact, become the responsibility of none" and sought to enlist naval personnel to "make a greater contribution toward the achievement of U.S. cold war objectives." These objectives included portraying a positive image of the United States "in our association of people of foreign lands" and making sure that even low-level members of the navy convey "useful ideas" to their superiors on how best to fight the Cold War against the "Sino-Soviet bloc."[12]

Federal laws like the NDEA, a law designed to bolster American education and boost the middle class, ended up promoting anticommunist fervor, as they bankrolled the formation of "Cold War seminars" across the country. Led by members of the military, private business, and government and financed by the DOD and probusiness groups such as the Chamber of Commerce, these seminars sought to inform seemingly apolitical Americans of the urgent threat of communism. Funding from the DOD provided the basis for Cold War seminars, as DOD paid for the speakers and venues and helped coordinate the logistics for the conferences. Meeting organizers relied upon federal dollars to finance their Cold War activism, as the seminars aimed to mobilize grassroots efforts to convert Americans to the cause of anticommunism.

Many of these Cold War seminars were held in locales that relied on defense spending. In 1961, at least fourteen cities convened "National Security" seminars, including Orlando, Las Vegas, Vallejo, El Paso, and Casper, Wyoming. Jointly sponsored by the Joint Chiefs of Staff (JCS), the Industrial College of the Armed Forces, and local chapters of the Chamber of Commerce, the organizers could boast that 224 seminars were held in 126 cities; consequently, approximately 24,800 certificates were given to civilians for completing the course. Cold War seminars were advertised to participants as a valuable resource for educating the average citizen on the global threat of communism. Like the 1958 NSC directive, the seminars emphasized that the Cold War was a household issue that one needed to confront on a daily basis. It was up to average citizens, regardless of political affiliation, to inform themselves in the ways they could protect national security. Comparing federal appropriations for defense to buying private insurance, seminar promoters complained that few Americans were knowledgeable about national defense issues, but no one "would think of buying an insurance policy without reading its terms . . . yet today the American taxpayer pays 75 cents out of every dollar for our national life insurance . . . the national security structure." The future of America at home was dependent upon the international context of the Cold War. "How secure is your future . . . your family's . . . your investments? . . . Think again! . . . It is only as secure as the position of the United States . . . and today our position is being challenged by the rapidly rising might of the Soviet Union and her allies and captive states," read the press release for one seminar. Americans must realize that free market capitalism is at stake as the "Soviet economic challenge is potentially more dangerous to the United States than the Russian military threat. They have declared a war to the finish between their system and the free enterprise system." Attendees left seminars prepared to defend "the interrelationship of the economic factors with the political, scientific, psychological, and military factors" of the Cold War.[13]

The seminars were also bipartisan led, as the organizers and speakers were a mixture of southern Democrats and Republican defense hawks. One typical Cold War seminar occurred in Little Rock, Arkansas, where the segregationist Democratic governor Orval Faubus was the keynote speaker. Faubus's key theme was the need for vigilance against internal communists seeking to subvert America's Cold War battle against communism. Fearful that Faubus's speech would be compared to the red-baiting tactics employed by Senator Joseph McCarthy years earlier, Colonel Williams Boaz—a scheduled speaker for a Cold War seminar in Vallejo—claimed that the seminars were "not a scare program" and had the approval of President Kennedy and former president Eisenhower. Boaz said that the seminars were merely educational and organized to highlight the "relationship between the national economy and the military power necessary to America's security in the face of perilous world conditions."[14]

The El Paso Chamber of Commerce also directed and financed its own National Security Seminar in 1961. The periodical *El Paso*

Today—an organ of the city Chamber of Commerce—claimed that over one thousand military and civilian personnel registered for the seminar that included in attendance "civic leaders, teachers, clergymen and women from El Paso." It was clear from the numbers of people present that "El Pasoans are smashing records in showing their interest in the important issues of the Cold War struggle between Freedom and Communism." General Albert T. Wilson told the audience that the "search for security transcends all other aims in our national life. Security must be foremost in our minds until the threat of communism is contained." Following its conclusion, organizers praised the seminar as "the most effective and important single effort our government has undertaken to weld a strong and united military-civilian team for national defense and survival."[15]

Accounts of seminars held in other cities echoed those in El Paso and Vallejo. In Minneapolis, the Twin Cities Citizens Council for American Ideals held a Cold War workshop in April 1961 composed of "businessmen, educators, clergymen, civic leaders, newsmen, students, youth leaders, and law enforcement officers at the United States Naval air station, World-Chamberlain Field." The workshop featured speeches on fighting against emotions such as "internal demoralization, political apathy, [and] spiritual bankruptcy" that the organizers felt characterized the broader public's outlook on the Cold War. Walter Mooney, a design engineer from Chattanooga, said that the seminar he attended provided an invaluable service to him and his fellow participants as it was the only program of its kind where one could "obtain such a concise factual representation of the struggle to come between the free world and the masters of the Kremlin." Local Minneapolis resident George Paluska said that the seminar explained "many of the problems and reasons" for conditions in Africa and the "riots on that continent." He only wished that more civil servants were there, including educators and religious leaders, for those individuals had "the ability and chance to pass along this information to hundreds."[16]

The popularity of Cold War seminars indicated the insidious ways the national security state shaped the political culture of the United

States following the Korean War—and reshaped the Cold War coalition. Cold War seminars reinforced the public's relationship to American military power, encouraging "ordinary" Americans to participate in the making of foreign policy; but they also provided opportunities for collaboration among anticommunist activists, high-ranking members of the American military, and defense workers. The economic and political structures of the American defense apparatus erected public forums to solidify a cultural consensus in support of America's Cold War objectives, allowing military personnel to function as partisan mobilizers of public opinion. Moreover, business elites and members of the military enlisted the taxpayer-financed national security state to promote a specific worldview that reduced the international conflict of the Cold War to a classic struggle between the forces of good and evil, one that could only be won by military superiority. The promotion of this worldview by participants of Cold War seminars consequently led more Americans to champion higher defense spending and a larger military presence abroad to eradicate global communism.

In addition to the Cold War seminars, right-wing activists held community events on military bases across the country to organize themselves against communist subversion. At these meetings, participants often conflated the fight against the Soviet Union with their hostility to liberalism. On February 15, 1961, Marion Miller and Paul Miller spoke on the communist threat at the Officers Wives Club luncheon at the Pacific Missile Range in Point Mugu, California. Marion was regarded as a hero within right-wing circles after she infiltrated communist organizations as an informant for the Federal Bureau of Investigation. Point Mugu was under the authority of Rear Admiral J. P. Monroe, who once arranged a viewing at the missile range of the John Birch Society movie *Communism on the Map* for local audiences. Monroe said that the Officers Wives Club in Point Mugu had invited the Millers to "help in our education about the Communist threat." Organizers of the luncheon encouraged members of the Officers Wives Club to invite guests and emphasized in gendered terms that "HUSBANDS will be especially welcome." When the local

Ventura County Democratic Control Committee discovered Monroe's involvement in spreading right-wing ideologies, Monroe agreed to stop showing *Communism on the Map* to nonmilitary personnel but said that the film would continue to be shown to members of the navy under his command.[17]

This activism went under the public radar until early 1961 when the Edwin Walker case captivated the nation's attention. Major General Edwin A. Walker had gone from leading the 101st Airborne Division during the Little Rock crisis (a position he abhorred having been a life-long segregationist) to the Twenty-Fourth Infantry in West Germany. It was in West Germany that Walker told men under his command that former secretary of state Dean Acheson and President Harry S. Truman—among other Democrats—were in fact communists who wanted to Sovietize the federal government. Walker even tried to instruct his soldiers on whom to vote for in the 1960 election: not the Democrats. After the allegations were reported in the media, Walker was investigated by the DOD, which found him guilty of indoctrinating soldiers under his command with propaganda published by the John Birch Society. Walker resigned his post after the publication of the DOD's report and turned the incident into a cause célèbre. His most outspoken supporters, including Senators Strom Thurmond and John Tower, William F. Buckley, and the right-wing evangelist Billy James Hargis, claimed that Walker had been a victim of "military muzzling" and was simply speaking the truth about American liberals and their sponsorship of global communism. Walker's supporters also included thousands of Americans who wrote letters and attended rallies in his defense. One woman from Indiana stated that the Walker case added weight to her opinion "that what masquerades as liberalism and a New Frontier is [not] progression, but an effort to take us back into Medieval days."[18]

The Walker case shocked the American public, and encouraged media outlets to investigate the hidden connections between the American military and DOD in the organization of Cold War seminars. In a series of articles published in August 1961, the *Washington Post* reported on the role of military officials in the Cold War seminars.

The paper argued that the true aim of the Cold War seminars was to portray New Deal programs as essentially communist, that communists were behind racial progress in the United States. The *Minneapolis Morning Tribune* editorialized that the seminars purposely exaggerated the threat of communism in order to attack liberalism: "Under the guise of alerting the country to communism, some of the right radicals have taken advantage of military help to attack the income tax, social security, and the civil rights guaranteed by the first 10 amendments to the constitution." The military's involvement in the seminars was reprehensible, and action was needed by the federal government to stop further Cold War seminars from taking place.[19]

The activities conducted in Cold War seminars were also detailed by Arkansas Democratic senator William J. Fulbright in a 1961 memorandum to Secretary McNamara. The Fulbright memorandum, as it came to be known, elucidated the military's efforts to disseminate right-wing propaganda to rank-and-file military men and contributed to the DOD's decision to forbid military involvement in Cold War workshops. Fulbright intended his memorandum to be confidential but published the memo in the *Congressional Record* after Walker's supporters targeted the Arkansas senator for General Walker's public downfall. Fulbright made clear that the seminars were not presenting objective information or diverse viewpoints on national security issues but that their "thesis of the nature of the Communist threat often is developed by equating social legislation with socialism, and the latter with communism." The seminars' organizers wanted the public to think a great deal "of the [Kennedy] administration's domestic legislative program, including continuation of the graduated income tax, expansion of social security (particularly medical care under social security), Federal aid to education, etc. . . . as steps toward communism." Citing various right-wing organizations and their connections to policy makers within Washington, D.C., Fulbright suggested that the "relationships between the Foreign Policy Research Institute, the Institute for American Strategy, the Richardson Foundation, the National War College, and the Joint Chiefs of Staff must be reexamined." To counter the power of the military, and prevent further cases like Edwin Walker, the senator proposed the seminars be placed "under civilian control."[20]

Fulbright's memo drew national criticism from an array of people who lauded Walker as a modern-day Cassandra unjustly persecuted for warning Americans about the lurking threat of communism. Support for Walker only increased after the Fulbright memo. A Pennsylvania woman wrote to her local newspaper to say that Walker's "only crime—one only—had been his open and realistic opposition to communism, expressed in an effort to teach the troops in his command the nature of the enemy we face. Make no mistake, if this could happen to General Walker, it could happen to us; to you and to me, our parents, and our children and our neighbors." Republican representative Edgar Hiestand, who represented the Twenty-First Congressional District in Southern California, rushed to defend Walker and the John Birch Society, asking, "Since when it is it wrong to advance the cause of Americanism?" Protests erupted in Hiestand's district six months later organized by Dr. Fred Schwarz and his Anti-Communist Crusade, who used the Walker case to pillory liberalism and its design to "substitute surrender for victory" in the Cold War. The Fulbright memo led to an acrimonious conflict between Thurmond and Fulbright as Thurmond decided to hold Senate investigations into the "military muzzlings." Fulbright was also personally derided by anticommunist conservatives as "the darling of the one-world-welfare state conspirators" and as "the red-wing Senator from Arkansas."[21]

Fulbright charged his right-wing critics with being outlandish and extreme and exaggerating the communist threat—and General Walker's assessment of that threat—to arouse attention to broader right-wing causes. In August 1961, at the height of the controversy over the Fulbright memo, Fulbright forcibly responded to these critics at the National War College and the Industrial College of the Armed Forces—which had sponsored the Cold War seminars—where he denounced "radicals of the right" for their cynicism toward the New Deal state and their simplistic outlook toward the conduct of U.S. foreign policy. Fulbright alluded to a contradiction among the anticommunist Right:

their persistent appeal to increase military spending to fight enemies abroad belied their argument that internal communists had subverted American democracy at home. If this was so, Fulbright believed the United States "would be wasting billions of dollars on the armed forces themselves, funds which instead should be transferred to the FBI to fight internal subversion." The Right was on a slippery slope in believing that government spending on any significant scale would lead to a communist state. Social progress and federal programs such as "the creation of the TVA, or the Arkansas River development program, [are] not, in my opinion, a step toward communism."[22]

Fulbright garnered supporters from the public and private sectors and sparked a national discussion about the proper role of the military in American society. The Fulbright memo also relaunched the discussion begun by Eisenhower several months earlier when the president warned Americans during his farewell address to guard against the "unwarranted influence" of the military-industrial complex. National commentators worried that the preponderance of American military officials "with extreme 'right-wing,' anti-democratic views" is enough "to make one wonder whether anything in a military career encourages this kind of divorce from socio-political reality."[23] Walker's extremism, critics claimed, was symptomatic of a larger problem that derived from the presence of the postwar military establishment.

Concerns about the undue influence of the military in public life would temporarily subside after the DOD announced it would not support future Cold War seminars. But the overwhelming criticism of the Cold War seminars after the Walker case did not prevent prospective ones from being organized and attended by anticommunist activists—and financed by federal institutions. While the federal government renounced its involvement in the seminars, other private individuals and organizations with military credentials continued to organize Cold War seminars in a more inconspicuous fashion. In 1963, a four-day Cold War Education Conference was held in Tampa, Florida, that was organized by groups such as the American Security Council, the American Legion, the Cold War Council, the Institute for American Strategy, Freedoms Foundation at Valley Forge,

Office of Civil Defense, and Project Alert. The governor of Florida, Ferris Bryant, was the leader of the conference that registered over four hundred individuals including teachers, congressional representatives, "corporate representatives," and "professional patriots." An entire day of the conference was even dedicated to "the subject of class-room teaching of anti-communism."[24] Activists, corporate leaders, and military officials involved in the national security state stepped in to take control of the seminars in the absence of overt federal involvement. Cold War seminars continued to take place at federally funded institutions and were attended by paid military personnel, but without the notoriety and scrutiny they received only months earlier. The seminars enabled anticommunists to spread their message about the need for a tough defense posture without occupying newspaper headlines. As late as 1974, Frank Barnett, president of the National Strategy Information Center, a group that had close ties to William Buckley Jr. and other right-wing intellectuals and activists, was organizing Cold War seminars at the National War College. Barnett even received a letter of appreciation from the DOD praising his recent presentation at the "Defense Strategy Seminar" and his "coverage of the principal issues involved in the mobilization of human and intellectual resources to support our national security objectives." The letter also thanked Barnett "for your contributions to the College over the years."[25]

The private-public connections between business and the military, and the financial and institutional support from sectors of the federal government, provided members of the Cold War coalition with an ability to influence both domestic and foreign policy in the early 1960s. Furthermore, national security politics gave the Cold War coalition connections to the American military, to foreign policy elites, to campaign for greater defense spending. The political economy of the Cold War thus provided the structure for organizing and mobilizing individuals who were opposed to the very state that financed their activism.[26]

Cold War seminars also heightened public concerns over America's vulnerability to the Soviet Union—and contributed to a political culture that compelled John F. Kennedy to run for the presidency in 1960 as a Cold Warrior. On the campaign trail, Kennedy claimed that Eisenhower had allowed the formation of a "missile gap," between the superpowers and accused the former World War II general of lacking diligence in the fight against communism. To close this missile gap, the United States needed to dig deeper into its pockets to pay for new weapons programs. Kennedy made sure he took this message to states where defense spending determined the futures of local communities. When Kennedy became president, he made good on his campaign promises and vastly increased military spending for innovative military weapons and furthered the space race with the Soviet Union. The American public's demand to "catch up" to the Soviet Union in space technology aligned with Kennedy's desire to increase spending for research and development in aeronautics and defense. In announcing his plan to place an American on the moon by the end of the 1960s, Kennedy argued that if the United States was going to "win the battle that is now going on around the world between freedom and tyranny," it must increase spending upward of $9 billion over course of the decade. Kennedy called not only for vast amounts of federal monies for the space program but also for the creation of new missiles such as the Rover rocket and communications and weather satellites.[27]

But once elected, Kennedy's adversaries worried he had not spent enough on defense in the early months of his presidency. Some of the opposition to Kennedy's defense policies was political grandstanding, as Republicans criticized the defense policies of a Democratic president. But hawkish voices from both parties felt that Kennedy was simply ignorant of Soviet intentions toward the United States. It was therefore up to them to educate the American public on the threat of global communism. Following the Cuban Missile Crisis, cuts in the United States defense budget further indicated to these Americans that the Soviet threat had become less of a concern to the public. As we shall see, to change these circumstances, the Cold War coalition sought to use the power and influence of the national security state to expand its power in the United States in the early 1960s.

* * *

Cold War seminars provided an infrastructure for the expansion of the Cold War coalition, but they also created a public platform for an antigovernment politics that combined a critique of civil rights, antipoverty programs, and various domestic reforms. This antistatist politics, however, did not dominate national politics in the early 1960s. Listening to speakers at the Cold War seminars, one would be unaware of the fact that by 1962, the Cold War had changed dramatically, that the Soviet threat had lessened. Since the late 1950s, the looming threat of nuclear warfare and the acceleration of the arms race spurred activists on the Left—and some policy makers in Congress—to work to ban the proliferation of nuclear weapons. The National Committee for a Sane Nuclear Policy (SANE) was formed in 1957 wanting "a permanent end to nuclear tests" as well as "comprehensive arms control." SANE was among a number of groups established during this time whose purpose was to eradicate nuclear weapons. The movement to abolish nuclear weapons was global in scope, as France, England, Australia, and West Germany all had significant antinuclear movements. Organizations such as the World Council of Peace were at the forefront of the international call for disarmament, helping to convene the World Congress for General Disarmament held in Moscow in 1962. "Disarmament—general, complete and controlled, including the destruction of nuclear weapons—is the most urgent need of our time," the council claimed.[28]

The Cuban Missile Crisis legitimized the concerns expressed by antinuclear activists over the escalation of nuclear weapons. The Cuban Missile Crisis in October 1962 offered the first significant challenge to the arms race and the viability of nuclear weapons to preserve what historian John Lewis Gaddis has called the "long peace."[29] After Soviet premier Nikita Khrushchev decided in 1962 to transport to Cuba missiles capable of launching nuclear weapons, it made very real the possibility that the two superpowers could kill a significant portion of the world's population over miscommunication and hubris. Nuclear war was fatefully avoided when a secret deal was arranged between Kennedy and Khrushchev—Kennedy would remove American missiles in Turkey the following year if Khrushchev took Soviet missiles out of Cuba. After the crisis was resolved, the world breathed a collective sigh of relief as it stepped back from the brink of nuclear war.

Many anticommunist figures were not satisfied with the Kennedy administration's resolution of the crisis, criticizing it for what they saw as its willingness to capitulate to Soviet intimidation. Groups such as the Committee for the Monroe Doctrine (CMD), headed by retired captain Edward V. Rickenbacker, were formed weeks after the conclusion of the Cuban Missile Crisis. The organization derived its name from the belief that Kennedy had "invented a Monroe Doctrine in reverse" by bargaining with Khrushchev over the missiles. Rickenbacker, along with *National Review* editor William F. Buckley Jr., formed the CMD to express their dissatisfaction with what they felt was Kennedy's decision to abandon Cuba to the communists. CMD members believed the crisis was far from over, as did activists who circulated bumper stickers in 1962 with the slogan, "Those Missiles Are Still in Cuba," to convey their suspicions that the missiles had not been removed from the island. The CMD also believed that communism would spread to other parts of Latin America after 1962. Charles Edison told fellow CMD members that the "tentacles of Communist subversion and sabotage have spread to every nation in Latin America" as communists have been "aided and abetted by all too many Americas—in government and out—who believe that the way to stop Communism in Latin America is through shoveling ten's [*sic*] of millions of our taxpayer's dollars into illusionary projects and schemes."[30]

The CMD waged a significant grassroots campaign to mobilize public opposition to the Kennedy administration's foreign policy after the Cuban Missile Crisis. Rickenbacker enlisted Richard Viguerie for his help in spreading the CMD's views. Viguerie was at that point an upstart political fundraiser and direct-mail strategist whose skills with a computer would later prove valuable in contributing to Republican victories in the 1978 midterm elections and Ronald

Reagan's presidential campaign in 1980. Viguerie and Rickenbacker launched a mass-mailing campaign to sway CMD members to obtain congressional support for its foreign policy ideology. Rickenbacker sent blank petition forms to CMD members urging them to "enlist the cooperation of your community to make this nation-wide petition campaign a success." John Franklin Hendon of Birmingham, Alabama, sent one such petition to his congressman, Homer Thornberry, after he collected over fifty signatures on the form, many of which were from Birmingham, but others were from Texas, Florida, and North Carolina. Members of the CMD claimed that one million signatures were sent to Congress by 1963 because of their direct-mail petitions.[31]

Others used the outcome of the Cuban Missile Crisis to argue that liberals had mismanaged foreign policy due to their preoccupation with civil rights and other domestic reforms. One woman from suburban Pennsylvania was furious that the United States, "while fanatically employing military force and violence" to carry out the "un-constitutional Supreme Court decision" in *Brown v. Board of Education* (1954), "ignored the Monroe doctrine, and allowed arms and ammunition to pour into Cuba from the Kremlin, in ships we 'loaned' them." Young members of the group National Association of Americans for Goldwater viewed the Kennedy administration as a collection of "welfare whiz-kids" that were in office "peddling their frosted over fertilizer under the appealing title, 'New Fronteer' [*sic*]."[32] These criticisms led to arguments that the Kennedy administration needed to spend more on defense rather than on social programs. One member of NAM, Joseph Borda, said it was "becoming more apparent every day" to him that federal money for social reform programs was expected "to come from a gradual cutback on expenditures on defense and from a hoped-for increase in revenues from an expanded economy."[33]

While often resorting to hyperbolic and racist rhetoric to express their concerns over the resolution of the Cuban Missile Crisis, the CMD and its followers highlighted a very real problem faced by American policy makers. During the last months of his life, President

Kennedy and members of his national security team were alarmed by their inability to verify that the Soviets had removed the entire arsenal of ICBMs shipped to Cuba. Kennedy also worried about the remaining Soviet troops in Cuba, receiving only the vague assurance from Soviet ambassador Anatoly Dobrynin that all Soviet personnel would be evacuated in due time.[34] Despite their misgivings about the resolution of the Cuban Missile Crisis, the Kennedy administration sought to make sure a similar event could not occur again. McNamara and Kennedy therefore reached the conclusion that a foreign policy based on mutual assured destruction was irrational and unrealistic. After October 1962, Kennedy's national security advisors operated on the presumption that the arms race was increasingly irrelevant within the changing context of the Cold War. The only means to deter nuclear war was through international agreements that limited the proliferation of nuclear weapons. White House officials did not arrive at this decision easily, but they reasoned that there were few options. Even after communist China tested its first atomic bomb in 1964, McNamara and Lyndon Johnson insisted that nonproliferation and disarmament were the best means to preserve peace.[35]

What a novel idea!

Policy makers like McNamara therefore decided that the creation of new weapons programs in preparation for an all-out war against the Soviet Union was a waste of federal dollars. The United States and the Soviet Union had achieved nuclear parity, McNamara argued, and allocating more monies to build conventional military weapons was not going to change these circumstances. It did not matter if the Americans had the Nike-Zeus (a proposed anti-ballistic missile system) and the Soviets did not. In the end, if war between the superpowers did come, it would surely come in the form of a nuclear war, and both countries would succumb to its consequences. Working from this premise, McNamara sought to reduce defense expenditures and overhaul U.S. foreign policy by squashing plans to fund extraneous weapons programs.[36] McNamara's decisions occurred just as United States' allies such as Great Britain responded to the Cuban Missile Crisis by trying to place pressure on Kennedy to push further for nuclear disarmament. Presidential speechwriter and Kennedy advisor Ted Sorensen claimed that Kennedy expressed "a desire to influence neutral and 'world opinion'" on nuclear disarmament, and the international pressure on Kennedy made him propose concrete plans for nuclear nonproliferation.[37]

As the Kennedy administration considered the virtues of nuclear disarmament, those financially wedded to the military-industrial complex, particularly in the Sunbelt South, were concerned about the economic repercussions. The federal government's investment in defense had led to vast economic growth in the Sunbelt, and few southerners wanted to return to a time when the region ranked last in per capita income, capital investment, and real estate values.[38] The political economy of the Cold War ensured that the South would continue to experience rapid rates of industrial development for decades to come. Moreover, in many parts of the South, the struggle against communism abroad meant maintaining big government policies in defense, while keeping government *out* of the region on local matters involving race.[39]

Indeed, the presence of the defense industry in strengthening the economic vitality of the Sunbelt also helped men like Barry Goldwater explain away the role of white racism in bringing southerners to the GOP. It allowed Goldwater as a presidential candidate to argue that his popularity in the South had nothing to do with his opposition to the 1964 Civil Rights Act. Southerners were growing increasingly conservative, Goldwater argued, because they "have roots in the new industrialization of a part of the country which from its earliest settlement has existed in an agricultural economy and society. They are related to the growing importance of business activity and concern for the interests of the business community." Sunbelt conservatism was "primarily an economic conservatism stemming from the growth in business activity." According to Goldwater, southerners had come to terms with "the fact that integration is coming and it is not an overriding issue with them." As historian Bruce Schulman has argued, federal investment in the defense industry in the South also served its residents by "maintaining the separation between military spending, which it approved, and social spending, which it reviled."[40]

Any talk of defense cuts therefore deeply disturbed former Dixiecrats turned Sunbelt politicians like Strom Thurmond. Known for
his outspoken support for racial segregation in addition to greater
military spending, Thurmond did not hesitate to tell leaders of the
defense industry that his state relied on the Cold War for its continued prosperity. "Defense business means better employment, bigger payrolls, and general economic improvement," Thurmond said,
and it was his political obligation to ensure that his constituents were
"not discriminated against in the awards of government contracts."
South Carolina's reliance on the defense industry was therefore tied
to Thurmond's and other southern politicians' political futures. The
economics of the Cold War also played a strong role in the development of postwar southern nationalism. Sunbelt conservatives
combined their opposition to liberalism with their ardent anticommunism when they railed against McNamara's nuclear détente
throughout the 1960s. Thurmond and other Republicans insisted
that liberals failed to comprehend that the weapons their constituents built did not exacerbate tensions between the United States and
the Soviet Union, but averted communist aggression. McNamara's
unwillingness to fund the Nike-Zeus, Thurmond told his South
Carolina constituents, exacerbated a "real and very dangerous gap"
between American and Soviet missile technology; but Thurmond's
references to preserving national security, according to one external report, disguised the boundaries of "where the 'national interest'
begins and self-interest leaves off."[41]

Another oft-cited critique of Kennedy's handling of foreign affairs
and national defense after the Cuban Missile Crisis was that the
federal government was not spending enough money on the right
programs. Paul Heilman, a businessman and Cuban exile, told the
Coconut Grove Rotary Club in Coconut Grove, Florida, on May 29,
1963, about the need to be educated about the nature of communism
because the greatest threat is "our own apathy" to the communist
menace." He went on to add that "unless the leaders of our nation
develop a will to win, a resolute plan to defend our interest against"
the threat of Soviet communism, "all other items in anyone's plan fall

flat." Adding to America's vulnerability, said Heilman, was the Kennedy administration's willingness to run up deficits for aid to the United Nations and the Peace Corps, two organizations that he felt did not deter the spread of communism. The only way to defeat the communists was to redirect federal expenditures away from these programs and develop "a policy of strength and firmness" based on military preparedness.[42]

Defense companies in the Sunbelt had perhaps the most to lose from a decline in the defense budget. Groups such as the Southern States Industrial Council (SSIC) that were composed of various southern manufacturers—many of which also received defense contracts—helped to finance efforts to expand American military forces and prevent defense cuts in the 1960s. Formed in the 1930s as a reaction to Franklin D. Roosevelt's New Deal, the SSIC billed itself as the "the Voice of the Conservative South" and argued for decreases in corporate tax rates, less government regulation, and a foreign policy reliant upon military power. While the SSIC represented southern business, it also solicited funds from corporate executives in the North. The leading contributor to the SSIC was Pierre S. du Pont III of the chemical manufacturer E.I. du Pont de Nemours Co., or DuPont, as it is more commonly called, based in Wilmington, Delaware. Pierre du Pont was the single largest donor to the SSIC. (Between 1958 and 1964, he gave the organization a total of $21,000.) An earlier generation in the du Pont family had founded the American Liberty League, an organization created in 1934 to overturn Franklin Delano Roosevelt's New Deal. Du Pont III's father, along with his uncle Irénée and grandfather Lammont, spent thousands of dollars to promote free market capitalism, at the same time making millions through defense contracts during and after World War II.[43] McNamara's cuts to the defense budget would hurt companies like DuPont as well as southern manufacturers. The SSIC also opposed reductions in defense on anticommunist grounds. In announcing their dislike of the "recently established United States Arms Control and Disarmament Agency," the SSIC said that the organization "will either prove utterly futile and a waste of taxpayers' money or it will impair in some degree this

Nation's security. In either contingency, this manifestation of governmental schizophrenia should be abolished."[44]

Other probusiness groups, afraid of a decline in profits if McNamara's plans for the military budget went forward, joined the chorus of forces opposing defense cuts. Organizations such as NAM and the Chamber of Commerce included members of the defense industry who feared a drawdown in the Cold War. Beginning in the 1960s, these defense executives collaborated with grassroots activists and former military officers (many of whom received jobs for defense companies following their retirement) to pursue efforts for more defense spending. These individuals converged in NAM and the Chamber of Commerce, as well as in groups with names such as the American Security Council, the National Security Industrial Association, the National Strategy Committee, and the National Strategy Information Center. These organizations were led by executives from companies that received numerous defense contracts including Motorola and General Electric and recruited individuals like William F. Buckley Jr. to attend conferences on the dangers of "relax[ing] our posture of readiness" for the sake of détente.[45]

Similar lobbying groups came out in force to oppose the 1963 LTBT that prohibited the atmospheric testing of nuclear weapons—and was the first major international treaty to signal a new era of reduced tensions between the United States and the Soviet Union. Stanley Andrews, a former advisor to the Senate defense hawk and Ohio Democrat Frank Lausche, created the group Americans for National Security because he thought American taxpayer dollars were wasted on the Senate Arms Control and Disarmament Agency. To Andrews, the agency was "being used as a tool of rash and fuzzy-brained pacifists in the State Department to unilaterally disarm the United States." Andrews told the Senate in hearings over the LTBT that the treaty would "enhance the opportunities which the Kremlin is seeking to achieve its ultimate design for world domination." By denying the passage of the LTBT, the Senate would "put a block in the way of communism's supreme objective—world domination." The euphemistic sounding Americans for National Security was an organizational offshoot of the Liberty Lobby, a notoriously racist organization that believed the federal government should stop financing federal education and civil rights reform and redirect its attention toward building a strong national defense. Other groups such as the Citizens Congressional Committee, headed by its legislative secretary Charles W. Winegarner, tried to rally Democratic and Republican conservative members of Congress against the "Treason Treaty." Winegarner stated in an issue of *The Cross and the Flag*—a magazine affiliated with the Christian Nationalist Crusade—that he had the support of over "50 Ambassadors or Legation representatives" for his antidisarmament agenda.

Some Cold War Democrats in Washington, D.C., also fought aggressively to defeat the treaty. Through their control of the Senate Preparedness Investigating Committee—a committee organized with the purpose of increasing military spending—Democratic Senator John Stennis from Mississippi and Thurmond held hearings where men like the hawkish General Curtis Lemay, who had close ties to the American Security Council, testified against the treaty. But the LTBT was approved in September 1963 by a Senate vote of 80–19, after being backed by considerable public support. The LTBT was unable to achieve a sustained détente between the Soviet Union and the United States during the 1960s, but it was a milestone in the Cold War. The treaty was the first major accord between the two superpowers in the postwar era whose intent was to ameliorate the arms race. For these reasons, the treaty's opponents viewed its ratification as the beginning of a process that would culminate with a communist takeover of the United States.[46]

Pentagon officials tried to downplay clams that the LTBT threatened the size of the defense budget and could compromise the financial status of the Cold War coalition. Maxwell Taylor and Roswell Gilpatric, chairman of the JCS and the assistant secretary of defense, respectively, urged Congress to restore proposed cuts to the defense budget as debate intensified over the LTBT—and many on the "radical right" tossed broadsides against those aiming for a Cold War détente. In statements before a Senate appropriations subcommittee, Gilpatric stressed that the LTBT must "not give comfort and encouragement to those people and nations who are all too easily convinced than an era of universal good will is at hand and that sacrifices for security are no longer necessary." Cutting defense spending would add to that image, he implied. The DOD had plans for building new aircraft carriers and the TFX fighter plane, allowing Americans to participate in the construction of "an indispensable new weapon," which was sure to bring "guaranteed prosperity and a gradual progressive increase in jobs."[47]

Anxieties over the state of national defense helped recruit members of the Cold War coalition to Barry Goldwater's 1964 presidential candidacy. The SSIC and other organizations that fought against the LTBT were part of the financial backbone of the Goldwater campaign.[48] The conservative business consultant F. Clifton White, who advised many defense companies in the 1950s through the Richardson Foundation, used the treaty as an issue to solicit donations to a redesigned Draft Goldwater committee. An executive at Weyerhaeuser Co., a company with ties to the defense industry, expressed interest in donating to the F. Clifton White committee because he felt liberals' abandonment of the free market and states' rights would have repercussions for America's vulnerability in the world. If liberals remained in charge, their domestic policies "move us inevitably toward less and less freedom and make us vulnerable to the development of ignorance and stupidity among our people, thus further weakening our national alertness and discernment so that we shall become easy marks for dictatorship and will ultimately lose spirit and fight and become a defeatable [sic] nation." While he did "not believe in a strong federal power, subsidizing weaker and weaker and less and less effective state governments," the U.S. government must provide security to Americans through "a powerful well-organized military adequately backed with the best possible research and development activities and receptive to innovations which will keep them in a position of leadership." Goldwater's supporters often reflected on the connections between local and international politics in backing the Republican's foreign policy. One Goldwaterite implied that the 1964 Republican National Convention should be viewed as another conflict in the Cold War, as the winner of "the 1964 Battle of San Francisco" would determine the course of international events for at least another four years.[49]

Goldwater's aggressive outlook on the role of the United States in the world also resonated with defense workers. Areas such as Southern California, where the defense industry dominated the economy since the 1950s, were rife with electoral potential for the Goldwater campaign. The *Orange County Industrial News* summed up the position of many county voters in 1961 with the statement "that there will be no agreements on disarmament or on limitation of nuclear weapons." Southern California continued to benefit enormously from defense contracts in the early 1960s but remained opposed to federal taxation and intervention in local race relations. Defense workers were present in the crowds at rallies held by figures such as Billy James Hargis of the Christian Crusade and General Walker. On their Operation Midnight Ride tour across the country, Hargis and Walker regularly lambasted plans of disarmament and the UN's control of U.S. foreign policy.[50]

California residents were not the only ones attracted to Goldwater's campaign because of his positions on defense spending. Boeing workers in Washington State were rumored to be supporting Goldwater in 1963 due to job losses from defense cuts. Bidding wars for the TFX fighter plane dragged on for much of 1962 between Boeing and General Dynamics, but by November, General Dynamics (and Grumman, based on Long Island) had won. Bethpage, Long Island, celebrated the award—even though "no major buildup" would arise from the TFX, defense workers were expected to keep their jobs with the expectation of "continued work"—and *Time* magazine contended that "Boeing's loss of the TFX fighter-aircraft contract and the state's loss of shipyard work to the East have irked both management and labor" and the combination of these factors "could be just enough to tip the state to Goldwater." Indeed, Goldwater sought access to traditional Democratic voters through the politics of the Cold War—as well as the politics of race, appealing to "law and order"—in 1964.[51] Democrats like Henry Jackson were on equal footing with Goldwater when he argued that the TFX was vital to U.S. national security and jobs in his home state of Washington. In the days leading up to the election, Goldwater made an appearance in nearby Oregon to speak to Boeing workers where he praised their efforts in contributing to American air power in previous conflicts and vowed they "will be doing so again," pledging to allocate more federal dollars to building new bomber aircraft.[52]

While cuts to the military budget generated criticism of the Johnson administration and favorable statements for Goldwater, the Arizonian still lost resoundingly in 1964. While some individuals within the Cold War coalition decided to support Goldwater—Orange County, California, remained an anomaly in 1964—the Arizonian failed to attract widespread backing for his policies outside of the Deep South. The years between 1953 and 1964 marked a shift in American defense policy but one that did not yet lead to widespread change in voting patterns among members of the Cold War coalition. In King County, home of Boeing—which employed 13 percent of the civilian labor force there in 1960—Goldwater lost by over twenty percentage points. A similar number separated Johnson from Goldwater in Nassau County, home of Grumman. In neighboring Suffolk County, Johnson won by fifteen percentage points. Right-wing politics did not flourish on Long Island after from Goldwater's trouncing; Democrats and moderate Republicans continued to hold sway in these areas for the next decade. In 1964, the First District of New York overwhelmingly went for Lyndon Johnson, as did the entire state of New York. In the House and the Senate, Democrats picked up significant gains in New York. Otis Pike, representing Nassau and Suffolk Counties, was elected by almost a two-to-one margin over his Republican challenger. And while the First District did not vote for Robert F. Kennedy as senator, Kennedy still won the election. Goldwater certainly stimulated antigovernment critiques with his criticism of post-Korea defense cuts and their impact on elements within the Cold War coalition, but they did not yet translate into large-scale victories for the Republican Party.[53]

Still, antistatist rhetoric resonated among the Cold War coalition throughout the 1960s. Feeling powerless to prevent job cuts created by fewer defense contracts, defense workers became disillusioned by the federal government's inability to offer protections against layoffs—or to stem the tide of continued cuts. The antilabor rhetoric propounded by corporate executives and Republican politicians like Goldwater since the 1950s created fissures among the Cold War coalition and its relationship to the federal government—which increasingly became the scapegoat for the problems plaguing the defense industry.[54] One Grumman employee complained that his senators and representatives failed to secure defense jobs for residents of Long Island. This same employee did not blame the company for the layoffs but rather the politicians in Washington, D.C. "I don't think they are doing everything they can to bring defense work to this area," he exclaimed.[55] One resident of Seattle, M. C. (Chuck) Snyder, said that layoffs at the Boeing plant made him feel he could not rely on the federal government anymore. "We can't sit here and demand economy in the federal budget everywhere but in our own backyards," Snyder said.[56]

Similar comments came from the mouths of defense workers in the Northeast. States like New Jersey, for instance, saw their percentage of defense contracts continue to decline, dropping by a third relative to the years of the Korean War, as more defense business continued to flow south.[57] After New York defense worker George Beecher lost his job in 1964 due to cuts, he suggested he was more likely to vote for Goldwater. After complaining that his congressman was "for the poverty program," even though he was "creating worse poverty right here," Beecher said the Democrats should "better look out in November." Other New Yorkers directed their anger to the federal government and its failure to bail out them out in times of trouble. In 1962, the DOD eliminated production of the F-105D fighter plane in favor of a more modern model. The F-105D was made by Republic Aviation, one of the leading military contractors in the nation (before being bought out by Fairchild Industries) and a major employer in Nassau and Suffolk Counties in New York. (In fact, defense contracts made up 100 percent of Republic's business.) The editors of Newsday wrote an open letter to President Kennedy on February 8, 1962, complaining that the cancellation of this one plane would potentially result in layoffs of thirteen thousand Republic employees, roughly 72 percent of the company's workforce and 40 percent of the people employed in the airline industry in Nassau and Suffolk Counties. The editors argued that the federal government "has an obligation to provide Republic with other contracts" in order to prevent job losses at Republic plants. While the paper upheld "the doctrine that national security is more important than any local economy," it also noted that "even before World War II, the government has encouraged Republic and similar defense plants to expand to the point where all of them represent a crucially important source of employment." The Cold War established a relationship between citizens and the federal government, and the president had "a responsibility to these people [in Nassau County] that extends beyond emergency help."[58] *Newsday* made clear that the business of the Cold War was bipartisan—it touched everyone in communities that relied heavily on defense contracts from the federal government. But the editorial did little good. Republic did not receive the contract, and just as predicted, by 1964, the company had laid off 75 percent of its workforce.

Criticism of the federal government's "abandonment" of the defense workforce continued after 1964 when the Johnson administration, like the Kennedy administration, failed to offer a substitute to military Keynesianism for unemployed defense workers. Some members of Congress tried to step in and resolve the crisis in defense employment. In response to job losses in defense—and the anger budget cuts engendered in workers, labor unions, and businesses—Senate Democrats attempted to redirect labor toward nondefense work. In 1964, George McGovern proposed the establishment of the National Economic Conversion Commission (NECC) to transition communities reliant upon defense contracts to nonmilitary work. McGovern saw the writing on the wall in 1964: an end to the military-industrial complex acting as a "gigantic WPA." In making his case for the NECC, McGovern argued that "reductions in defense spending can provide a very hopeful opportunity for the people of the United States"; and he had ambitious "plans for exciting and hopeful alternatives where those resources and that manpower can be used." The

Senate Committee on Commerce, chaired by Washington senator Warren Magnuson, held hearings on the NECC at a time when the Civil Rights Act took up much of the Senate's time and attention. Magnuson, like Senator Jackson, was an avid supporter of Boeing and defense spending. His support for defense labor in Washington State made conversion more urgent, as the number of military contracts for his constituents declined since 1961. In opening the Senate hearings on the NECC, Magnuson commented that "roughly 50 percent of the total Federal Budget and about 9 percent of our working force is directed toward the national defense effort" and its future was therefore of grave concern to Americans. The goals of the NECC were also supported by many local politicians in Washington State who were "attempting to lure new nondefense industries, but continuing layoffs at Boeing eradicated jobs twice as fast as [they] could secure new ones."[59]

McGovern's plan was bold and necessary, but the NECC folded months after initial Senate hearings. When Vietnam, like Korea ten years earlier, restored prosperity to defense business—again, temporarily—defense conversion became low on the list of priorities for the industry. Embroiled in a soon-to-be quagmire in Southeast Asia, the Johnson administration pilloried McGovern's NECC as unrealistic and claimed McGovern's ideas for drastic defense cuts (approaching $300 million) were "radical." The NECC burned out by 1965, with members of the Cold War coalition—particularly those financially invested in the Cold War economy—placated by the uptick in military spending generated by Vietnam and the Johnson administration hostile to any plan for wholesale reform of the military-industrial complex.[60]

But the collapse of defense conversion entailed job losses without a structural overhaul of the defense economy—which predominantly affected unskilled or uneducated workers in the defense industry, many of them black and working class. Take Long Island, for instance. In 1950, only 16,964 blacks resided in Nassau County, and a thousand fewer lived in neighboring Suffolk. Nassau and Suffolk Counties were 96.4 percent white in 1950, a number that had increased only by

0.4 percent since World War II—and the percentage of blacks went mostly unchanged between 1940 and 1960. Moreover, black defense workers historically had little protection from racist hiring practices in the defense industry, even in a unionized workforce in companies like Republic Aviation. This was particularly the case once the federal government financed Cold War weapons that required fewer blue-collar defense jobs—jobs where African Americans predominated—to design and make them, leading to increased layoffs for blacks.[61]

Empowered by civil rights legislation, particularly the 1964 Civil Rights Act, African Americans looked to challenge the long-standing discriminatory practices of the defense industry. Among the most well-known was the case of African American civil rights activist Percy Green. When Green was laid off by McDonnell Douglas in 1964 as a technician, the company cited "a reduction in force" as the excuse for his dismissal. Green suspected his earlier civil rights activism, the company's racially biased hiring practices, and its failure to diversify its workforce were, in fact, the root cause of his termination, and organized protests outside the plant in response. And when the St. Louis–based company refused to hire him back, even when the company rehired workers after receiving fresh contracts from the Pentagon, Green filed suit with the federal government for protections under the Equal Employment Opportunity Commission. Green's case echoed demands levied by the Congress of Racial Equality (CORE) against Grumman in 1965. After decades of rampant job discrimination, the Long Island chapter of CORE pressed Grumman to create an internal grievance panel as a platform for black workers to advocate for more jobs and to hire more African Americans—Grumman had increased its numbers of skilled black craftsman by over 200 percent and skilled black clerical workers by 1,320 percent in 1965, but blacks remained a minority in the industry—among other demands. Green in St. Louis, and CORE on Long Island, demanded that defense contractors in their communities create more jobs for African Americans, that job recruitment for blacks be the focus for the industry.[62]

But by 1965, there were fewer defense jobs to win back—for blacks or whites. In 1964, unemployed defense employees across the country were working as ice cream truck drivers and selling milk door to door; they worked as office janitors or took part-time jobs in cafeteria service—jobs that paid half of what they formerly earned in defense. Some saw their jobs reappear after a few months of unemployment, but others felt rushed into unfamiliar employment sectors, forced to feed their families. Workers felt that in such an unstable economic climate for defense, any job was a good job. In the words of one defense worker collecting unemployment, "My three kids can't eat stones." And even after Grumman, McDonnell Douglas, and most defense contractors embarked upon a hiring spree in the first two years of the Vietnam War—between 1965 and 1967 (a subject discussed at greater length in the next chapter)—Grumman still cut eight hundred jobs in 1967 due to production delays for fighter jets and fewer orders from the Pentagon. Moreover, protests by those fighting against the defense industry hiring practices, like Percy Green—who later lost his case against McDonnell Douglas in 1973—and CORE fell flat in an era of employment losses; the tactics of boycotting and picketing with signs outside Grumman—"At Grumman, blacks are the last hired and the first fired"—did not result in leverage over the federal government, and the jobs that did return in defense after 1964, in the words of one scholar, "favored skilled workers and a leaner workforce." In sum, campaigns to force defense contractors to hire more blacks, or create more jobs overall, failed.[63]

Robert McNamara's public comments, and approach to dealing with defense cutbacks, did not help matters for black—or white—workers employed in defense. With defense jobs disappearing, and few federal plans for defense conversion, McNamara put the problem of a bloated military-industrial complex onto its victims: those communities, and Americans, dependent upon defense spending. With the economy growing, and overall unemployment falling in 1964 (despite job losses in defense), McNamara had tough words for the defense industry: diversify or perish. In a speech to Long Island defense workers in 1965, McNamara said the warfare state circa World

War II and the Korean War was gone and localities should shift to nondefense work since "the defense industry is a highly erratic industry and you should not try to build an economy on it." McNamara therefore left defense conversion in the hands of those least able to carry it out. McNamara made the captives of the military-industrial complex responsible for its destruction; he released the federal government from a comprehensive role to remake the defense economy for civilian uses. As historian Timothy Keogh argues, McNamara's message to defense workers on Long Island (and the country)—that "the defense boom is over"—failed to offer an answer or address systemic unemployment in defense that could satisfy a democratic public.[64]

McNamara's defense policies had stark political ramifications in the early 1960s. The defense secretary simply aimed to undo superfluous and uncompetitive defense contracting, but the results yielded an untenable political situation. McNamara mandated the defense industry downsize without an economic policy to replace the jobs lost from his decision, creating anger and unrest among Americans who ultimately blamed the federal government for their problems, not the industry that cut their jobs. McNamara set a precedent for the federal government to be the face of the defense industry's decline, for the abdication of the federal state in the lives of defense workers, and for the government to inadequately support them.

McNamara's policies—carried out in both the Kennedy and Johnson administrations—allowed corporations to escape blame for job losses. Defense business was, in many ways, like other business: it sought profits in the most expedient and cost-effective manner. And like other corporations, labor made up most of the company's costs—and defense executives consistently looked for ways to reduce those costs. Job losses were therefore inevitable when the industry felt pinched by shareholders or a bad procurement market. But when jobs were cut, the industry could fall back on the DOD as the cause of its instability. The Cold War coalition's hostility toward government, not corporations, was compounded by McNamara's outright dismissal of the defense industry—and its history—as a federally subsidized path to full employment. McNamara rejected the notion that the military budget should ever generate full employment, despite a twenty-year precedent for being a New Deal–like jobs program. Moreover, the fact that McNamara had little to offer defense workers but caustic comments for their addiction to defense dollars—and not a policy to replace that "gigantic WPA"—made the government appear, more than the industry itself, the callous arbiter for the fate of thousands of Americans. "We elected a Democratic President in 1960, and now we find out a Republican Secretary of Defense is running the country," said one defense worker. Such comments spoke to how McNamara's defense policies remade American politics, giving fodder to Republicans who said McNamara represented "false economy" and a threat to American security.[65]

The remaking of the military economy at home thus occurred while elements of the national security state mobilized against the new era of international stability. New individuals (right-wing activists like Edwin Walker) and groups (organizations such as the SSIC and the American Security Council) joined forces with a confederation of preexisting Cold Warriors in both the public and private sectors in the early 1960s. A conglomeration of anticommunist activists, defense executives, Democratic and Republican hawks, union leaders, defense workers, and military personnel discovered each other in Cold War seminars, in opposition to McNamara's defense policies or the LTBT, or in rallying behind Barry Goldwater's presidential campaign. Constituents within the Cold War coalition therefore found new allies within the institutions of a federal state that provided them significant financial and organizational resources to attack the direction of American foreign and defense policies—which expanded the ideological and financial connections among the coalition.

Right-wing elements of the Cold War coalition also prospered by employing the warfare state as a cudgel against the welfare state. Lyndon Johnson's efforts to pass civil rights legislation made groups like the SSIC, for instance, expect increased government regulation, an expanded welfare state, and "support of the Negro Revolution" for the foreseeable future. The SSIC forecasted that domestic reform would come at the cost of national security, as Americans should be prepared for more "accommodations with Russia and China" as well as "unilateral disarmament and U.S. adherence to a world government"—which the group said amounted to "Fabian socialism." Other right-wingers—writers, intellectuals, and activists—echoed the SSIC. Editors at *Human Rights* magazine, for instance, feared Great Society legislation distracted Americans from the Cold War. The magazine posited that "the Soviets have been making great strides forward" in military capabilities throughout the 1960s because the federal government "has been focusing on social welfare programs."[66] Reactionary members of the Cold War coalition thus relied again on anti-statist positions to convince Americans that the federal government sought to divert military spending into domestic programs. In making these claims, politicians, corporate executives, and activists channeled anticommunism into a material justification for a strong military, arguing the federal government had to reorganize its priorities in an era still threatened by the Soviet Union and its allies. This line of reasoning would continue to prove powerful to parochial interests in the Cold War coalition as the federal government scaled back defense spending following the Vietnam War.

The political economy of the Cold War, and the changes it engendered from the mid-1950s to early 1960s, reinforced the anticommunist, antistatist tendencies that emerged within the Cold War coalition during the first decade after World War II. The Eisenhower and Kennedy administrations' defense and foreign policies remade the ideologies and economics of the Cold War coalition in ways that complemented its various constituents, offering an overlapping—if not always integrated—set of ideas and interests that made the members of Cold War coalition both active builders and perceived victims of the national security state. But despite echoing each other—in their criticism of the federal government and their parochial and political program to increase military spending—the Cold War coalition experienced unequal results from its activism, from its collective backlash against a thaw in the Cold War. Indeed, American defense polices, and their economic effects in the 1960s, jarred the political and economic stability of the Cold War coalition without offering an alternative, particularly to its most vulnerable members. Architects of Cold War foreign policy, in their desire to cut defense spending while strengthening the welfare state, and to establish a U.S-Soviet détente while continuing to adhere to Cold War anticommunism, left Americans uncertain of their future and clinging to the material and ideological structures that benefited them most since World War II. The Cold War coalition therefore remained committed to militarism at home and abroad—albeit to different degrees, and for different purposes. And once the Americanization of the Vietnam War produced prosperity and peril among the Cold War coalition, and animated members of the coalition anew, the consequences would keep the national security state thriving in times of economic duress.

CHAPTER THREE

Vietnam and Antimilitarism in the 1960s

In 1970, William R. Wilson, Vice President of Public Relations for Lockheed Aircraft Corporation, wrote an article in *NAM Reports* (the official magazine of the National Association of Manufacturers [NAM]) to convey his concerns over the reputation of American foreign policy and the defense industry. In the article entitled "How to Get Rid of a Complex," Wilson stated he had grown tired of what he felt were the thoughtless attacks against the defense industry by congressional liberals and the American Left. As a self-described "member of the industrial side of the military-industrial complex," Wilson believed the defense industry's image as war profiteers was misleading. The criticism levied on the national security state, Wilson argued, threatened the military strength of the United States and was therefore responsible for a decline in American military power that left the nation vulnerable to an onslaught by communist aggressors. Alluding to the Vietnam War, Wilson claimed that the liberal critics of the defense industry wished that the United States could simply "point our magic wand at the . . . Communist turmoil in Southeast Asia" and thereby rid themselves of the military-industrial complex. Wilson urged his colleagues to fight the "scorn from the new left activists" and defend the reputation of private industry for what he claimed was its important role in protecting the United States from communism.[1]

Wilson's article offered a neat summation of the defense industry's reaction to a political culture of antimilitarism in the United States during the late 1960s and early 1970s, one brought on by the Vietnam War. By the time he wrote his article in 1970, the lessons of Vietnam were palpable to the American people: U.S. Cold War foreign policy produced an endless and meaningless conflict that resulted in the deaths of thousands of Americans and Vietnamese—and the United States needed to take measures to prevent further Vietnams. After the coordinated ambush on American military installations and major cities in South Vietnam by the Vietnamese insurgency during the Tet Offensive in January 1968, opinion polls showed that a near majority of Americans were opposed to the Vietnam War. A Gallup poll conducted in March 1968 claimed that 49 percent of Americans felt "the United States was wrong to become involved militarily in Vietnam." This number only increased during the 1970s. By 1971, 61 percent of Americans agreed the war was a disastrous blunder, while polls also showed that Americans were less likely to classify themselves as "hawks" on the war, as 42 percent of the public saw themselves as "doves." When polled, more Americans also suggested that the United States must scale back its role in the world—and federal monies spent on defense should be shifted to social welfare programs.[2]

The war also mobilized antimilitarism among the Left who feared the gains made in civil rights and antipoverty legislation would come undone in the jungles of Vietnam. Civil rights leaders such as Martin Luther King Jr. and Stokely Carmichael, for instance, highlighted the relationship between Vietnam and the decline of the Great Society in justifying their antiwar positions. In publicly announcing his opposition to the Vietnam War, King told an audience at Riverside Church in Harlem on April 4, 1967, that he "knew that America would never invest the necessary funds or energies in rehabilitation of its poor so long as adventures like Vietnam continued to draw men and skills and money like some demonic destructive suction tube. So, I was increasingly compelled to see the war as an enemy of the poor and to attack it as such." Carmichael went further: "We [African Americans] will not support LBJ's racist war in Vietnam."[3]

By the early 1970s, public opposition to the war, combined with the prominence of the antiwar movement and a resurgent Left, succeeded in altering the politics of Cold War foreign policy in favor of anti-militarists. Congress responded to this culture of antimilitarism with demands for defense cuts, military restraint, and a political rhetoric that called for a rethinking of American foreign policy. Indeed, the failed war in Vietnam generated interest in slashing defense expenditures and drawing down America's military to an extent unseen prior to World War II, as critics of the defense establishment, or antimilitarists, waged a collective struggle against the commanding power of the national security state.[4]

To marginalize the antimilitarists, and public disaffection toward America's war in Vietnam, defense hawks and national security activists—within and outside of government—exploited the entrenched institutions of the Cold War state to protect their ideological and economic interests—and sway the public to their cause. Defense company executives, local politicians, military officials, and assorted national security activists continued their crusade to maintain exorbitant military spending. But in the late 1960s and early 1970s, they did so under a more hostile political climate. In response, defense companies, rather than focusing on profits and letting groups like Southern States Industrial Council speak for their politics, launched attempts to defend their industry to the public, castigating their infamous image as the "military-industrial complex." The industry also actively courted defenders of the military-industrial complex, including right-wing politicians and activists. As they had in their campaign against defense cuts and nuclear disarmament in the 1960s, the Right sought allies among dependents and proponents of the national security state to promote a hawkish defense policy.

But whereas Cold War seminars helped fuel right-wing politics and ideologies on national defense in the early 1960s, during the Vietnam War, and particularly from 1968 to 1975, the avenues for coalition-building among the Right narrowed. By 1968, movement conservatives were one of the last remaining political constituencies who unequivocally supported the war. They had quarreled with President Lyndon Johnson over his policy of gradual escalation, but believed that the war was a moral cause that the United States needed to fight and win. Despite the public consensus against Vietnam, the activist Right continued its support for the war and for a more stringent policy toward the communist powers. Even the election of a Republican president in 1968 proved unfavorable to the prowar Right. President Richard Nixon had little patience for right-wing activists, finding them a nuisance and a constraint in his efforts toward opening diplomatic and economic relations with China, ending the Vietnam War, and establishing arms agreements with the Soviet Union. Nixon and his national security advisor (and later secretary of state) Henry Kissinger sought to cajole and prod the Right into supporting the administrations' foreign and domestic policy, but to no avail. After several activist conservatives suspended their support for Nixon in 1971 (including William F. Buckley), pessimism dominated right-wing circles; a return to Cold War containment—a renewed confrontation with communism—appeared impossible.[5]

Vietnam also raised dilemmas for Cold War liberals (and Democrats). With their relentless defense of the Vietnam War, and the greater fight against communism, Cold War Democrats like Senators Hubert Humphrey and Henry Jackson became an anachronism within their party and among the public. Labor unions such as the AFL-CIO that represented, and were affiliated with, Cold War liberals—who also possessed similarities with conservative Republicans and Cold War Democrats on defense spending and the war—felt frustrated that the public, and increasingly more Democrats, repudiated military Keynesianism, the foundation of full-employment policy during the Cold War. At odds with increasing antiwar and antidefense positions of their party, Cold War Democrats played a significant role in the creation of organizations such as the Coalition for a Democratic Majority and the Committee on the Present Danger and who rallied Cold War liberals and conservative Democrats against the antimilitarist shift in American politics during the 1970s—and who would then form alliances with hawkish Republicans looking to return America to a pre-Vietnam foreign policy.

As Vietnam created schisms within American politics, the backlash against the war offered the possibility that the postwar state created to fight communism would be remade in ways that would benefit the social welfare of Americans. This did not happen. While the eradication of the military-industrial complex was difficult, if near impossible to conceive, the late 1960s and early 1970s were a critical time for the Left in postwar American politics, one that provided them with a platform to restrict the power of the military and defense corporations to an extent unseen prior to World War II and Henry Wallace's campaign in 1948. But the collapse of the American economy in the mid-1970s prevented efforts by the anti–Cold War Left to drawn down the national security state with any significance. Moreover, several economic forces aligned in the 1970s to frustrate the agenda of anti-militarists and the anti–Cold War Left. Declines in productivity and wages at the end of the "American century" strengthened arguments made by defense hawks that military spending was needed to supply Americans with jobs at a time when they appeared to be dwindling— and made members of the Cold War coalition defend the military-industrial complex and the jobs it provided.

The Lockheed loan crisis in 1971 ultimately exemplified how the relationship between defense spending and economic austerity determined the fate of antimilitarism—and its influence on national politics in the 1970s. After poor investments in costly technological prototypes during the late 1960s, Lockheed requested several hundred million dollars in federal loan guarantees to prevent the company from going bankrupt. The potential collapse of Lockheed led its workers (and the communities that depended on the defense contractor) to petition and lobby their local, state, and national leaders to keep the company solvent. Companies had received bailouts and federal loan guarantees before, but the size of the loan, and the reasons for Lockheed's request, ignited opposition among left-wing antimilitarists and right-wing deficit hawks who bonded together to prevent the federal government from saving the private corporation. When the debate over the Lockheed bailout ended, however, the aftermath revealed the severe limitations antimilitarists confronted when trying to undue the ways the Cold War economy affected the lives of Americans for decades.

The Lockheed loan crisis also shaped the politics of the Cold War coalition in the early 1970s as its members (those employed by defense industries) confronted defense cuts unseen since the Korean War. The proposed bailout of Lockheed generated a debate not only over the solvency of one of the nation's largest defense contractors, but also over whether the private defense industry—on such a massive scale—served a public good. As the debate ensued over the matter of Cold War militarization—and whether military contractors benefited or harmed American democracy or furthered national security interests—two ideological camps emerged: those who believed in military Keynesianism—or, at the very least, that the federal government must continue to provide prosperity and military hegemony through massive defense spending—and those who did not. As one camp emerged victorious over the other in 1971, the Cold War coalition was, in many ways, back to where it started before Vietnam: committed to an unstable economic regime, one intellectually sustained by Cold War militarism and anticommunism.

Instead of a federal bailout to save workers, one that permanently preserved jobs or rescued workers from the war economy, the outcome of the crisis did little to rectify problems within or change the defense industry—and proved to be a stopgap measure on the road to greater economic austerity, a signpost of a coming neoliberal era. The outcome of the Lockheed loan crisis ultimately delayed the inevitable: more pink slips for working-class defense workers (without new jobs to await them) and greater economic security for highly skilled, elite employees. Corporate executives in defense also enriched themselves at the expense of their workers. As we shall see, the bailout was a victory for Cold Warriors and hawks of all political stripes who argued that an expansive military budget remained paramount in fighting the Cold War, even amid the Vietnam War. The bailout therefore entailed—in economic and ideological terms—that the Cold War coalition remain stratified in its composition, but still united after the Vietnam War. Indeed, the Lockheed loan fight exposed how the contradictions and diverse politics within the Cold War coalition worked to the advantage of the coalition overall, but against the interests of its least powerful members: those precariously wedded to the military-industrial complex for job security.

* * *

The Vietnam War provided the catalyst for antimilitarist politics in the United States during the 1960s. In February 1965, President Lyndon Johnson made the fateful decision to send American marines to Vietnam, thus expanding a protracted conflict whose origins reached as far back as World War II. Johnson felt trapped by twenty years of American commitment toward Vietnam but reasoned that if the United States did not confront communism in the region, U.S. credibility around the world would be jeopardized. Johnson therefore made a series of decisions in 1964 that made the escalation of the Vietnam War nearly a fait accompli. Even prior to the Gulf of Tonkin incident, the president was predisposed to favor escalation rather than alternative courses of action. Once Johnson made the decision to Americanize the war, however, he realized that escalation was not a panacea. Johnson predicted that American firepower, particularly the bombing campaign of Operation Rolling Thunder, would overwhelm the Vietnamese communists. He was wrong. What Johnson hoped would be a quick war dragged on for weeks, then months, and eventually years. Even early on in the war, Johnson sensed that a resolution to the conflict was far from his reach. "There ain't no daylight in Vietnam," Johnson told his longtime friend and Senate colleague Richard Russell in March 1965. "The more bombs you drop, the more nations you scare, the more people you make mad."[6]

When Johnson widened the war in 1965, his actions vitalized an emergent antiwar movement and a group of activists known as the New Left. Composed of students, clergy, and social activists, the origins of the New Left lay in the 1948 Henry Wallace campaign, the antinuclear movement, Beat culture, and the civil rights movement of the 1950s. The New Left railed against the "corporate liberalism" of the Democratic Party and its inattention to those Americans left behind during the postwar economic boom. The New Left also criticized the direction American foreign policy had undertaken since

World War II, arguing that American intervention abroad was impe-
rialist in its design and outcomes.[7] While the New Left remained frac-
tured by a multiplicity of interests and ideas, its members were joined
by the common desire to end the Cold War and, in the wake of the
civil rights and women's rights movements, achieve social justice for
those on the margins of American society. This goal, they believed,
was impossible if the United States was entrenched in a Cold War
with the Soviet Union.

By 1967, the New Left and antiwar movement galvanized larger
numbers of Americans upset over the rising troop levels in Vietnam,
the persistence of the draft, and mounting casualties. In the spring of
that year, antiwar activists under the banner of the National Mobilization Committee against the War marched in New York and San
Francisco to show support for an American withdrawal from Vietnam. Over thirty thousand antiwar activists gathered on the steps
of the Lincoln Memorial in the March on the Pentagon in October,
hoping, in the words of antiwar activist Abbie Hoffman, to "levitate"
the Pentagon. Hoffman's promise to raise the Pentagon was a stunt,
but one that attracted considerable media attention.

The New Left—and its critique of American global hegemony—
obtained greater attention by the media, policy makers, and the public after 1965. What started as a fringe movement gathered momentum in the second half of the 1960s as the Vietnam War dragged on
and protests against the war grew. College campuses erupted in protest as students energetically spoke out and demonstrated against the
war. In addition to colleges and universities, the New Left and the
antiwar movement took the fight against the war into the streets in
major American cities. Antiwar protesters then obtained greater support from leading public figures such as Senator William Fulbright,
who conducted congressional hearings on the war from 1966 to 1971,
some of which were televised. Antiwar South Dakota senator George
S. McGovern spoke at the National Mobilization Committee against
the War in 1967, despite objections by members of his staff.[8] The antiwar movement also garnered assistance from leading intellectuals
during the late 1960s. Throughout 1968, as young men of the group

New England Resistance burned their draft cards in public in Boston, famed pediatrician Benjamin Spock, Martin Luther King Jr., and MIT professor Noam Chomsky all signed the "Call to Resist Illegitimate Authority" as a sign of solidarity with indicted draft resisters. [9]

The broader American public then turned against the war after January 1968, when the Tet Offensive discredited the claims of President Johnson and his advisors that the United States was winning in Vietnam. By the spring of 1968, the Vietnam War was lost in the eyes of the public. Undersecretary of the Air Force Townshend Hoopes admitted to Secretary of Defense Clark Clifford that the war was "eroding the moral fibre of the nation, demoralizing its politics, and paralyzing its foreign policy." Once Americans saw footage of the Tet Offensive broadcast into their homes, the war ended President Johnson's political career, as he bowed out of the 1968 presidential race after barely defeating antiwar candidate and Minnesota senator Eugene McCarthy in the New Hampshire primary. The popularity of McCarthy's antiwar platform sent the very clear message that Americans had had enough of Vietnam. [10]

But the public turn against the war did not resolve the nation's underlying compulsion toward imperialism, argued members of the New Left. Ending the war would not be a panacea; only a demilitarization of the Cold War ensured America against future Vietnams. Vietnam could not be disaggregated from the broader context of the Cold War, as the conflict was a corollary of a "significantly militarized" society, wrote Tom Hayden of the Students for a Democratic Society (SDS), one that resolved international tensions through armed conflict. Since 1945, the decision to go to war was "the property of the military and industrial arms race machine, with the politicians assuming a ratifying role instead of a determining one." Hayden implied that the Cold War diverted resources for social reform toward American imperialism abroad. Only by eliminating the arms race and the tensions between the two superpowers could the United States achieve racial, gender, and economic equality. [11]

In making their case against the militarized nature of the Cold War, the New Left appropriated the ideas and writings of thinkers like the sociologist C. Wright Mills. Before his premature death in 1961, Mills authored works such as *The Power Elite* and *The Causes of World War III* in the 1950s that singled out a "military elite" as having a growing influence in the conduct of American politics. Mills envisaged the concept of the military-industrial complex long before the term was spoken by Dwight Eisenhower in 1961. Mills argued that a cadre of military figures and corporate elites threatened the sanctity and security of the American republic by their ability to undermine the wishes of the electorate through the possession of unprecedented economic and political power. Mills posited that the Cold War gave birth to an intrinsic relationship between the military and the economy that leeched the United States of its financial resources and democratic values. Corporations came to rely upon military leadership for ensuring profits, and the military thereupon depended on corporations for employment. "Without an industrial *economy*, the modern army, as in America, could not exist; it is an army of machines. Professional economists usually consider military institutions as parasitic upon the means of production. Now, however, such institutions have come to shape much of the economic life of the United States."[12] Mills's writings took on greater salience after 1968 as it seemed to many Americans that defense corporations were the primary benefactors of the Vietnam War.

Mills provided the intellectual context for opposition to the warfare state in the 1960s, but antimilitarists did not rely upon Mills's broadsides against a permanent warfare state (alone); they possessed ample empirical data that corporations profited substantially from the war. During the early years of the Vietnam conflict, defense spending increased to 9 percent of GDP in 1966 from 7 percent in 1964, and private industry saw significant gains from this uptick in military expenditures. One economist, George Cline Smith, told defense executives in September 1965 that it was hard to believe that only months earlier, business was concerned that a steep recession loomed on the horizon. An economic downturn was improbable now as the Vietnam War had alleviated these worries. Cline stated that the primary impact of the war "has been the sharp shift toward optimism over the business outlook." Indeed, "the war in Vietnam has given the defense industries a badly needed stimulus," economists at Northeastern University concluded. While rising inflation and interest rates were long-term preoccupations, it was clear that the war had a "stimulative effect."[13] The increase in military spending due to the Vietnam War provided the national security state with what they had wanted for years: growth in the industrial defense sectors and a steady stream of federal contracts. Executives of defense companies had long complained that cuts to military spending since the Cuban Missile Crisis imperiled American interests abroad and at home and had wounded them financially. Vietnam seemed to offer a solution to their concerns as profits continued to rise for many defense companies in the 1960s. For instance, the Grumman Corporation in Nassau County, Long Island, attained substantial profits in its nine-month earnings balance sheets due to Vietnam. During the first year of the Vietnam War, Grumman employed 31,600 workers, only 3,400 shy of the 35,000 employees hired by the company during World War II.[14]

Antiwar groups therefore targeted leading defense contractors throughout the country as sites for protests in the late 1960s and early 1970s. The organization Women's Strike for Peace demonstrated outside the corporate headquarters of Dow Chemical, the maker of napalm. The labor union United Electrical, Radio, and Machine Workers, protested at a General Electric plant because the corporation took a significant sum of money from the government for defense contracts. SDS members and student radicals "occupied" buildings of Columbia University demanding the school cease funding departments that conducted research for the military.[15]

As the New Left disparaged the military-industrial complex, the term resurfaced in American culture for the first time since the Edwin Walker scandal and the public controversy over the military's involvement in Cold War seminars. Books on the subject of the military-industrial complex proliferated in the late 1960s and early 1970s. With titles such as *The Economy of Death* and *The War Business*, these books revivified debates over the relevance of the military-industrial complex in American life. Vietnam proved that

Eisenhower's warning against the power of a permanent military establishment went unheeded throughout the 1960s, these books argued; and now that Americans have witnessed the dangers of a military-industrial complex, they were prepared to eradicate it. In a review of economist's John Kenneth Galbraith's 1969 book *How to Control the Military*—which argued that the federal government should nationalize the defense industry—the *New York Times* noted that the book sounded the alarm against the bloated largesse of the Pentagon but that Galbraith's work was premised on the belief that Americans "have escaped the cold-war psychosis; the American people are ready to prune the military industrial complex."[16]

In addition to the publication of books and a number of newspaper articles, in 1969, magazines such as the *Atlantic* and *Time* dedicated space to articles on the military-industrial complex. Military personnel, many of them retired, felt the context provided them the opportunity to speak out against American foreign policy. General David M. Shoup, who served in World War II and was regarded as a hero for his role in the Battle of Tarawa, published an article entitled "The New American Militarism" in the April issue of the *Atlantic* in 1969. Shoup declared without equivocation that "America has become a militaristic and aggressive nation." In contrast to the militarism of the Axis powers in World War II—which thrived on nationalism and racism—American militarism was contingent upon unfettered capitalism, on a private, for-profit defense industry. Cold War anticommunism allowed the military-industrial complex to profit endlessly from war, Shoup argued—and Vietnam revealed the interdependency of defense executives, labor, and military officials in keeping militarism alive for financial gain.[17]

Television stations also aired programs on the military-industrial complex in the later 1960s and early 1970s, a sign of how widespread the public's concern was about its influence on American life. One of the most popular was the documentary *The Selling of the Pentagon*, which CBS aired in February 1971 to great controversy. *The Selling of the Pentagon* discussed the lengths military personnel had gone to in order to promote the Vietnam War. The documentary revealed how employees of the Department of Defense, with taxpayer money, made speeches across the country equating patriotism with militarism to try to ramp up public support for the war. While groups such as the American Security Council (ASC) and policy makers such as Secretary of Defense Melvin Laird cited flaws with the film, *The Selling of the Pentagon* went on to win a number of awards, including an Emmy. Trying to attract greater ratings for its own network, ABC aired a documentary one year later entitled *Arms and Security: How Much Is Enough?* that relied on interviews with critics of defense spending who argued the military-industrial complex had perpetuated the arms race.[18]

Vietnam therefore generated a broad public questioning of the military-industrial complex and its consequences for American society that was entirely new to the postwar era. Newfound public awareness—and interest—in the military-industrial complex expanded the antiwar movement's critique of American military power beyond the campus and the streets and into the homes of Americans, as the heightened attention to the size and effects of the military state—and the corporate powers that gave it life—mobilized opposition against a culture of militarism in the United States. Vietnam therefore revived and popularized the critiques of the U.S. foreign policy made by the anti–Cold War Left during the years of Henry Wallace.

This public scrutiny of the military-industrial complex would eventually force policy makers in Congress to reevaluate the need for new weapons programs during the latter half of the Vietnam War. Congress took new measures to limit the imperial presidency by defunding expensive military projects beginning in the late 1960s. The anti-ballistic missile defense system (ABM) proposed by President Richard Nixon in 1969 became the main target of antimilitarists in Congress. Plans to build an ABM were not new. The project to construct a missile defense shield dated to the 1950s and went through several forms and name changes. But up until Nixon, an ABM system was never more than an item on the wish list of defense hawks. Many in Congress viewed the ABM project as overwrought with problems, including its potential expense and technological feasibility. Nixon himself was at times unenthusiastic about his ABM program entitled Safeguard. From the ABM's inception, Nixon expressed worries over whether it was even possible to create such a missile defense shield. In the end, however, these concerns became irrelevant to the president. Nixon believed that the ABM was useful in negotiations with the Soviets—whether it could be built or not. The ABM could be used as leverage to cajole the Soviets into accepting the demands of the United States when both countries met at the bargaining table over the Strategic Arms Limitation Treaty (SALT I). The ABM also offered the Nixon administration an opportunity to neutralize right-wing objections that it was too soft on communism.[19]

Congress once again reacted negatively to proposals for an ABM. Much of the criticism of the ABM was contextualized within the debate over the Vietnam War; the war became a metaphor for the unforeseen, unexpected costs of the ABM. As William Miller, an assistant to the antiwar Republican and Kentucky senator John Sherman Cooper, wrote, "The Vietnam experience shows that a 'commitment' to a massive ABM system will involve a further draining of energy both intellectual and physical."[20] In opposing the ABM, congressional antimilitarists also had to confront pressure from constituents and social movements who lobbied lawmakers to kill the missile defense shield. Groups like SANE argued that the ABM would intensify the arms race, while residents in Grenville, Illinois, passed a resolution stating their opposition to the presence of any ABM sites in their town.[21]

While many antimilitarists had reservations over the ABM, the missile defense system had sweeping support among Cold War hawks—both Democrats and Republicans. The nation must put cost aside in order to protect American lives from Soviet aggression, supporters of the ABM argued in the late 1960s and early 1970s, as they claimed the Soviet Union had overtaken the United States in military superiority and a missile defense shield was the country's last line of defense. The American Security Council (ASC) came out in force to support the ABM. Composed of defense executives, former military brass, wonkish strategists, and anticommunist academics, the ASC warned Americans that the Soviet Union maintained the upper hand in the arms race because of its planned economy. The ASC was consistent in its belief that America was perpetually behind the Soviet Union in the arms race and that Congress and the president needed to authorize the production of a missile shield to deter a nuclear war. Nixon's announcement of the ABM thus gave the ASC an opportunity to push for increased defense spending. In a 1969 report entitled "The ABM and the Changed Strategic Military Balance" and published in booklet form, the ASC argued that it was indisputable "that the Soviet's military objective is strategic superiority because they have passed 'parity' and are still building" up their nuclear arsenal. Using various graphs and charts that indicated that the United States trailed the Soviet Union in numbers of bombers, civil defense, and military expenditures, the ASC argued that the Soviet threat continued to loom large, and thus the ABM provided "the American people a seamless garment of security in an age of acute danger." The ABM was far from perfect, but it was "a method of deterrence which will save lives."[22]

The right-wing media stood steadfast behind Nixon's plan for an ABM as well. *Human Events* and *National Review*, the two main literary organs of the Right, published several favorable articles on the ABM. *National Review* even felt that the ABM did not go far enough in its capability to protect the United States from the Soviets. The magazine worried that the ABM could "be overwhelmed by a sufficiently large number of warheads and/or decoys arriving in a short enough time interval."[23] Despite the shortcomings of the program, the magazine agreed the ABM was "a practical system for shooting down hostile H-bombs."[24]

The ABM also received support from longtime Cold Warriors such as Paul Nitze, the coauthor of NSC-68. As deputy secretary of defense under President Johnson, Nitze defended American policy in Vietnam and lobbied Johnson to increase defense spending. Now in May 1969, Nitze helped form the Committee to Maintain a Prudent Defense Policy (CMPDP) to counteract attempts to defeat the ABM.

The CMPDP recruited members from the public and the private sector, including leaders within the defense industry. General Electric executive Daniel J. Fink wrote to former secretary of state Dean Acheson (also a member of CMPDP and Nitze's former employer in the State Department) wanting to join the CMPDP and fight for the ABM. Fink claimed that his pro-ABM stance had nothing to do with him being an employee for the third largest defense contractor in the nation that had a financial stake in the ABM. In fact, Fink was concerned he would an ineffective supporter of the ABM because he was part of the "self-serving element of the military industrial complex. His concerns did not prevent him, however, from writing to Senator John Stennis with his opinion that the ABM was necessary to deter Soviet capabilities in the event of a nuclear strike.[25]

Richard Perle and Paul Wolfowitz, staffers for Senator Henry Jackson, wrote policy papers on behalf of the CMPDP to push the ABM through Congress. They faulted Democratic senators like Maine's Edmund Muskie for relying on anti-ABM scientists to justify their positions that Safeguard will not work, that it was superfluous, and that it would renew the arms race with the Soviet Union. Perle and Wolfowitz rejected Muskie's contention that the United States "ought to convince the Soviets that we are interested in stabilizing the arms race." This can only be achieved through the ABM because it "acts to insure stability" by strengthening U.S. capabilities to strike first during a nuclear war.[26]

Much to the chagrin of its backers, however, the ABM never saw the light of day in Congress. Missouri Democratic senator Stuart Symington, a once vociferous Cold Warrior turned skeptic of greater military spending, led the campaign in the Senate against the ABM. Symington and antimilitarists in Congress were not persuaded by claims that the ABM was vital to national security. The Cooper-Hart amendment, sponsored by Senators John Sherman Cooper and Philip Hart in 1968, aimed to stop the ABM in its tracks. The amendment polarized Congress into two warring camps, ones that did not necessarily break down along party lines. The anti-ABM coalition contained antimilitarist, antiwar members of Congress but also some budget hawks who opposed further spending on costly defense and technological projects. The proceeding fight over Cooper-Hart between proponents and critics of the ABM was unprecedented, and the sizeable opposition to the ABM generally stunned its backers. ABM supporter Henry Jackson resorted to threatening his colleagues who did not fall in line with the ABM, going so far as to warn Senator Mike Gravel that "if you vote against the ABM, it's going to cause you problems around here."[27] While the antimilitarists lost the first significant battle over the ABM in a 51–49 vote against the ratification of the Cooper-Hart amendment, as a significant minority, they prevented the ABM from going forward in subsequent votes.

Additional Pentagon projects such as the supersonic transport plane (SST) and the C5-A met the same fate as the ABM. SST proponents hailed the plane as a vital contribution to American economic and military power. The plane promised to break the sound barrier, cutting travel time from Paris to New York down to a few hours. The SST was far superior to the Soviet equivalent of the supersonic plane, the Tupolev Tu-144, and was sold to the public as a vital contribution to U.S. supremacy in the fields of technology and weapons development. The SST was also billed as a solution to joblessness in the defense industry. Corporate backers of the SST promised that a majority of the expenditures for the plane would be spent in areas whose percentage of unemployment exceeded the national rate. Representatives from Boeing (who won the contract to build the plane) claimed "that the minor economic stimulus of the SST prototype program would be preferable to the cost of temporary, avoidable dislocations and the resulting lack of stability" for defense workers. Furthermore, at a time when issues regarding balance of payments dominated discussions over American economic policy and relations with Japan and Europe, sales of possible SSTs would reverse the deficits.[28] A memorandum to George S. Moore, a Boeing executive, argued that the SST would generate jobs, dominate world aviation markets, and lead to more efficient air travel. More importantly, it would provide an additional fifty thousand jobs to skilled white-collar workers who were presently unemployed.[29]

Antimilitarists, however, were alarmed by the prospective cost of the SST, passenger safety, and the negative atmospheric impact the plane would have upon the environment. Individuals opposed to the SST represented a diverse group of men and women, including environmentalists, consumer advocates, and scientists. In December 1970, with a final roll call vote of 52–51, the United States Senate voted against additional appropriations for the SST. The death knell to the SST came in March 1971 when the House finally voted to terminate all funding for the project. The House vote made certain that the SST would not be flying in American skies. After the SST was rejected, Barry Goldwater criticized the vote as a victory for the antiwar Left. Rather than blame nonpartisan scientific experts and government officials who felt the SST was cost prohibitive and detrimental to the environment, Goldwater impugned liberal Democrats who he felt were on a crusade to weaken American might. Goldwater argued that the "same people who found it easy to understand the reaction of the liberal doves to the War in Vietnam found their attitude on the SST."[30]

The C5-A plane was felled by the rising surge of antimilitarism in the United States as well. Designed in the mid-1950s by the Lockheed Corporation to transport planes and other large equipment to battlegrounds like Vietnam, the C5-A was plagued by cost overruns and poor construction from its inception. The C5-A proved to be a symbol of that war when it rolled off assembly lines in the 1960s. With a 223-foot wingspan and a six-story tail wing, the C5-A could only be contained in a space about the size of a football stadium. The plane's grandiose size did not equate to functionality. After several dozen planes proved deficient due to cracks in their wings—and antispending hawks in Congress such as Wisconsin Democrat William Proxmire protested—future production of the plane was canceled. The C5-A also had a fair number of proponents from both sides of the aisle. Democrats and Republicans defended the C5-A to preserve the jobs that depended upon production of the plane. Senators Herman Talmadge from Georgia and Alan Cranston from California, Democrats at opposite ends of the ideological spectrum, were outraged that the federal government was willing to put thousands out of work in their states that relied upon the C5-A for employment.[31]

The jobs argument, however, did not succeed in saving expensive military projects like the C5-A plane or the SST. By 1971, antimilitarists had gained the upper hand in Congress and looked to be presiding over a new era in the Cold War. The Vietnam War tainted the respectability of the defense establishment to the extent that a new consensus on U.S. foreign policy began to take shape, one that rebuked the pervasive presence of the Cold War military in American political culture. Defense programs once deemed vital to the health of national security were now attacked as expensive, anachronistic, and unnecessary. Marred by disrepute and financial setbacks, the defense industry would go on the offensive in the late 1960s to repair its image and grow its profit margins. In making its arguments against antimilitarists and the New Left in the late 1960s, the defense industry would have an ally in the White House: President Richard Nixon.

* * *

When Nixon won the 1968 election over his Democratic challenger Hubert Humphrey, he did so at a time of uncertainty and unrest over Vietnam. Discussion of Vietnam had radically changed since the previous presidential campaign. The debate was no longer over what course of action the United States would take in Southeast Asia but over how the country would extricate itself from the conflict. The war was the primary issue on voters' minds during the election, as a Gallup poll taken in August claimed that 52 percent of Americans believed it was the overriding issue in the campaign.[32] Ever the consummate politician, Nixon realized that voters wanted a definitive conclusion to the Vietnam War and told the American public that he had a "secret plan" to end the conflict that he would reveal once elected.

In articulating his views on the Vietnam War, Nixon transformed his reputation from Cold Warrior to peacemaker during the campaign. Prior to his second run for the presidency, Nixon had stellar credentials as an ardent anticommunist. As a California representative in the 1950s, Nixon investigated and targeted suspected communists like Alger Hiss. When he was vice president under Dwight Eisenhower, Nixon was arguably best known for his "Kitchen debate" with Soviet premier Nikita Khrushchev at the American National Exhibition in Moscow, where Nixon proudly touted the virtues of capitalism over communism. Nixon was also a hawk during the early years of the conflict in Vietnam, having urged President Johnson to adopt a tougher approach to prosecuting the war. Indeed, in December 1965, Nixon wrote in *Reader's Digest* that the United States must be resolute in winning the war and there should be no attempt at negotiation with the North Vietnamese. "There can be no substitute for victory when the objective is the defeat of communist aggression," Nixon wrote.[33] In 1968, however, Nixon shed his hawkish past and portrayed himself as the man who would bring "peace with honor" in Vietnam. Nixon waged a presidential campaign that united suburbanites in the Sunbelt and moderate, Rockefeller Republicans in the Northeast on his claim that he would end the war in Vietnam and restore "law and order" in the United States, a coded message that appealed to opponents of the civil rights movement.[34]

[margin note: Nixon changes tunes]

When Nixon took office in January 1969, Americans were hopeful that he would uphold his campaign promise to end the war and achieving a lasting peace. Antiwar liberals in Congress even withheld criticism of Nixon in early 1969, waiting for the president to stay true to his word that he would bring American troops back home. The armistice between Nixon and Congress was short-lived, however, as the president expanded the war into Cambodia in March 1969 through Operation Menu, a secret aerial campaign intended to disrupt communist supply routes from North to South Vietnam. When Operation Menu failed, Nixon then sent ground troops into the country, an event that Nixon made public on a televised address to the nation in May 1970. The announcement of the Cambodia operation propelled antiwar activists out into the streets again, with deadly consequences. Four students were killed and eight were wounded at Kent State University on May 3 after the Ohio National Guard opened fire on peaceful student protesters. The shock of Kent State led to further antiwar demonstrations, as the Cambodia operation revitalized

[margin note: Cambodia]

[margin note: Kent State]

calls for an immediate evacuation of American troops from Southeast Asia.

The American intervention in Cambodia provoked further criticism of the national security state. The Nixon administration was all too aware of the negative public perception of the military and defense apparatus in the early 1970s. Henry Kissinger wrote in his memoirs that he and the president felt confronted by an antidefense climate that (to him) indicated the revival of American isolationism. Faced with the crisis of Vietnam, one that upended the Cold War consensus, Kissinger concluded that Americans in the early 1970s aimed to retreat from international affairs and divest the country of its responsibilities as leader of the free world. Demands for defense reductions and foreign policy retrenchment were "symptomatic of the bitter and destructive mood of the period and of the substantial breakdown of national consensus," according to Kissinger.[35] "The passionate critique of the war in Vietnam spread to an attack of the defense establishment as a whole," Kissinger wrote, as more Americans believed the Cold War military apparatus should be dismantled to pay for social programs. Intellectuals too had embraced the idea that the military-industrial complex had finally succeeded in exerting a "disproportionate influence on American life."[36]

As critiques of the military-industrial complex reached their apex in the late 1960s and early 1970s, the defense lobby sought to wage a campaign to dispel the negative image of its industry and its role in perpetuating the Vietnam War. After the 1967 protests against Dow Chemical, the defense industry was compelled to change its image as militaristic warmongers. While they did not expect to convince the "Weathermen of SDS" of their viewpoint, defense contractors hoped to engage critics who claimed the defense industry was an inherently destructive force in American life, that "society is in the grips of the Military Industrial Complex."[37] In 1969, the National Defense Committee of NAM launched a public relations campaign to overturn Americans' negative perceptions of the defense industry. In a pamphlet entitled "What Eisenhower Really Said about the Military-Industrial Complex," NAM argued that Eisenhower was misquoted in his 1961 Farewell Address where he warned Americans about the threat the military-industrial complex posed to American democracy.[38] NAM felt that it was "ironic" that liberals and the New Left referenced Eisenhower in making their case against Vietnam and for spending on expensive weapons systems such as the ABM. While Eisenhower did warn the country about the military-industrial complex, NAM argued that he made more statements supporting the need for a strong defense against the threat of communism.[39]

The makeshift public relations effort organized by the defense industry indicated just how ill prepared it was to confront such extensive negative criticism. From the end of World War II to the early 1960s, as was the case for much of the Cold War, defense contractors focused on winning contracts and maintaining a close relationship with Congress and the Department of Defense. Executives did not think long term in their financial projections, working from contract to contract without applying proper attention to antimilitarist politics surrounding their business.[40] Defense companies had a coordinated infrastructure for lobbying that emerged out of World War II but at the same time prided itself on not needing one.[41] Up until the late 1950s, the industry saw the Pentagon and Congress on its side, and there existed little need to engage in hostilities with either the executive or the legislative branch. Open insubordination to the acting presidential administration and Congress would be consequential for contract procurement. The industry relied on the presumption that it could maintain seamless connections with the federal government without complication.

That is, until Vietnam. Whereas NAM's previous public relations efforts primarily targeted federal regulators, NAM's new enemy was the American public. The Vietnam War and its critics compelled NAM to relaunch a renewed effort to convince Americans that the defense industry suffered from undeserved condemnation and libelous statements from fringe radicals in order to save its reputation. Defense executives feared that lawmakers would abandon their industry if popular opinion reflected the arguments made by the antiwar Left and thought a public relations campaign could be a bulwark against further damage to their reputation.

The main organization that represented the defense industry in the early 1960s was the Council of Defense and Space Industry Associations (CODSIA). Formed in 1965, CODSIA was dedicated solely to matters of procurement. The membership of CODSIA was a list of who's who in the defense business. The organization included United Aircraft, General Electric, Lockheed, and Texas Instruments among others. It also included organizations such as NAM and the National Security Industrial Association (NSIA), which contained representatives from defense companies throughout the country who were ardent proponents of greater military spending. The role of CODSIA changed, however, after the Vietnam War. Several defense corporations broke with CODSIA in the late 1960s for its unwillingness to confront critics of the national security state, once the industry's focus began to shift from procurement to public relations. Both NAM and the NSIA resigned from CODSIA in 1969 with an eye toward changing "the current climate of public opinion regarding national defense affairs" after CODSIA refused to do so. Some members of CODSIA were concerned that dropping out of the organization would be counterproductive. Apprehension about resigning from CODSIA stemmed from the fear that NAM would sacrifice a close relationship with the White House and its allies in Congress to go after antimilitarist lawmakers. These hesitations, however, were dismissed as insignificant to CODSIA's defectors.[42]

Utilizing its vast financial resources, and the support of organizations like NAM and NSIA, the defense industry tried to sway policy makers to their side. Defense contractors targeted Secretary of Defense Melvin Laird, Deputy Secretary of Defense David Packard, Assistant Secretary of Defense James Schlesinger, and Admiral of the Navy Elmo Zumwalt. Each one of these men had voiced concern over the culture of antimilitarism among the public and in Congress. Laird garnered particular attention because of his position and influence on Capitol Hill. A former representative from Wisconsin, Laird had close connections to many in Congress and used them to great advantage: he obtained much of what he wanted in the defense budget. As secretary of defense, Laird argued that vast sums for defense were needed to restore American superiority, which he believed had been squandered because of the Vietnam War.[43]

During the early 1970s, NAM sent Laird letters praising his call for an increase in the defense budget to fight Soviet communism. Daniel Z. Henkin, an aide to Laird, even spoke at a NAM conference, flippantly claiming to represent the "Commander in Chief of the Military Industrial Complex." At the conference, Henkin called for a federal program that would silence "critics aiming for the front pages of major newspapers," rehabilitate the image of the military, and stress the vital contribution enrolled service members were making to the safety of the American people. Laird himself gave speeches to defense contractors keeping them abreast of administration policies. In 1970, Laird told executives of the electronics industry that his demand for $80 billion in defense was an "austere, rockbottom, barebones budget." Even so, critics assailed the military budget as excessive. Laird then called for greater coordination between defense companies and the government to ensure American prosperity in the face of lean times—and unrelenting criticism from the Left.[44]

The defense industry also looked for allies among Cold War Democrats and Republicans in Congress. In a speech delivered before defense industry executives at NAM's Seventy-Fifth Annual Congress of American Industry meeting, Arizona senator and 1964 Republican candidate Barry Goldwater told those present at the meeting that the overwhelming condemnation of American military power was "carefully timed by the critics of American defense to coincide with an understandable disenchantment and irritation on the part of the American public with the long, dirty, frustrating war in Indochina." Goldwater said he did "not have to explain to this group the nature of the liberal assault which has been made over the past two years against the portions of American industry which contribute so materially to the American defense establishment." He warned those in attendance that "the tremendous hue and cry about the so-called Military-Industrial Complex" has further contributed to American capitulation in the face of a Soviet military resurgence.[45] Goldwater's colleague, South Carolina Republican Strom Thurmond, spoke at a

1967 NAM meeting for its National Defense Committee, where he was warmly announced as a strong supporter of the Vietnam War and "military preparedness." NAM members said Thurmond had also played an important role in the 1960s denouncing the "muzzling of military officers in their anti-communist statements" and was instrumental in "troop education programs and cold-war seminars for reservists and the public."[46]

Denigration of the New Left and the antiwar movement also came from right-wing activists who had ties to the defense industry. Representing the National Security Industrial Conference, a right-wing think-tank, Frank Barnett warned the University of South Carolina graduating class of 1970 about the New Left and its call for an immediate American withdrawal from Vietnam. Along with the internal threat of the New Left, the greatest external threat remained global communism. Barnett critiqued the direction of American foreign policy in the 1960s, stating that the United States had allocated its resources to "social inventions that range from Head Start to the Peace Corps" and had not been attentive to the Soviets, which he claimed outmatched the United States in "strategic weapons, and, by 1972, may even be ahead."[47]

While working with White House officials and hawkish politicians, defense industry executives also took it upon themselves to change popular opinion through public speeches and newspaper articles. Edward G. Uhl, president of Fairchild Industries and chairman of NAM's National Defense Committee, echoed hawkish sentiments when he commented that the "Soviet buildup" of its military arsenal "has been completely over-balanced by the unpopularity of the war in South Vietnam." The war was merely the excuse liberal doves needed to implement their long-term goal of reducing the size of the military, Uhl argued, as he was sure the Left would reduce the military status of the United States to that of "a second or third rate nation."[48]

Defense contractors also tried to distance themselves from involvement in the Vietnam War. Executives of defense contractors argued that the failed war in Vietnam adversely affected the prestige of American military power and had made the United States a

weaker nation. Charles B. McCoy, president of the chemical manufacturer DuPont, gave an address to the annual business meeting
of the Manufacturing Chemists Association in 1970 where he said
that the "Vietnam war is tearing at the whole fabric of our social and
political and economic life." After antiwar demonstrations increased
throughout college campuses following the invasion of Cambodia,
McCoy said he realized the extent to which Vietnam had polarized
the nation. McCoy went on to say that the war had not only led to
numerous American deaths but endangered the health of the American republic. It was "hard to see how we can apply adequate resources
to domestic needs, and restore a feeling of national unity and confidence, until we reach a settlement of this conflict in Southeast Asia,"
McCoy said. Quotes from McCoy's address appeared in editorials in
newspapers such as the *Hartford Times* and *Press-Gazette of Green
Bay* that likewise favored withdrawal from Vietnam. The *Daily News
Record* noted McCoy's address with disbelief, a reaction that elicited
a letter from DuPont executive Samuel Lenher. Lenher criticized the
paper for acting as if McCoy's comments on peace in Vietnam "were
surprising, presumably because Du Pont is thought to benefit from
war-related sales." Lenher added that his company would "prosper
only as the country prospers, and the waste of war with its terrible
social and economic effects is extremely costly to us, as a Company
and as individuals."[49]

But whether disavowing their image as warmongers, denouncing their left-wing critics, or wrapping themselves in patriotic statements, the defense lobby had difficulty convincing the public that its
members were engaged in virtuous economic enterprise during the
Vietnam era. Defense executives gained allies in power in the late
1960s and early 1970s but not enough to overturn the culture of antimilitarism in the United States. As long as the conflict raged in Vietnam, defense companies had a hard time convincing a skeptical public they did not profit from war. Vietnam was a cancer that ate away
at public confidence in the military and defense structure, making
the prowar factions within the defense industry a besieged minority.
Where the defense industry failed in its lobbying campaign, other

elements of the Cold War coalition conducted their own efforts to convince policy makers (and the public) that the United States must maintain its overwhelming military power if the Cold War went on.

* * *

With the military—and its corporate connections—in disrepute, as well as the reigning foundations of Cold War foreign policy, the Nixon administration was pressured to rethink how the United States fought the Cold War. The antiwar movement and the New Left placed limitations and constraints on the actions of policy makers following Vietnam. Once in office, the Nixon administration operated under the perception that the American people had revolted against the Cold War order and longed for a new foreign policy strategy.[50] Nixon's solution to dealing with these post-Vietnam constraints was through détente with the Soviet Union and China. As a grand strategy, détente accepted the limits placed on U.S. foreign policy due to the conflict in Southeast Asia and the reality that it was impossible for the Cold War to carry on as it had been since the late 1940s. The main architect of détente, Henry Kissinger, avoided assigning value judgments to foreign regimes, as he preferred not to conduct relations with countries based on their internal characteristics. What mattered to Kissinger was whether countries had the best interests of the United States in mind, not their governing ideology, no matter how repressive or undemocratic. Nixon and Kissinger avoided direct intervention in the developing world, preferring to offer indirect assistance through arms sales and economic aid to allied countries in Africa and Asia.[51] The increase in arms sales helped keep the defense industry in business during the Nixon years and circumvented the military-industrial complex argument prevalent in New Left circles, as they funded internal rather than external conflicts. Détente served domestic ends as well. Détente would mute those voices on the Left who had called for a reduction in the arms race and better diplomatic relations with the Soviets. The goals of détente were threefold: to silence domestic critiques of foreign policy, impose order on the chaotic environment of global politics, and preserve America's status as a superpower.[52]

[margin handwritten note: Goals of détente]

The Nixon administration foresaw diplomacy with the Soviet Union and China as providing the basis for détente. Triangular diplomacy, the White House predicted, would widen the Sino-Soviet split that had its origins in the mid-1950s following the death of Joseph Stalin. Nixon hoped that a friendlier relationship with China and the Soviet Union would cause both countries to compete for aid and attention from the United States. Détente was also a possible path to peace in Vietnam, as Nixon and Kissinger felt it could force the communist superpowers to place pressure on the North Vietnamese to end the war. To achieve this, in 1969, Nixon began making plans to be the first president to visit the People's Republic of China and thereby "open" the country to a better economic and diplomatic relationship with the United States. At the same time, Kissinger created a secret backchannel to Soviet ambassador Anatoly Dobrynin to conduct negotiations for reducing nuclear weapons.[53] These policies, the Nixon administration hoped, would allow the United States to pursue the policy of containment under different terms.

It was to no surprise of Nixon that when his grand strategy of détente was made public, it angered the conservative element within the Republican Party. Negotiations with the Soviet Union and China were anathema to conservatives' received wisdom about the reasons for the Cold War. *National Review* writer James Burnham could not understand why Nixon and Kissinger still perceived the Soviet Union to be an enemy but pursued negotiations with the country nonetheless. To Burnham, the Nixon administration seemed schizophrenic in its relations with the Soviet Union. On one hand, Nixon encouraged reductions in intercontinental ballistic missiles through SALT I, arguing that mutual assured destruction was antiquated and nuclear escalation and brinkmanship must come to an end. But on the other, the administration campaigned for an ABM whose logic was situated on the basis that the Soviet Union had sufficient and credible nuclear power that deterrence was still needed. Furthermore, Kissinger's willingness to separate communist ideology from state behavior was evidence of cognitive dissonance. Conservatives still believed that foreign policy decisions made by the Kremlin emanated from the

[handwritten margin note: or rationality "doing business" at arms length]

doctrine of Marxism-Leninism, and Vietnam had not changed this. The same was true of any communist power. The Soviets were still an expansionist empire, and the only way to deal with them was through a show of force.[54]

But right-wing activists failed to see their views toward the Soviet Union and communist countries represented in the decisions of White House policy makers. Their disagreement with Nixon over the need for a stronger defense budget contributed to their gradual falling out with the president. Discontent among movement conservatives (at least among the leadership) toward the administration finally came to a head in the summer of 1971. Nixon knew the suspension of conservative support for his administration was coming. In a meeting with Kissinger and his chief of staff H. R. Haldeman, on July 28, Haldeman noted that the president was ruffled because "Bill Buckley and his troops, plus the other *Human Events* types met on Monday and decided to issue a statement of nonsupport of the P."[55] Nixon was stunned that Buckley and his cohorts would go so far as to repudiate his administration. With an eye toward reelection in 1972, Nixon would rest easier if he knew he had conservatives' support, realizing it played a role in his election in 1968. Nixon said this much to Buckley in 1967 as Nixon prepared to run again for the presidency. Referring to his loss to Pat Brown for governor of California, Nixon privately told Buckley, "I found out in 1962 that you can't win an election without the right wing."[56]

Nixon cared enough about pressure from the Right in 1971 that he ordered Henry Kissinger to play the role of unofficial ambassador to conservatives. Indeed, Kissinger personally met with leading conservatives to assuage their concerns over détente. Present at the meeting were Allan Ryskind and William Rusher, editors of *Human Events* and *National Review* respectively, and representatives from the ASC, Young Americans for Freedom, and the American Conservative Union. New York State was well represented in the meeting, as Dan Mahoney from the New York Conservative Party and Bill Schneider, a defense expert and a staff member of New York's conservative senator James Buckley, also attended the meeting. Kissinger wanted the meeting to remain off the record because he had "never spoken with this degree of candor before" and therefore insisted that "none of these matters can appear either directly or indirectly in print." Kissinger began by reiterating what he felt were the obstacles the administration faced. Kissinger told the men in the room that "this Administration came to office at the end of a period of substantial collapse of foreign policy theory," which resulted in "vicious isolationism" and an "extreme attack on general principles of authority, and in particular, on the Defense establishment—the military." The Cuban Missile Crisis, Kissinger said, led to the cancellation of new weapons programs and a subsequent deterioration in military superiority, an argument that Kissinger knew would appeal to the Right. "This erosion of power was compounded by a domestic crisis arising from the existence of the Vietnam War," and Kissinger urged the men in the room to have sympathy for the president. The national security advisor defended SALT, played up Nixon's support of the ABM, and portrayed the Congress as the real enemies of defense spending, not the White House. The president has "implemented the maximum Defense budget possible, without raising taxes in a[n] election year." Nixon had too many enemies on the Left, and he could not afford them on the Right. "This administration, gentlemen, is the loneliest administration imaginable," said Kissinger.[57]

But Kissinger's passionate defense of the administration did not win over his guests. "Defense is the key issue here," said Bill Schneider. The president had to make a concerted effort to convince the American people that military superiority "was the *sina* [sic] *qua non*" issue in American politics. If the president was willing to do this, he "would chase Senator Proxmire up the road." Dan Mahoney told Kissinger that Nixon was a deep disappointment and that he was disturbed that "in the current intellectual and political context that the White House can see itself clear to take the minimum now on the Defense issue." The sole means of reversing course and "to turn the Establishment and the nation is with Presidential leadership," and the president had thoroughly failed in this task. Stan Evans acknowledged Kissinger's candor but said that his "prior opinion still holds," regarding Nixon's foreign policy. Exasperated, Kissinger replied that conservatives were far too critical of Nixon. Kissinger concluded the meeting saying, "I just hope you will stop yelling at us, and start yelling at our enemies."[58]

Despite the attention he paid to conservative leaders, Nixon privately brushed them off as inconsequential to the success of his presidency. At the July 28 meeting, Nixon expressed agitation but not extensive worry over the defection of conservative intellectuals. "The P is not too concerned" about the *National Review* declaration, noted Haldeman at the time. Haldeman wrote that Nixon wanted "answers communicated to [conservatives], but he makes the point that we don't need to worry too much about the right-wing nuts on this." Indeed, the chief of staff told his boss that there was no "conservative revolt" against his administration with the exception of "about 300 people."[59] Nixon barked at Haldeman to tell Henry Kissinger to "get off his ass" and speak to William F. Buckley Jr. about the declaration, but Buckley was the only conservative that mattered to Nixon, as all others were simply "doctrinaire rightists."[60]

What bothered Nixon more than the Right's opinion of his foreign policy were the political attitudes of the American worker. Indeed, the activist Right, like the defense lobby, made little headway in changing the culture of antimilitarism in the late 1960s and early 1970s. The "silent majority," as Nixon dubbed working Americans in 1969, had more sway in the perceptions and decisions of Nixon's political thinking than right-wing intellectuals. Nixon saw the future of his reelection prospects—and the Republican Party—in working and middle-class Americans disenchanted with a stagnating economy.[61]

* * *

By 1971, the popularity of the defense establishment had suffered immensely due to the culture of antimilitarism. The winding down of the Vietnam War and the scrutiny of the military-industrial complex meant that the defense budget declined from 10 percent to 7 percent of the GDP. The public relations campaign by the defense industry failed to make significant inroads into the public's and Congress's opposition to militarism and support for détente, and conservatives, Cold War hawks, and other proponents of massive defense spending had little influence on American political culture.

The recession that hit the country and the developed world by 1970 proved more detrimental to the defense economy. From 1969 to 1970, unemployment soared from 3.5 percent to 6.1 percent; and inflation stood at 5.6 percent, only a 0.5 percent drop from the previous year, and still high for a recession. Cuts to the defense budget since 1965, combined with the recession, struck the defense industry with a vengeance, as those in the industry worried that the end of the Vietnam conflict "contributed to a slowing of the economy." Since 1968, 2.3 million overall jobs were cut in the defense industries, with the private workforce in defense declining from 3.6 million to 2.3 million in three years.[62] In addition to the drop in employment due to the end of the Vietnam War, corporations outsourced more defense jobs in the late 1960s, hastening the process of deindustrialization in the United States. While Massachusetts Democratic senator Ted Kennedy led efforts in Congress to pass legislation to aid out-of-work engineers and scientists employed in the technology fields (many working at Harvard, MIT, or for defense companies along Route 128 in Massachusetts), he feared it would only provide short-term assistance. Officials in Washington, D.C., knew that the elimination of defense programs such as the SST affected the political allegiances of "so many scientists and engineers out of work in key electoral states like California, Florida and Texas," which would then influence the coming election year.[63]

Scientists and engineers were not the only ones affected. Layoffs in aerospace particularly affected the blue-collar workforce. Defense manufacturing on Long Island, New York, faced severe cuts in 1971. Along with cuts in manufacturing in the defense sector, manufacturing overall lost jobs. Grumman Corporation reduced its workforce by five thousand jobs in 1970 alone; it was scheduled to cut another three thousand in 1971. This came at the same time that the New York State Department of Labor predicted that "cutbacks in the manufacturing industries can be expected to continue until at least June 1971," forcing unemployment up to 5.2 percent from 4.5 percent, most of which "will be persons displaced by defense cutbacks and [who] will tend to be unemployed for long periods of time." Such working-class employees had less mobility or options than their upper-class counterparts and therefore had little economic opportunities once their jobs disappeared.[64]

In addition to New York, California was also hit hard by the drop in the defense budget. Governor Ronald Reagan argued that the federal government should assist the aerospace industry in the area, which had remade the region after World War II by spurring high-paying jobs, upper-class suburbs, and a significant base of tax revenue for the state. While Reagan professed to be committed to the free market, his antistatist ideology was qualified by his larger need to keep defense jobs in his state. Nixon advisor Harry Dent noted that Reagan in 1970 had "a very strong desire to personally talk to the President about his interest in another Air Force contract for California" and had tried repeatedly to contact the president over "getting the Freedom-Fighter contract for Northrop Aviation in California."[65] Reagan also hoped to get the B-1 bomber contract—even while an organization entitled the National Campaign to Stop the B-1 Bomber mounted a campaign to squash it. When entreaties to Nixon did not make sufficient headway, Reagan wrote to Kissinger in June reiterating his plea for additional defense contracts. Without the contract for Northrop Aviation, Reagan feared cuts to businesses and job losses, including his own as governor. "Without this 'building block' seven plants in the L.A.-Long Beach area will close," Reagan warned, as Southern California contained "35% of the states [sic] manufacturing and our unemployment is already far above the national average." Reagan emphasized that "the socio-economic elements (and for that matter the political) weigh heavily in Californias [sic] favor." Referring to the self-immolation of Buddhist monks in protest of the Vietnam War, Reagan crudely joked that if California did not receive a fresh infusion of money from the Pentagon, "It isn't that important—but I have a yellow Monks robe and a can of gasoline if it doesn't go through."[66]

Unemployment in the defense industry provided a backdrop to the heated debates over the proposal to bail out the Lockheed Corporation in 1971. Founded in 1912 and based in Burbank, California, Lockheed had been a major employer and industrial force in Southern California since World War II. In the 1960s, however, Lockheed had mismanaged government funds and overspent on expensive and unwarranted defense projects. Among these programs were the C5-A plane and the L-1011 Tri-Star airliner, a civilian aircraft whose costs per plane engine had doubled. Lockheed had partnered with the British company Rolls-Royce in building the L-1011 engine, but Rolls-Royce went bankrupt in February 1971, leaving Lockheed holding the deficit for the engines. In response, the company laid off 9,200 employees working on the L-1011. By May 1971, the banks reeling from the fallout of Lockheed's bad investments promised they would not allocate additional credit to the company if the federal government did not guarantee the funds. If the government refused to back billions in loans that Lockheed wanted to keep production of the L-1011 (and the company) going, it was expected that Lockheed would default, declare bankruptcy, and liquidate its operations, leaving its ninety thousand workers across the country unemployed.[67]

Few were more concerned with the future of Lockheed than Richard Nixon. Unlike the controversy over the SST, the C5-A, or the ABM, the discussion over the Lockheed loan guarantee was not about whether to fund a potentially unnecessary project but about whether to save a large corporation that employed tens of thousands. Indeed, the Lockheed bailout debate centered on whether to save preexisting jobs, not on creating new ones—a far more heated topic.

At a time when the United States had witnessed the collapse of the Bretton Woods system and was experiencing increased competition from overseas markets and rising inflation and unemployment rates, the Nixon administration believed it could not afford to allow an additional economic catastrophe and rushed to save Lockheed. Lockheed was not any ordinary company, Nixon said, but one of the largest employers in the defense industry and "one of the Nation's great companies." Lockheed offered "an enormous employment lift to this part of the country," and Nixon was determined "to see to it that southern California—after taking the disappointment of not getting the SST, which would, of course, have brought many, many jobs to this part of the country—that California does not have the additional jolt of losing Lockheed."[68]

The chief proponent of the bailout in the House of Representatives was California representative Barry Goldwater Jr., the son of the conservative icon. Goldwater Jr. was an unequivocal supporter of the loan guarantees, as Lockheed's headquarters was in his district. In the Senate, the conservative Republican from Texas John Tower emerged as the main advocate of the bailout. In the abstract, both Tower and Goldwater Jr. were free market, antiregulation conservatives who normally fumed at the prospect of government intervention in the economy. But the Cold War defense economy did not enter into their concept of the free market. In the minds of Goldwater and Tower, Lockheed and similar companies were exceptions to the laissez faire rule.

While the supporters of the bailout were numerable, the anti–loan guarantee forces were just as large, and thought to be insurmountable. Antimilitarists in Congress, New Left activists, and Lockheed's competitors were staunchly opposed to the loan guarantees, even while noting that the employment situation in the defense industry was a difficult one. Senator William Proxmire resumed the role he maintained in the SST and C5-A battles as chief deficit hawk in the Senate. Proxmire had a long history of opposing the wastefulness in the defense industry, which he conveyed in his book entitled *Report from Wasteland: America's Military-Industrial Complex,* published in 1970. Democrats like William S. Moorhead of Pennsylvania echoed Proxmire's concerns over profligacy among military contractors and argued that Lockheed's threats of bankruptcy held the government hostage to its mismanagement. "This is like an 80-ton dinosaur who comes to your door and says, 'if you don't feed me I will die and what are you going to do with 80 tons of dead stinking dinosaur in your yard,'" Moorhead stated.[69]

Joining Proxmire and the antibailout Democrats were right-wing, libertarian-leaning senators like James L. Buckley and Barry

Goldwater Sr., who stood stalwart against the Lockheed bailout, citing what they believed was its unconstitutional interference in the
free market. In an official statement on the Lockheed loan, Buckley
said he would only support reimbursement of Lockheed if the federal
government incurred a "moral obligation to Lockheed" for its defense
work. Only then would Congress entertain creating "a proposal to
reimburse Lockheed for its expenditures made in good faith." Also
in the antibailout mix were representatives from Rockwell, Boeing,
and General Electric. All three lobbied to defeat the loan guarantees
knowing it would hurt a strong competitor in the aerospace industry. Indeed, the Nixon administration had difficulty finding another
aerospace company to support the loan guarantees during the summer of 1971.[70]

Once the legislation was put forward, California residents engaged
in a massive media effort to convince Congress to pass it. As *Time*
magazine noted, white-collar and blue-collar employees of the aerospace industry served "as amateur lobbyists" in pressing for the legislation, some of whom had been out of work because of the SST vote.
Defense workers published ads in newspapers and urged Americans
to boycott Wisconsin beer and cheese as an affront to Proxmire. Members of the International Association of Machinists (IAM) launched
a lobbying campaign that would see over five hundred thousand letters written to members of Congress and eventually spend $55,000 to
support the bailout.[71]

Supporters of the Lockheed bailout cited national security and the
Cold War as the reasons for the federal government to step in and
rescue the company. The city of Campbell, California, also adopted a
resolution on behalf of the proposed loan guarantees. Campbell was
"one of fifteen incorporated cities in Santa Clara County which is the
home of Lockheed," and the company should be saved as the "concentration of development skill, technology and scientific talent . . . must
be considered of fundamental importance to both this nation and to
the entire Free World." Keeping Lockheed afloat meant not only saving jobs, local tax revenues, and a suburban community whose future
rested on the company's success but also maintaining the security of

the United States and its allies.[72] The *Marietta Daily Journal* likewise urged citizens of Cobb County, Georgia, to support the proposed federal loan guarantee to prevent the Lockheed Corporation from going bankrupt. The article requested that residents "come into any of the three Cobb Federal offices . . . and sign the resolution to tell Congress and the nation Cobb County is behind Lockheed." County members were also encouraged to write letters to their congressional representatives and to relevant committee members to convince them that Lockheed needed to stay in business because "Lockheed-Georgia has been a business citizen of Cobb County for 20 years, contributing substantially to our economy." Not only was Lockheed vital to keeping skilled, middle-class jobs in suburban Georgia, but the company served the interests of American foreign policy in keeping the nation safe from communism. Indeed, the loss of Lockheed would mean "irreparable harm" to the state of U.S. "national security."[73]

Facing pressure from their constituents, Governor Ronald Reagan and his lieutenant governor Ed Reinecke were concerned that the loan guarantee would not make it through Congress. When the loan guarantee was up for debate in the House, Reinecke asked for a meeting with Nixon over the layoffs in the aerospace industry and the possible "re-employment of California engineers and scientists." Nixon refused to meet with Reinecke, offering the excuse that his schedule did not accommodate his request, but an aide to Nixon reassured Reinecke that the president shared his concerns over aerospace unemployment in the state.[74] Ever the political opportunist, Nixon sought to use the Lockheed crisis to gain favor from the company's workers and the labor unions that represented them. Deputy Assistant to the President Dwight L. Chapin wrote to Haldeman that because "the Administration is on the line regarding this loan, we might as well milk it for what it is worth in Southern California." Hoping to add additional members to Nixon's Republican "New Majority," Chapin proposed that the president, "drive up to Los Angeles via the Freeway and stop at one of the Aerospace plants." Nixon should engage in a conversation with the workers and "assure them that he was going to see that they keep their jobs and that their friends are rehired."[75]

The fight over the Lockheed bailout ensued over the course of the summer and pitted members of Congress against one another. Congress heard testimony by Lockheed CEO Daniel Haughton that the loan guarantees were needed to employ the over thirty thousand workers "in 35 states" working on the L-1011, figures that included the various subcontractors working on the plane. Democrat Alan Cranston, like he did over the C5-A controversy, defended Lockheed for responding to the "call to arms to help equip the nation for national defense," saying that the United States relied on the weapons Lockheed built during the Cold War, "for national defense and security." Cranston's antimilitarist colleagues argued that monies were better spent on public infrastructure projects and that by passing the bailout legislation, the government would be funding Lockheed's irresponsibility. The pro- and antibailout factions continued to war with one another throughout June. By the end of July, there was still no clear sign that the legislation would pass.[76]

The Lockheed loan fight also divided labor; union leaders who did not represent Lockheed workers argued that the bailout did not serve the long-term interests of workers. IAM President Floyd E. Smith—and the leadership of the AFL-CIO—lobbied Congress to approve the bailout. But Joel Jacobson of the United Auto Workers cited the need for defense parts to be made at home rather than abroad, like they were for the L-1011. In an implicit critique of capital flight and globalization, Jacobson argued that the death of Lockheed would mean that McDonnell Douglas would pick up the work in defense production with its DC10 aircraft, made with General Electric and Pratt and Whitney engines, and would keep more jobs in the United States. The death of Lockheed, to Jacobson, "would be highly advantageous to the American aerospace worker." Divisions among labor over the benefits and disadvantages of the Lockheed bailout to union members led to fissures that prevented an interunion and interlabor effort to challenge the deleterious effects the bailout had on defense workers (particularly blue-collar workers) across the country. [77]

Following heated debate—and compromise—the House approved the bailout legislation, but only after the amount of the loan guarantees was reduced to $250 million dollars. The Senate then finally agreed to vote on the legislation on August 2, 1971. Nixon dedicated hours of his day before the Senate vote to obtain last-minute support for the loan guarantee, telling potential converts that the legislation was crucial to his presidency. Nixon called Republicans Barry Goldwater Sr., Caleb Boggs, Carl Curtis, and George Aiken to see if he could sway them to his side, claiming he had spoken to Reagan who was anxious for Congress to approve the bailout—and that if it were defeated, Republicans' chances in California in the following presidential election were imperiled. Nixon recited this argument to the four senators, stating the 9 percent rate of unemployment in California was second in the nation, and with "the SST being knocked out," a failure to pass the loan guarantees would adversely affect "the situation of '72."

Nixon had limited success in convincing the congressmen. Goldwater refused to budge, saying the issue was a "matter of principle." If the federal government guaranteed loans "for Lockheed, we're going to have to do it for everybody," Goldwater said. Aiken and Curtis were noncommittal. Curtis said he would "see what [he] can do" for Lockheed, while Aiken—from the state of Maine—expressed the concern held by many in the Northeast that the bailout was a boon to the Sunbelt, which would receive federal help from the legislation. There was "hardly anyone up our way in the Northeast . . . that wants it," Aiken told Nixon. If it was not discriminatory and encompassed the entire defense industry, Aiken would support it, but not if it benefited Lockheed alone. Hoping it would seal Aiken's vote, Nixon told the senator to "let me know whenever we can do something" for those plants in his state.[78] In the end, Aiken balked in supporting the bill—but his vote was not needed. The legislation passed in the Senate by one vote, and Lockheed received the $250 million in loans backed by the federal government. Both its liberal and conservative opponents were wounded, as Proxmire told James Buckley that the "loan guarantee loss was a heartbreaker," even though "the razor-thin margin of one vote makes it clear that this should be no easy, quick precedent in the future."[79]

But the Lockheed bailout did set a precedent for the federal government's efforts to enfranchise employers to the detriment of defense workers, as passage of the loan guarantees saved Lockheed but hurt many of its workers. Less than half of Lockheed's workforce affected by the layoffs in February returned to work. The same unemployed workers who sided with Lockheed in support of the bailout legislation therefore still found themselves without a job. Indeed, unemployment continued to plague Southern California and much of the Sunbelt. After the Senate vote, the Nixon administration still wondered how "to absorb the 2 million people that we've released from the defense industries."[80]

Seven months after the loan guarantees were approved, Goldwater Jr. wrote to Nixon advisor Clark MacGregor that residents of Southern California continued to express unease "with the status of the aerospace/defense industry employment situation." Goldwater Jr. acknowledged that Nixon had helped defense workers in his district in the past, but it was simply not enough—and implied that austerity measures would coincide with any gains in defense employment. "My constituents see their taxes rise, and at the same time, watch the mounting unemployment problem among their families and friends. The President's efforts on the Lockheed loan guarantee are not forgotten, but more needs to be done," Goldwater wrote.[81] Ted Antonich, a photography studio owner from Canoga Park, California, wrote to Goldwater saying this much. Antonich was not a conservative ideologue. Antonich favored a more stringent clampdown on crime and drug use in California but supported Nixon's China visit and sought the government's help in limiting inflation through wage and price controls. But the most important local issue to him was national defense and federal spending in the aerospace industry. "What this valley and state needs are Aerospace and National defense contracts which will put people to work," Antonich wrote. The high unemployment levels in the defense industry, which affected the entire region of Southern California, translated to a loss of revenue for Antonich's business. "In fact if something doesn't happen soon to boost the employment situation I'll either have to go bankrupt or go on welfare, neither of which I want to do," Antonich said. "There must be some way to put people to work so that we can hold our heads up again and look the landlord in the eye as well as our other creditors, which I can't do now." Antonich concluded his letter demanding Goldwater "get [his] ass in gear and do something about it."[82]

Just a few months after they passed Congress, the loan guarantees proved to be a short-term response that disproportionately benefited company executives to the detriment of workers. Donald Douglas Sr., chairman of McDonnell Douglas, deviated from the bloc of defense companies against the bailout to offer his full support to Lockheed. To Douglas, Lockheed deserved the federal government's help because he felt the company faced hard times due to the "unreasonable wage demands from labor unions that have forced and are forcing aerospace companies out of business."[83] The resolution of the Lockheed crisis gave Douglas and his colleagues the opportunity to limit the power of labor, which they felt was the real problem, not careless spending. In January 1972, Phase II of Nixon's New Economic Program, part of the president's response to rising inflation rates, allowed the appointed federal Pay Board to cap wage increases in the aerospace industry at 8.3 percent, the figure executives had wanted, rather than the 12 percent that labor wrested out of the early negotiations with employers. Lockheed employee Robert Englander, who ran the company's research laboratory, best summed up the feelings of the company's workers when he said, "The Nixon Pay Board has hurt my pocketbook. First they cut my wages 17 cents from last year's raise and now they are dragging their feet in approving our raises for this year. Meanwhile prices keep going up and interest rates remain sky high."[84]

The American public soon noticed that the largest beneficiaries of the loan guarantees were Lockheed executives and the bankers who financed the corporation's malfeasance. Amid the bailout, Hal Troeger from Grand Marais, Michigan, complained to the *Chicago Tribune* about "the parade of bankers now pleading the Lockheed cause before congressional committees," as he pondered "if their concern is jobs for aircraft workers or jobs for bankers." In the same paper, Glen

Ellyn, Illinois, resident Katherine Moore said that instead of bailing out Lockheed executives, the Senate should be more concerned about "the unemployed coal miners in southern Illinois and throughout Appalachia," who have faced unemployment "for years and no bolstering of the industries which hired them. These people need help worse than do the aircraft workers, who have comparatively healthful working conditions and are not suffering from chronic blacklung disease."[85]

The government's decision to back Lockheed's loans ultimately angered Americans who believed the federal state was operating against their interests, fomenting political divides to the benefit of capital and executives within the defense industry and the Cold War coalition. Indeed, the Lockheed bailout created fissures within the electorate later exploited by hawkish political candidates and pro-defense spending advocates. Defense communities in Long Island, New York, and Seattle, Washington, who had also experienced the financial pinch of post-Vietnam cutbacks, felt the loan guarantees were unfair to exclude other defense workers. In Farmingdale, New York, the home of Grumman, the impact was palpable. Daniel J. D'Addario, a Farmingdale subcontractor who depended on business from Grumman, believed the economic downturn in his community was a consequence of the federal government turning its back on the Cold War. Long Islanders like D'Addario concluded that anti-Vietnam liberals were the reason why the American dream promised to suburbanites was evaporating in the early 1970s, not Nixon's policies. "The elected officials have chosen to be expedient, hacking at the defense budget—not welfare where there are 14-million votes," he said. D'Addario saw both his output and workforce cut in half. In Seattle, home of Boeing, unemployment climbed to 15 percent, while Nixon denied the city additional federal funds for antipoverty programs, forcing residents to rely on local charities and foreign aid for feeding the hungry. After Japan shipped one thousand pounds of rice and other foodstuffs to feed unemployed aerospace workers in the city, Democratic senator Warren Magnuson—who had supported aid to Lockheed in June before voting against the loan guarantees in August—exclaimed, "This administration can see great humanity in providing a $250 million loan for a hungry Lockheed Corp., but can't see spending another dime on hungry human beings."[86]

Even with sizeable criticism toward the military-industrial complex in the early 1970s, the Lockheed loan crisis exposed the lasting grip of a militarized economy on the American electorate. Challenges to the Cold War economy from the Left—and antimilitarists—ultimately collided with the material reality of the national security state, with the fact that efforts to draw down American military spending did not transform the Cold War economy; they did not detach Americans from the financial tentacles of a permanent war economy. The late 1960s and early 1970s would, in retrospect, be the height and nadir of antimilitarism, as the bailout provoked the full weight of the Cold War coalition behind the political economy of American military power: executives from Lockheed, defense workers, labor unions, community activists, and political representatives from California—and other states where Lockheed plants and headquarters were located.

The economics and parochial politics behind Cold War defense spending ultimately became the vital counterforce to antimilitarism. For jingoism (alone) could not dilute antimilitarist politics in the United States—the Vietnam War remained unpopular and Americans prioritized restraint over engagement during this time. Moreover, lobbying by the defense industry and right-wing activism on behalf of greater defense spending defused, but did not obstruct, the political climate hostile to the military-industrial complex. It took the full weight of the national security state—its economic and political appendages—to demonstrate the limitations of left- (and some right-) wing opposition to a political economy of militarism. The unlikely bloc of antimilitarist Democrats incensed by the seemingly unstoppable growth of the military-industrial complex and free market Republicans apoplectic over the intrusiveness of the federal government in market functions found that governing from the basis of ideology was difficult when faced with the public's vested interests in the warfare state—particularly economic interests.

And as the country crawled into the economic doldrums of the 1970s, antimilitarists and antibailout Republicans faced further structural obstacles, as the jobs and federal benefits the military-industrial complex provided to the Cold War coalition became scarcer. While members of the Cold War coalition were able to pressure their political representatives to support legislation like the Lockheed loan guarantees, their power proved limited in strengthening the social compact between citizens and the state that emerged in World War II. Claiming to be victims of the international dynamics of the Cold War, the Cold War coalition rallied once again to support the military-industrial complex in the name of national security, only to resume the same struggle throughout the 1970s and 1980s as plant closures and job losses persisted in the political economy of the Cold War. As a bailout, not a restructuring of the industry, the loan guarantees revivified antistatist and militarist politics in the Cold War coalition—and the body politic.

Moreover, in trying to save jobs lost to an economic recession and the drawdown of the Vietnam War, those in the Cold War coalition who campaigned for the bailout inadvertently furthered divides between the federal state and the public—divides that supplied fodder for a right-wing politics. The growing decline of defense spending as a portion of GDP in the 1970s spelled disaster on the horizon to Cold War communities, particularly those communities that did not profit from the bailout of companies like Lockheed (one bailout to one corporation could not stop structural changes to the Cold War economy). Defense workers regularly feared they would lose their jobs in the 1970s—while inflation eroded their earnings—and were drawn to reductive arguments and election-year posturing by politicians and political actors who promised them a better tomorrow in some form. As poor economic conditions left the financial dependents of the military-industrial complex subject to forces seemingly beyond their control, they turned to political elites who promised to keep the spigot of defense dollars flowing—elites who often employed anticommunist, if not militarist, language to justify a bigger military budget and were all too happy to align their politics with critiques of a bloated, federal state they claimed was uninterested in the financial health of its citizenry and unwilling to spend money where it is needed most: on national security. As the country approached an era of growing austerity, the Cold War coalition therefore refocused— and strengthened—its militaristic qualities.

CHAPTER FOUR

The Cold War Returns

On June 28, 1976, Ronald Reagan wrote to Southern Chairmen's Association member Clark Reed to explain his differences with President Gerald Ford on domestic and foreign policy. When Reagan challenged Gerald Ford for the Republican presidential nomination months earlier, it seemed like a hopeless cause; but it was now shaping up to be a battle that the former California governor could win. Reagan captured Texas in May and California in June, and he needed Reed on his side as he headed into the Republican convention. Reagan told Reed the reasons why he was the better Republican: For starters, he opposed mandatory school busing (which he said should be settled by "local communities"), a national health insurance program, and the Humphrey-Hawkins bill. But in addition to telling Reed his stance on the major issues in the race, Reagan also took stock of how his campaign evolved since the previous November, noting that the months of "campaigning has convinced me as well of something I didn't know when I began: the American people are ready to halt the retreat of the last several years that has gone under the name of detente."[1]

Public opposition to détente—and Ford's foreign policy—jump-started Reagan's campaign after a series of defeats in early primary elections. Reagan did not intend to make foreign affairs the cornerstone of his candidacy but focused his attention on national security issues after audiences (and voters) responded enthusiastically to his call for expanding America's global reach to fight communism.

Reagan told Reed that Americans wanted to refight the Cold War, since they believed the "best guarantee for peace—the guarantee our Soviet adversaries understand—is military strength."[2]

As Reagan hinted in his letter, the Cold War coalition provided momentum for his campaign strategy in 1976. Eastern European immigrants upset over the Helsinki Accords and the Strategic Arms Limitation Treaty (SALT), defense workers and military personnel who lost their jobs to budget cutbacks, right-wing activists, anti-Castro Cuban Americans, and southern Democrats angered over American involvement in southern Africa all gravitated toward Reagan in 1976 to support his call to increase defense spending and roll back détente. But partisan mobilization alone did not make Reagan's campaign—the Cold War coalition acted in a specific historical moment.[3] The end of the Vietnam War, the Watergate scandal, and the decline of the American economy created a heady and combustive political and cultural atmosphere in the United States, one that formed the context for changes to national security politics in the mid-1970s. Reagan's supporters also exploited new campaign finance laws and tectonic shifts in American electoral politics (particularly the increasing advantage special interests and activists exerted over the party system).[4]

The 1970s therefore created opportunities for a figure like Reagan to remake the Cold War coalition—and for the coalition to change political culture—in ways that transformed American democracy. Voters' distrust of détente, and their interest in adopting tougher national defense policies, convinced the former California governor that the country would embrace an interventionist, aggressive, and uncompromising foreign policy agenda were he to be elected, one that entailed massive defense increases. While Reagan was a conservative ideologue, he was also a politician willing to modify his political agenda to attract and maintain public support. Reagan promulgated a Manichean anticommunist ideology throughout much of his life but was restrained on his critique of American foreign policy during the early months of the primary election. He took a cautious stance against détente throughout 1975, stating that he was not opposed to détente in principle but to détente as conceived, practiced, and advocated by President Ford. Reagan even promoted the policy goals of détente as an envoy to Europe and Asia during the years of the Nixon administration. But after winning states like North Carolina and Texas on a hard-line foreign policy stance in 1976, Reagan was able to capture voters in other areas of the country, expanding the influence of the Cold War coalition during and beyond the presidential race.

Reagan therefore relied on the Cold War coalition to push American politics to the right in the 1970s. As détente and defense cuts threatened the financial stability of defense workers, executives, labor leaders, and business interests—many who voted for Democrats prior to 1972—the political makeup of the Cold War coalition changed. Reagan's 1976 campaign garnered new constituencies for the Republican Party on national security issues, including Democratic voters in the Northwest, Midwest, and South who relied on the defense industry—which the Democrats wanted to scale back. Reagan's campaign also appealed to Republican-leaning areas of the Sunbelt where national defense issues and the Cold War economy animated local politics. National defense thus solidified the base of the Republican Party but also attracted moderate voters to Reagan's campaign and his vision for the country, enabling political realignment in the 1970s.

Reagan also succeeded in reshaping American politics because many members of the Cold War coalition felt Democrats failed to respond to their collective concerns. Antimilitarist Democrats increasingly dominated the Democratic Party after Vietnam, with Cold War liberals leaving office or marginalized in Congress. But as the country moved into the 1970s, antimilitarism fell out of favor. Angry voters confronted Democrats with tough questions about how across-the-board defense cuts would affect their jobs and how the United States waged the Cold War. Moreover, Democratic calls for trimming the defense budget in the 1970s coincided with economic decline in the United States. The combination of these two factors was disarming to voters in the Cold War coalition, and Democrats lacked a satisfactory solution to them. While Reagan and other right-wing Republicans championed Cold War militarism and a hike in the defense budget as a resolution to both—a simple yet efficacious policy for an election season—Democrats offered long-term conversion to civilian work. But Democrats' proposals for defense conversion had little appeal to workers (both working class and middle class) who saw their job security disappear altogether in the early 1970s, leaving them in a tenuous position. As defense plants and military bases closed or downsized due to the winding down of the Vietnam War, members of the Cold War coalition argued that defense employment and American military power were needed immediately to ameliorate the economic crisis. Conversion would have to wait.

While revealing the electoral advantages available to Republicans in the 1970s, Reagan's 1976 primary campaign also offers insight into the limitations and obstacles faced by the American Right in the 1970s. As historians Meg Jacobs and Julian Zelizer have shown, Reagan's approach to governing—his designs for deregulation, reducing taxes, limiting social welfare benefits—were not always well received by the public.[5] The limits of Reagan's conservative ideology, however, were on full display well before his presidency. Reagan was confronted in 1976 with the fact that Americans liked the New Deal and Great Society programs that right-wing conservatives wanted to cut. Americans favored a reduction in the size of the federal government as long as it did not threaten programs from which they benefited. Part of the story of Reagan's rise to the presidency is how national defense and foreign policy allowed Reagan and his supporters to respond to this disconnect between the public's reliance on federal programs and its antagonism toward big government.

By combining austerity and national defense politics in ways that united a cross coalition of voters behind his primary campaign, Reagan found a solution to this dilemma. Reagan mobilized economic anxieties with the Cold War coalition to justify a politics of austerity, a politics that fed into and furthered his Cold War anticommunism. It was a political strategy that Democrats and Republicans would employ more frequently as the country saw jobs in defense—and the Cold War economy overall—decline in the 1970s, particularly in defense manufacturing. As a case study, the 1976 Republican primary also shows how the political choices made by individuals within the Cold War coalition contributed to economic inequality among its ranks. The Cold War coalition thought Reagan was the answer to unemployment in defense and Cold War retrenchment, but Reagan's policies reinforced their problems. As defense expenditures declined after Vietnam and the United States faced new international challenges, the Cold War coalition expanded to include new constituencies—ones that competed for their respective interests in the military-industrial complex, and once again, to the detriment of many coalition members.

* * *

When he ran for reelection in 1972, President Richard Nixon finally aimed to realize his goal of creating a Republican "New Majority." Nixon hoped to wed blue-collar labor, blacks, and white ethnic groups to his base of white suburbanites that got him elected in 1968, fracturing the Democratic coalition for generations. Standing in his way was South Dakota Democratic senator George S. McGovern. A dark horse contender, McGovern, was thought to be too far to the left of his party to be elected. Few political pundits gave McGovern more than cursory attention in the early months of the race, as the senator was given a 200-to-1 chance to win the nomination.[6] McGovern overcame these odds by expertly tapping into the culture of antimilitarism that pervaded the United States in the late 1960s and early 1970s. McGovern's criticism of the Vietnam War quickly distinguished him from the field of leading Democratic candidates including Edmund Muskie, Hubert Humphrey, and Henry "Scoop" Jackson. McGovern also proposed cutting nearly $87 billion from the defense budget in 1972 and transferring the monies saved to social welfare programs.[7] Even though national defense was low on the list of voters' priorities, McGovern made it a salient topic of discussion. Cutting the defense budget was a priority for McGovern, one that was a close second to ending the Vietnam War. The Nixon campaign too noted there was "strong support for the idea that we need to spend a large portion of our resources on our own domestic problems" and a significant number "of voters are in favor of cutting the defense budget."[8] Cold War liberals like Jackson bristled at McGovern's politics, but the American public supported them. Indeed, Jackson experienced a barrage of attacks from his Washington State constituents over Vietnam and his Cold War liberalism. Since the Americanization of the war in 1965, Washingtonians urged Jackson to renege on his support for the war, arguing that the United States could not rely solely on its military power to remedy global conflicts.[9]

Washingtonians were not alone in telling their elected representatives they opposed the Vietnam War—even while profiting from it. In the suburbs of Boston, many residents were professionals employed by the defense industry, but ones who self-identified with the peace movement and supported defense cuts. Even when companies like Raytheon cut their workforce by twenty-five thousand jobs, and ten thousand engineers and scientists in suburban Massachusetts alone lost their jobs in 1969, some residents celebrated the losses. While other Massachusetts suburbanites decried the fact that they were now forced to "just live day by day," others were happy that they now had to search "outside of the military-industrial complex" for employment.[10]

In addition to the predominance of antiwar politics within the party and its constituents, McGovern rose to the front of the Democratic pack by taking advantage of new delegate rules instituted by the Commission on Party Structure and Delegate Selection, more popularly known as the McGovern-Fraser commission. Created in 1968 following the Democratic National Convention in Chicago, and headed by McGovern and Democratic representative Donald Fraser of Minnesota, the McGovern-Fraser commission remade the structure of the Democratic Party. The commission tried to unite the reformers and regulars within the Democratic Party, making it more inclusive of new constituents while redistributing power away from the party elites (labor leaders, senior congressmen, and state bosses) who dominated the procedures for selecting the party's presidential candidate—and who in 1968 picked Vice President Hubert

Humphrey as the nominee, despite Humphrey not running in one single primary. The McGovern-Fraser commission abolished rules and regulations that placed restrictions on public influence on primary elections, including the selection and composition of delegates, and embraced the civil rights revolutions of the 1960s by mandating that delegates to the convention consist of minorities, women, and young people relative to their state populations.[11]

Partly due to the commission's reforms, McGovern's core supporters were not the Democratic elites who dominated conventions in the past but young activists assembled from the New Politics movement still upset over Humphrey's nomination and Lyndon Johnson's Vietnam War. The New Politics movement—composed of students, civil rights figures, women's liberationists, antiwar figures, and members of Ralph Nader's consumer movement ("Nader's Raiders")—coalesced around McGovern in 1972, attracted to his antiwar position and his detachment from the Democratic Party machine. The ratification of the Twenty-Sixth Amendment in 1971, which lowered the minimum voting age to eighteen, also helped bring young voters to McGovern. The administrative composition of the McGovern campaign was therefore unprecedented in terms of its age, race, and gender diversity. While tensions existed between the activists and McGovern, this conglomeration of left-wing support supplanted the need for the Democratic candidate to cater to labor bosses and the machine politics of the 1960s associated with men like Chicago mayor Richard Daley—who would be tossed from the convention floor in 1972. By July, McGovern had sealed the Democratic nomination, shocking the political punditry and the party regulars.

The surprise success of the McGovern campaign represented the success of the New Politics movement in remaking the Democratic Party after 1968, but the revolution in the Democratic Party came at a price. McGovern's nomination opened fissures within the party, ones lingering since Humphrey's loss in 1968. These rifts were not necessarily McGovern's fault. Cold War liberals and southern Democrats were horrified by McGovern's antiwar agenda. Instead of rallying to McGovern's side after he received the nomination, his former opponents preferred to watch his candidacy implode. McGovern's opponents portrayed the senator as being in favor of "Amnesty, Acid [and] Abortion," and when McGovern won the nomination, some of his fellow Democrats—including Henry "Scoop" Jackson—gave him an endorsement that was less than enthusiastic.[12] Labor unions such as the AFL-CIO also had little respect for McGovern. They despised his opposition to the Vietnam War and his role in party reforms; they also hated McGovern's call for massive defense cuts. But the idea of undoing the Cold War economy angered the AFL-CIO, which since the 1940s believed that Cold War defense spending prevented the spread of communism and provided economic security to American workers. Indeed, after the July convention, McGovern faced stringent opposition from AFL-CIO president George Meany and organized labor. Meany was just one man, but a powerful representative force for organized labor and the Vietnam War.[13]

Yet despite hostility from trade union leaders, Cold War liberals, and party regulars, McGovern (at first) seemed to be an appealing candidate to some members of the Cold War coalition. McGovern's platform rejected defense spending as a New Deal–style jobs program and thought defense jobs could be repurposed for peacetime work, with military expenditures curtailed in favor of increased spending on domestic programs. McGovern's talk of trimming the military-industrial complex was not simply election-year posturing. Since his election to the Senate in 1962, McGovern was a leading voice for defense cuts on Capitol Hill. Shortly after taking office, he proposed a National Economic Conversion Commission that would divert workers in defense to peacetime jobs. Under McGovern's plan, scientists and engineers in defense would be reemployed to serve civilian purposes including working on solutions to "water pollution, air pollution" and building public works projects.[14] McGovern also argued that defense companies should receive government funds to aid them in the transition process. "I believe the Federal Government has a clear obligation to these companies, communities, and individuals that have become dependent on our defense budget for their income, and that we must create the necessary governmental machinery to prevent changes in our Defense Establishment from resulting in an inevitable loss of employment and income," McGovern said in 1964.[15] Some white-collar workers in the Cold War coalition found McGovern's ideas attractive. Robert Englander, in charge of a research laboratory at Lockheed, thought McGovern "would work hard to switch defense-oriented companies to peacetime production whenever possible and perhaps even increase the number of jobs."[16] McGovern was not just antidefense, but projobs.

In 1972, however, McGovern failed to articulate his ideas on reconversion in a more convincing manner. In response to an African American defense worker's concern that "whenever the war is over, then there'll be more layoffs," the South Dakota senator stated that if the United States "had to depend on war, we're in sad shape in this country" and talked vaguely about full employment and reinvesting defense dollars in environmental and housing programs. The subject of defense conversion was not mentioned.[17] Attacks on McGovern's defense budget also escalated in the months before the election. The *National Review* claimed McGovern's defense cuts reduced American military forces without heeding threats from the Soviets, making his defense budget "the first step down the rather short road to a Carthaginian peace for the United States." The cuts would also mean reductions in military pensions, the editors warned.[18]

Members of McGovern's own party eviscerated his defense budget as well. McGovern's chief Democratic rival, Hubert Humphrey, pounced on his proposals for defense reductions, stating McGovern was detached from the problems faced by American workers—who relied on defense jobs. Trying to win votes among aerospace employees in California during the Democratic primaries, Humphrey implied that if McGovern were elected, further job losses would ensue. When McGovern criticized Humphrey's endorsement of the Lockheed bailout, his campaign struck back by saying, "When we talk about Lockheed and the space shuttle, we're really saying: who was really concerned about the working-man in California?"[19] The group Democrats for Nixon—an organization led by Republicans—even used Humphrey's critique of McGovern's defense budget in a provocative television commercial against the Democratic nominee. The ad quoted Humphrey's claim that McGovern's defense policies were "cutting into the very security of this country." The leader of Democrats for Nixon, former Nixon treasury secretary John Connolly, believed Democrats had largely defected to Nixon because of McGovern's plans for "large cutbacks in defense spending."[20]

While McGovern's campaign provided evidence that defense cuts meant net job increases in the future, not job losses, his message failed to gain traction among the electorate. McGovern made several key mistakes when discussing his defense policy and its impact on American jobs, but his biggest problem was his honesty. McGovern was not shy in identifying the specific military installations he would eliminate, angering members of the Cold War coalition who faced job losses. For instance, McGovern was bold enough to tell defense workers in central Florida that he would do away with the space shuttle program, ending Cold War jobs that depended on it. As journalist Hunter S. Thompson fantastically imagined, "This is not the kind of thing people want to hear in a general election year—especially not if you happen to be an unemployed anti-gravity systems engineer with a deadhead mortgage on a house near Orlando."[21]

But underlying Thompson's flippant comment was McGovern's major problem: convincing the Cold War coalition (in an election year, and in an era of economic decline) that the military-industrial complex did not serve their long-term interests. This was the issue that would taunt antimilitarist Democrats throughout the 1970s. While McGovern's alternatives to the Cold War economy were nuanced and feasible, they relied on future policies. Unemployed workers, or workers concerned for job security, particularly blue-collar defense workers, wanted immediate action, not "a systemic analysis of what caused this unemployment situation."[22] As one defense worker (a cabinet finisher) put it in 1972, "I've been struggling as far as pay is concerned."[23] Therefore, despite the potential appeal of his conversion policies, his antimilitarist populism, and his efforts to guarantee jobs for unemployed defense workers, McGovern still had difficulty relating to unionized defense workers and the working class: a traditional constituency of the Democratic Party and postwar liberalism. In the 1972 election, McGovern saw his glowing prolabor, antidefense record in the Senate overshadowed by the difficulties he faced in explaining how he would transition the defense economy to peacetime status—in terms that translated to votes.[24] McGovern ultimately left voters questioning where the Democratic Party stood on Cold War defense, creating what political scientist Bruce Miroff has called an "identity crisis" in the Party.[25]

McGovern's missteps, attacks from Cold War liberals and the Right, and the absence of a broader structural solution to war capitalism hamstrung the candidate. In the months leading up to the election, many defense workers, particularly blue-collar workers, admitted to being unenthusiastic about McGovern. While a fair number of unions supported McGovern's defense budget and his recipe for ending the military-industrial complex, including the United Auto Workers and the Communication Workers of America, members of the International Association of Machinists (IAM), which was affiliated with the AFL-CIO, did not. In September, the New York Times went to Burbank, California, and interviewed employees whose jobs were rescued by the Lockheed bailout a year earlier to ask them their thoughts on the election. The newspaper found that few supported Nixon, but not many more liked McGovern. Times reporter Philip Shabecoff wrote that those "who work in and around the Lockheed plant here have very few good things to say about George McGovern," especially on economic issues. "Nixon has tried to kill us off, but we've got nothing from McGovern for nine years but a lot of talk," said Gerald Sklarsky, president of local Lodge 727. Their union, the IAM, endorsed McGovern, but the decision inspired neither celebration "or howls of outrage." Some workers were going to vote for Nixon, others McGovern, saying that the president failed to "do something for us working around here," even though he was from their home state. "I don't care much for McGovern, but I'll take him over Nixon," echoed one Lockheed worker. However, the overwhelming sentiment among the workers was apathy. As Sklarsky told the *Times*, "I'm going to sit this election out. I can't say either one of them [Nixon or McGovern] has done us any good."[26]

Comments from blue-collar defense workers like Sklarsky represented their disenchantment with politicians who failed to provide job security in a period of economic decline. Months earlier, defense workers failed to gain concessions on wage increases from Nixon's Pay Board—the federal body created by Nixon to regulate federal pay and reduce inflation—echoing trends in collective bargaining agreements nationwide.[27] Defense jobs declined by over 30 percent in six sectors of the defense economy, with defense manufacturing losing six hundred thousand jobs between fiscal year 1968 and fiscal year 1971.[28] As S. A. (Tex) Newman, a Lockheed worker, put it, "When Nixon took office there were 242 tool and die makers at the plant. Now we are down to 115."[29] The winding down of the Vietnam War added to workers' concerns. Like many Americans in 1972, defense workers were opposed to the Vietnam War; but the Paris Peace Accords left them concerned about their jobs. One such worker was Patricia Ash. Ash made bombs at the Crane Naval Ammunition Depot in Crane, Indiana, for $3.84 an hour and wanted to keep her job after the war was over. Ash said a "cease-fire worries me" as it would surely lead to layoffs within the plant. While she would "just as soon have a cease-fire, like anyone would," since she had a young son who could potentially be sent to fight in Vietnam, she also said she would "hate to lose [her] job." Ash, like many workers in her situation, was irresolute toward future job prospects. She tried to convince herself that when the Vietnam War ended and she lost her job, she "could always find another one, I guess."[30]

McGovern's troubled relations with defense labor were compounded by the attitudes of his most dedicated supporters, who felt defense workers contributed to America's overseas empire—and were part of the problem, not the solution. McGovern's New Politics base consisted of middle-class activists who saw little distinction between union workers and the labor bosses responsible for the old ways of doing business in the Democratic Party. The Democrats (and soon

the Republicans) were morphing into a party that was more attentive to the ideological proclivities of elite activists who saw political
bargaining, patronage, and quid pro quo exchanges as thwarting the
participation of the masses.[31] The antiwar movement that supported
McGovern also disdained defense workers, lumping them into the
"military-industrial-labor complex . . . [that] is locking itself into the
structure of our country."[32] The larger critique of American militarism in the late 1960s and early 1970s therefore took on an antilabor
tenor, as labor unions (and defense workers) were seen as complicit in
the escalation and atrocities of the Vietnam War. Such critics of labor
failed to recognize (or downright ignored) the history of the early
Cold War where the transition to the defense economy stifled the
social democracy of the 1930s, making labor depend on the national
security state for its continued livelihood.[33]

Intraclass tensions within the Cold War coalition also contributed
to McGovern's and the Democratic Party's woes. Indeed, as tough
times grew worse in the Cold War economy, skilled defense workers shied away from working with their unionized, working-class
counterparts to end volatility in the defense workforce, claiming that
"unions kill creativity" and that "engineers want to be and should
be individualists," a message that deviated from unions' purpose to
"cater to the masses." Many of these antiunion defense workers were
McGovern supporters in Massachusetts who gave the senator his
only state in the general election. As the Democratic Party catered
more to these upper-class suburbanites than its working-class base—
and further embraced defense cuts rather than defense increases—
some Cold War defense workers searched for a new political home.[34]

Without the support of a broad-based coalition behind the Democratic Party (including a unified labor movement), and with the
Nixon campaign dividing the Democratic base along cultural and
racial lines, McGovern lost the 1972 election in a landslide. In addition to winning Massachusetts, McGovern also captured three electoral votes from the District of Columbia. That was all. As historian
Jefferson Cowie has pointed out, McGovern managed to obtain a
significant portion of the labor vote and lower-income voters, even

more so than white-collar workers and college-educated Americans, but so too did Richard Nixon. Votes for Nixon among defense workers helped Nixon win all of Southern California, and in the case of Orange County, nearly a two-thirds majority. While Democrats picked up many seats in Congress in 1972, Nixon had a clear mandate. The president captured the economic and cultural anxieties of the American voter better than McGovern in 1972. Nixon's new Republican majority seemed to be a reality after the results of the 1972 election were in.[35]

But Nixon's triumph was short-lived as the Watergate scandal unfolded in 1973 and into 1974. The Watergate crisis overshadowed the midterm elections in 1974, leading to huge Democratic gains in Congress. Democrats picked up forty-three seats in the House and gained four in the Senate. These new Democrats hailed from wealthy Sunbelt suburbs and northern districts once held by liberal Republicans. George Wallace Democrats were replaced by Sunbelt moderates, and few of these Democrats stood a chance of being elected prior to 1974. The freshmen class rode the anti-Washington fervor straight onto Capitol Hill, promising to tackle the corruption and cronyism that they told Americans were so cancerous to lawmaking. Having come from upper-class, wealthy districts, these Democrats were a new breed of liberals, different from their New Deal predecessors. As the former McGovern campaign manager and newly elected Democratic senator Gary Hart said about his colleagues, "We're not just a bunch of little [Hubert] Humphreys."[36] Many held moderate views on economic issues and liberal views on foreign policy. These so-called Watergate babies were also progenies of interest groups and identity politics; they were concerned about environmentalism, consumers' rights, and reducing the inflation rate and felt little connection to the traditional base of the Democratic Party including labor and labor unions. Kenneth Young of the AFL-CIO lamented that "the freshmen Democrat today is likely to be an upper-income type, and that causes some problems with economic issues. It's not that they don't vote what they perceive to be working class concerns, but I think a lot of them are more concerned with inflation than with unemployment."[37]

In regard to fighting the Cold War, Watergate babies favored restrictions on American conduct abroad and wanted a leaner defense budget. Many opposed the Vietnam War and wanted to avoid the mistakes made by Cold War liberals—whom they held responsible for Vietnam.

The political economy of the Cold War, however, interfered in the Watergate babies' attempts to reduce America's military posture. These new Democratic legislators came from districts and states that relied heavily on defense spending and leaned Republican prior to Watergate. It soon became apparent that Democratic freshmen wanted to withdraw America's presence overseas but keep Pentagon funds flowing to defense contractors and military bases in their districts. Post-Vietnam, post-Watergate Democrats therefore found themselves trying to separate their antimilitarism from their relationship to the political economy of the Cold War—with little success. Representative Philip Hayes was among the Democrats elected in 1974, representing the Eighth District in Southern Indiana. Hayes opposed defense increases but felt pressured to prevent the Department of Defense from closing a local naval munitions depot in his district, leaving several hundred Indianans unemployed. Hayes admitted that his antimilitarism only went so far as he faced "strong pressure to maintain what is euphemistically called a 'strong national defense position' as are other members who have military bases and defense contractors in their areas."[38]

The remaking of the Democratic Party in 1974 exacerbated the question faced by McGovern in 1972: How could liberals curtail defense expenditures without sending large numbers of Americans into unemployment? This dilemma ultimately led to an evolving centrism within the party on national defense—and other issues. Moreover, since post-Watergate Democrats had few good answers to Americans' economic dependency on the Cold War, they were left exposed to right-wing political candidates who claimed they were "weak" on foreign policy and national security in future elections. Post-1974 Democrats were increasingly caught between the political economy of the Cold War and their commitment to reducing

America's military presence abroad, creating opportunities for the political Right in an age of anxiety over the direction of the country.

*   *   *

When Vice President Spiro Agnew resigned on October 10, 1973, Richard Nixon appointed Michigan representative Gerald Ford as his replacement. Nixon's own resignation in August 1974 then left the presidency to Ford, who became the first unelected executive in the nation's history. Ford was also the fourth president to inherit the war in Vietnam, which would end in April 1975, but not before an acrimonious debate with Congress over the funding of the South Vietnamese regime. In terms of dealing with American's chief rival, the Soviet Union, Ford vowed to continue Nixon's policy of détente and leaned on secretary of state and national security advisor Henry Kissinger for guidance in managing foreign affairs.[39] Once in office, however, Ford found that in a post-Vietnam, post-Watergate America, détente had difficulty withstanding attacks on its legitimacy. Détente had its share of detractors for years, but now those critiques resonated with a wider audience. After 1974, Ford and Kissinger confronted charges from the Left and Right that détente neglected human rights and appeased communism. The passage of the Jackson-Vanik Amendment—which restricted trade with the Soviet Union after it placed restrictions on Jewish emigres to the United States—and the fall of South Vietnam made Americans question whether the means of détente served appropriate ends. Détente also seemed to be tainted with the politics of Watergate. The secretive nature of Kissinger's diplomacy, his backdoor channels and negotiations with foreign leaders, made Americans wonder what Kissinger was up to and whether he had the country's best interests at heart. No longer was Kissinger "Super K," but instead a cagey and devious diplomat whose policies would lead to Soviet hegemony. Kissinger tried to dismiss the vitriol, but détente continued to unravel during the second half of the 1970s.[40]

One of the first domestic challenges to détente involved the visit to the United States by the writer and Soviet dissident Alexandr

Solzhenitsyn. In his book, *The Gulag Archipelago*, Solzhenitsyn chronicled his eight-year detention in a Soviet labor camp, and after its publication in 1973, he was deported from the Soviet Union. The book was received well in the United States, and the Right (and Cold War liberals) lauded Solzhenitsyn for his outspoken criticism of the Soviet regime. North Carolina Republican senator Jesse Helms hoped to bring Solzhenitsyn to the United States in March 1974, after he wrote to the author that he was a "citizen of the world" who was poised "on the threshold of a new phase in your struggle for truth and freedom in your own native land and in the entire world."[41] Solzhenitsyn declined the offer in 1974, but he did make a visit to the United States in June 1975 where he met with his most ardent admirers in Congress including Helms, Strom Thurmond, and Henry Jackson. Solzhenitsyn then spoke to members of the AFL-CIO, where he demanded a "true détente" between the United States and the Soviet Union that was not "based on smiles, not on verbal concessions, but . . . based on a firm foundation." Détente, as carried out by Ford and Kissinger, was leading the United States "down a false road," Solzhenitsyn said, that would inevitably lead to American weakness in the eyes of the world. He urged America to "try to slow down the process of concessions and help the process of liberation," of those suffering under communism.[42]

Helms and Thurmond requested that Ford meet with Solzhenitsyn, but Ford refused. Kissinger also discouraged Ford from meeting with the recent Nobel Prize winner, believing it would imperil détente. Other prominent members of Ford's staff disagreed; Deputy Chief of Staff Richard Cheney fired off a memo on July 8, 1975, to Chief of Staff Donald Rumsfeld expressing his anger over Ford's refusal to meet with Solzhenitsyn. Détente could not conceal the fact that the United States and the Soviet Union still perceived each other as enemies, Cheney wrote, and it was "important that we not contribute any more to the illusion that all of a sudden we're bosom buddies with the Russians."[43] On July 7, 1975, Helms declared on the floor of the Senate that Ford's decision not to meet with such a "dedicated exponent of freedom" was a shameful moment for the nation. The rebuff of Solzhenitsyn proved that détente was a "deceitful device" that would allow the Soviets to continue to "throttle and enslave countless millions of people all over the world."[44] The Solzhenitsyn affair also angered the Soviet dissident's admirers within the conservative movement. William F. Buckley, writing in the *National Review*, commented "that the conservative Right has embraced" Solzhenitsyn for "his tactical and strategic intuitions about the futility of the policy of détente." Buckley even felt compelled to "salute the leaders of the AFL-CIO" for inviting him to speak. Ford's staff also received complaints from voters for his handling of Solzhenitsyn. One letter writer, Carol Hummel, said she was "deeply disappointed in the treatment that Ford and the Congress gave to one great Russian citizen, Alexandr Solzhenitsyn."[45]

Ford was in trouble again only weeks after the Solzhenitsyn incident, when he signed the Helsinki Accords on August 1, 1975. Ford had anticipated the domestic reaction to the Helsinki Accords would be mild at best, since they represented the stated goals of détente: freer trade relations, concern for human rights, and recognition of sovereign countries to regulate domestic affairs. To certain people in Eastern Europe, and the United States, this last provision amounted to the United States accepting past and possibly future Soviet intervention in Eastern Europe. Kissinger, never enthusiastic about the Helsinki Accords, failed to understand this argument and was baffled by the subsequent controversy over Helsinki.[46] The agreements did not endorse the Soviet takeover of Eastern Europe but rather codified the boundaries of the Soviet Union that existed since the 1940s, Kissinger argued. He told Ford to disregard criticism of his participation in the negotiations, as the accords were favorable to "the interests of the Baltic American community." Ford did not intend to surrender Eastern Europe to the Soviet Union, and any suggestion otherwise was absurd.[47]

Americans of Eastern European descent felt differently. The Polish American Congress warned Ford that he confronted a growing number of "meetings, demonstrations and petitions" among Eastern European immigrants in opposition to the Helsinki Conference. One protest was held in Ford's home city of Grand Rapids, Michigan, in July 1975. Western Michigan University student Silins Gunlis led two hundred Baltic Americans in a demonstration against the Helsinki Accords. Gunlis said that he and those in attendance were "asking people to stand up and say that the Helsinki Pact is morally wrong." Protesters carried signs with slogans such as "There Are No Small Countries," and after the protest disbanded, activists went around the city with a petition seeking "U.S. recognition of Latvia, Estonia, and Lithuania," which Western Michigan University student Ruta Ozols said she had no trouble getting people to sign. With seemingly no end in sight to the protests, national and local politicians tried to convince Ford to rethink his commitment to the treaty.[48] Democratic congressman Charles Bennett told Ford that he was approached by several constituents on the "proposed agreement to recognize the boundaries of Russian domination in Europe" and felt the treaty was "not an asset" for the United States. A local Republican leader from Tulsa, Frank A. Wallace, wrote to Ford that he was "getting weary of trying to defend your administration and its actions" to residents and wondered how the president could champion the "aspirations of all peoples for self-determination and liberty" and at the same time authorize the Helsinki pact.[49]

Others were angered by Ford's policy in Africa, which to some Americans, reflected the overreach of the federal government at home. Ruled by the white minority since 1965, Rhodesia exhibited the dying gasps of Western colonialism in Africa. As a bloody civil war raged between the ruling whites and black nationalists in the early 1970s, President Nixon remained unconcerned with the status of Rhodesia. Nixon's indifference angered southern Democrats in Congress, who sympathized with the white regime led by Ian Smith and worked to gain international recognition of the country. Southern Democrats rallied to obtain passage of the Byrd Amendment in 1971 (sponsored by Virginia segregationist Harry Byrd) that allowed shipments of chrome ore to the United States from Rhodesia, defying UN sanctions against trading with the white minority government. But after the collapse of Portuguese control over Mozambique and

Angola between 1974 and 1975, Kissinger recognized that white rule in Rhodesia was untenable. Touring the country in 1976, Kissinger said that U.S. sponsorship of the black nationalists in Rhodesia was in the interest of "racial justice."[50] Among former George Wallace supporters and southern Democrats, U.S. policy toward Rhodesia was compared to desegregated busing in public schools. Memphis resident Leslie Birchfield wrote to Ford that he would not vote for the president unless he "fires Henry Kissinger" over his policy toward Rhodesia. "The way I see it," said Birchfield, "our role in southern Africa duplicates the role of the Federal Government in bludgeoning of the Southern people into accepting School Integration against its will. The same evil effects will come in southern Africa as has already come to our public school system."[51]

The compilation of public grievances toward détente, defense, and American national security in the first half of the 1970s galvanized the Cold War coalition. As the Cold War coalition grew disenchanted with both political parties on national defense issues, they looked for answers among figures outside the party system. As more jobs were lost to cuts in defense spending, the mainstream wings of both parties continued to advocate for demilitarization (on the Democratic side) and continued rapprochement (from the Republicans). This was unacceptable to Americans with personal connections to the Cold War, who wrote letters and marched in protest against the policy of détente. As historian Fredrik Logevall has pointed out, Americans were never enthusiastic about negotiating with their communist enemies during the Cold War, viewing détente as necessary, rather than desired, after the Vietnam War; but a critical mass of Americans now deemed détente (and Ford's foreign policy) contrary to U.S. interests at home and abroad.[52]

By late 1975, Ford's staff feared that defense cuts and foreign policy crises collectively jeopardized his support from members of the Cold War coalition who were pivotal to his reelection in 1976. Republicans thought Ford was now undoing Nixon's efforts to build a new Republican majority, as they had "worked very hard during the last decade to cement the allegiance of many East European ethnic groups to the

Republican Party" and feared that Ford might lose these voters due to "negative coverage in the American ethnic press for his participation in the [Helsinki] conference." Ford had also not done enough to reach out to various ethnic groups "who feel no identity" with the president and his policies.[53] Internal polling by Ford's staff in December 1975 showed that the public had shifted rightward on foreign policy, as Americans professed to be more conservative on foreign policy than Ford or Congress and were less inclined to favor future diplomatic consultation with the Soviet Union.[54]

Republicans upset at Ford's foreign policy—and Ford overall—wanted a conservative figure to challenge Ford for the Republican nomination in the 1976 presidential primary, someone who would refight the Cold War in the name of American hegemony. They wanted a new direction in foreign policy and decided that Ronald Reagan should be at its helm. Reagan contemplated running for president even before his second term as governor of California expired in January 1975. In the days after Nixon's resignation, Reagan met with a cadre of political operatives, including former Nixon staff member John Sears and his press secretary Lyn Nofziger to determine the viability of a presidential run. They told Reagan that Ford was unpopular and vulnerable. He was an unelected, moderate president, marred by the legacy of Watergate and an economic recession, and would have difficulty maintaining credibility within the Republican Party. Reagan agreed, whereupon his advisors soon formed the committee Citizens for Reagan, headed by the Republican senator from Nevada, Paul Laxalt. While Citizens for Reagan began to raise money and coordinate an infrastructure for a Reagan presidential campaign, Reagan made sure to keep himself in the public eye, waiting to see if a primary candidacy was still in the works. He wrote a syndicated newspaper column, gave a regular radio address, and made speeches across the country touting his philosophies on government spending, taxes, and foreign affairs.

Ford's advisors knew there were rumblings over a Reagan campaign in 1975 but were unconcerned. Internal polling showed voters believed Ford to be the better person to tackle inflation and the economy. Reagan's strength was in foreign policy, but the Ford campaign predicted that foreign affairs would not be a factor. "Only in some areas of foreign policy does Reagan beat Ford, and foreign policy is a distant fourth among voter concerns this year," they wrote. They saw no scenario where Reagan would defeat Ford.[55] Members of Reagan's staff realized too that Ford had the upper hand. Political history and the incumbency were on Ford's side. "No one since the Civil War has successfully challenged an incumbent president for the nomination and gone on to win the general election," wrote Reagan fundraiser Jaquelin H. Hume in an internal memorandum. If Reagan lost, he "and all his supporters will be persona non grata with the [Ford] administration. Since this will include most conservatives, this can seriously reduce conservative influence."[56]

On November 20, 1975, Reagan officially announced his candidacy. Dennis Dunn, chairman of the King County Republican Central Committee in Seattle, typified right-wing thinking in his hope that the primary campaign would revolve around foreign policy. "It may well prove to be that Ford's most serious blunder was the inexcusably crude fashion (and politically dumb) in which he treated Alexandr Solzhenitsyn. I doubt that anything in recent years has enraged the true American conservative anymore than this most recent display of the Rockefeller-Kissinger type of mindless gaucherie."[57]

But Reagan largely ignored individuals like Dunn. Reagan had discussed foreign policy issues repeatedly in his radio addresses and in speeches to groups such as the Veterans of Foreign Wars, where in August, he called the withdrawal of American troops from Vietnam a tragedy and claimed the Ford administration had not done enough to confront the threat of communism.[58] However, in the early days of the campaign, Reagan largely ran on a platform of reducing the size of the federal government, not foreign affairs. While the Ford campaign believed foreign policy was Reagan's strength, big government appeared to be the most salient issue to Reagan's more ideologically conservative advisors such as the American Conservative Union's (ACU) Jeffrey Bell. In his first speech as a presidential candidate, Reagan said he was running to change the corruption and cronyism in Washington, D.C., that originated from the "root" of America's problems: government largesse.[59] The economy was also an overriding concern for Reagan. In the summer and fall of 1975, polls showed that Americans were overwhelmingly distraught by rising taxes, inflation, and unemployment. In states like Wisconsin, Reagan was told by advisors that domestic issues were of the utmost interest to voters, where anxiety over high taxes meant "taxpayer groups have been springing up like weeds," while "national security and the social issues are less important" than the economy.[60]

In September 1975, Reagan put forward a specific plan to stimulate the economy by reducing government spending. In a speech in Chicago, Reagan proposed to transfer federal expenditures for areas such as housing, health care, public education, welfare, and transportation to state governments, while most areas of defense spending, the second largest budget item behind entitlements, would be untouched.[61] Reagan claimed his program would ultimately reduce the federal budget by $90 billion, giving local governments more control and streamlining government services to Americans who deserved them. Once Reagan announced his candidacy, however, his redistribution plan did not stand up to scrutiny. Office of Management and Budget analyst James T. Lynn wrote that it "would, by necessity, result either in a significant increase in the tax burden on the American people, or in a radical reduction in the transferred programs which would leave recipient groups worse off than they are now."[62] A preponderant number of primary voters in New Hampshire relied on government benefits and worried about insinuations that local taxes needed to be raised and government benefits slashed to pay for Reagan's program.[63]

When he lost the Iowa caucus in February, Reagan tried to distance himself from the $90 billion program. In press conferences, Reagan avoided discussion of the plan's details, albeit unsuccessfully. When questioned by reporters about how he chose the government programs to cut, Reagan said he "never did pay any attention to that list. That was just some stuff the economists gave me."[64] The "$90 billion gaffe" plagued Reagan's campaign in New Hampshire, where he lost to Ford. Moreover, the American economy began to recover in late January after a prolonged recession. Increases in consumer spending and stock market prices discredited Reagan's claim that Ford had mismanaged the economy and made domestic issues less resilient as the weeks went on.[65]

After falling in Iowa and New Hampshire, Reagan lost the next four primaries: Massachusetts, Vermont, Florida, and Illinois. After Illinois went to Ford, journalists Rowland Evans and Robert Novak felt the president had all but sealed the nomination.[66] Even Reagan's advisors, groping for a coherent campaign strategy, cautiously urged the former governor to reconsider continuing in the race after May.[67] If Reagan did not win the next primary in North Carolina, his quest for the White House was over. To win North Carolina, Reagan's advisors reasoned that he had to assemble a new coalition of supporters on issues other than big government. Attacks on federal programs would not be enough to carry Reagan into the White House. David Keene, in a memorandum to Reagan, noted that building a coalition in North Carolina meant attracting white-collar suburbanites from urban areas in the Piedmont region, "disaffected Wallacite Democrats" from the eastern part of the state, and voters in the western mountains who occupied the base of the party since the Civil War. Keene recommended to Reagan that they put a coalition together that wedded the "sectional and social" factions within the North Carolina Republican Party between the metropolitan suburbs and the rural areas of the state. In 1968, Nixon captured a significant portion of the vote in Raleigh (from which Jesse Helms emerged as a senatorial candidate) and dominated in the surrounding suburbs of Charlotte. Reagan had to repeat Nixon's performance and court right-leaning voters in the counties that elected Helms.[68]

In North Carolina, Reagan received much needed help by well-coordinated, well-funded grassroots activists hoping to revive his chances of victory. One resident of Charlotte wrote to Paul Laxalt—even before Reagan announced his candidacy—that she was eager to volunteer for the governor, as she "will work day and night for Regan [sic]. I can type, answer the phone, get out mail or whatever I can do to help," because Ronald Reagan was "the only one I think could help the U.S. now."[69] The political machine that elected Helms to the Senate in 1972 backed these grassroots activists. Helms defeated the Democratic nominee, Representative Nick Galifianakis, by uniting the western base of the Republican Party with the traditionally Democratic eastern part of the state, where he attracted former followers of Democratic presidential candidate George Wallace. Helms's understated sympathies for the racial politics of the past, along with his hostility toward the federal government, sent him to Capitol Hill. Helms's election in 1972 led to the creation of the North Carolina Congressional Club, an organization that wielded money and influence on behalf of Helms and the collection of right-wing groups and individuals that backed his Senate campaign. Helms's close advisor and avid Reagan enthusiast Tom Ellis ensured that the Reagan campaign had the full patronage of the North Carolina Congressional Club, which used its money and members to mobilize campaign workers, gather crowds for Reagan's speeches, and assemble a media presence for Reagan on local television stations throughout the state.[70]

The main issue that made North Carolinians gravitate toward Reagan was not big government or the economy (alone), but national defense. National defense issues enticed defense workers near Greensboro, who were employed by Western Electric to build the anti–ballistic missile system. They also attracted voters in the eastern part of the state, which since 1969 had "produced a larger percentage of volunteers for the Army and other military services than any other part of the country." National defense also interested voters near Camp Lejeune and the Fort Bragg Army base in the southern part of the state, which voted overwhelmingly for Nixon in 1972 because of McGovern's proposals to cut military spending. Military spending in North Carolina—as in many Sunbelt states—was intrinsically connected to other economic and social issues dependent upon military spending, including veterans' benefits and military pensions. American military superiority, the fate of the Panama Canal, and the inadequacies of détente were issues that voters throughout the state were vested in for ideological, personal, and material reasons.[71]

Sunbelt voters' interest in Cold War politics was first recognized by the Reagan campaign during the Florida primary. On March 4, Reagan gave his first major speech on national defense, sounding like Solzhenitsyn when he said "all our smiles, concessions, and toasts of détente have not brought genuine peace any closer" and that Ford had "shown neither the vision nor the leadership necessary to halt and reverse the diplomatic and military decline of the United States." Requests for the text of the Florida speech poured into Citizens for Reagan. Unemployed aerospace workers and Cuban Americans angry over the president's policies toward Castro liked the speech and asked for copies. Out of fifty Republicans polled by the Reagan campaign, twenty-eight supported Reagan, and of that number, twenty said they liked Reagan for his opposition to Castro and his call for a stronger defense. After the Florida primary, David Keene geared the campaign toward an "attack strategy" against Ford, believing that the "Reagan attacks on détente" helped the campaign to build energy with the Republican electorate.[72]

Campaign manager John Sears and the rest of his staff did not anticipate the sizeable response to Reagan's address on national defense in Florida. The Reagan campaign's polling company, Decision Making Information, had not extensively polled voters on foreign affairs in early primary states such as New Hampshire and Illinois.[73] Reagan was also cautious on foreign policy in New Hampshire. Reagan claimed he was not opposed to détente entirely, but to a détente that failed to take into account the history of Soviet aggression toward the United States. Détente established a foundation to pursue peace with the Soviet Union, and the United States "should continue to do so," Reagan said, while remaining skeptical of Soviet intentions.[74] In a February speech at the Phillips Exeter Academy in Exeter, New Hampshire, Reagan was sufficiently critical of détente, but not dogmatic. "We are told that Détente is our best hope for a lasting peace. Hope it may offer, but only as long as we have no illusions about it," Reagan told the audience. He went on to claim that, "Détente, if it is a one-way street, will fail. As a two way street it may succeed."[75]

Reagan also glossed over his background as a proponent of détente during the Nixon administration. Hoping to bolster his image among conservative Republicans, Nixon sent Reagan on a tour of Southeast Asian nations in October 1971, where Reagan offered "very helpful explanations of the Nixon Doctrine" to Southeast Asian leaders skeptical of the president's efforts toward "opening" China to the United States.[76] Eight months later, Reagan was sent as an envoy to Europe—after Nixon and Soviet premier Leonid Brezhnev signed the SALT treaty—to assure Western European leaders that the United States would continue working to reduce tensions with the East through negotiation and diplomacy.[77] Along with his muddled positions on foreign affairs during the beginning of the primary, Reagan's role within the Nixon administration indicates that he lacked a grand strategy prior to 1976 and was unprepared to respond to voters' concerns with national defense and American foreign policy.[78]

Various independent right-wing groups also helped the campaign's shift to national defense—while retaining Reagan's focus on federal spending and the size of government. Reagan's campaign received much needed help from the Supreme Court with its January 1976 ruling in *Buckley v. Valeo*, which allowed unlimited contributions to independent organizations that lobbied on behalf of political candidates. The court's decision gave rise to the proliferation of political action committees (PACs) that supplemented funds from Citizens for Reagan, which often had trouble paying its creditors.[79] With money flowing from independent groups such as the ACU and the Conservative Victory Fund, movement conservatives bought time on radio and television airwaves emphasizing Reagan's hard-line stance on national defense. The ACU began placing ads in approximately ten local newspapers in Florida; by North Carolina, that number had grown to thirty-three. A major focal point of the radio advertisements for Reagan was his opposition to the Panama Canal treaties that ceded control of the waterway to General Omar Torrijos. Over eight hundred radio commercials were sponsored by the ACU that criticized the Panama Canal treaties and blamed Secretary of State

Henry Kissinger for coddling the Soviets. The ads also announced that "Ford stands for continued drift with the liberal policies of big government and détente," while Reagan was the embodiment of "new initiatives in freedom based on limited government, personal liberty, and peace through strength."[80] The theme of the ACU ads also supplemented the attacks levied on Ford by Helms, who equated federal welfare programs with the Panama Canal treaties, implying that the federal government was transferring its resources to socialistic projects at the expense of national security.[81]

On March 23, Reagan defeated Ford in North Carolina by six percentage points. In Guilford County, where Greensboro and hundreds of defense workers were located, Reagan won by 418 votes. In Onslow County, home of Camp Lejeune, Reagan beat Ford by a 640–319 margin. In the four counties that occupied Fort Bragg, Cumberland, Harnett, Hoke, and Moore, Reagan won the first three and lost Moore.[82] Reagan also took the entire eastern coast of North Carolina except for Dare County, where Ford prevailed by merely five votes.[83] Bruce Wagner, in charge of advertising for the Ford campaign, noted that national defense had won the election for Reagan, lamenting "this effective change in campaign tactic" that allowed Reagan "to seize the campaign momentum that had previously belonged to President Ford." Wagner wrote to Ford campaign manager Rogers Morton that Reagan's use of media to promote his ideas on national defense was the reason for Ford's defeat. Wagner argued that "Ronald Reagan has demonstrated his ability to revitalize his campaign with a series of highly personalized half-hour television addresses," which highlighted Reagan's differences with Ford on national defense policy. Campaign worker Peter Kaye was also upset that Ford had not used television effectively as Reagan. He believed the campaign should have made an extended television commercial prior to the North Carolina primary to counter Reagan's assertions. Reagan now had the upper hand as "the issue is defense and détente," wrote Kaye.[84]

After North Carolina, Reagan promoted a hawkish image to Republican primary voters opposed to the current direction of American foreign policy. The challenge for Reagan's advisors was to avoid comparisons to Goldwater's presidential campaign in 1964, when Goldwater was portrayed as irresponsible and reckless in his foreign policy to the extent that it would imperil global security. In selling Reagan's image abroad as a diplomat and statesman, the campaign had to confront the "notion spawned by some in [the] U.S. press that RR is a warmonger, bomb–thrower and recklessly belligerent," impressions that marred Goldwater in 1964.[85] Goldwater's endorsement of Ford exacerbated the perception of Reagan as an extremist on foreign policy. In explaining his decision to support Ford, Goldwater said he saw little difference between Ford and Reagan on substantive issues and believed a change in leadership would delay austerity reforms and hurt the Republican Party in the long term. He thought it unnecessary to "finally come so close to achieving what we set out to achieve three elections ago [in 1964] and risk it all now over a hair-splitting debate within the party about which of two genuine and bona fide conservative candidates is the more conservative."[86]

While careful to avoid a repeat of 1964 (in the context of a Republican primary), the campaign pressed on with Reagan's new strategy as national defense and U.S. foreign policy emerged as the core issues in the primary. Seeing the success national defense played in turning North Carolina to Reagan, his supporters and campaign staff replicated the strategy in the next major primary state, Texas. Before the Texas primary, Citizens for Reagan enlisted the Houston-based advertising and public relations firm Chamberlain-Frandolig for its help in assessing a profile of the typical Texas voter. The report claimed there was no other state "more critical to the Reagan campaign than Texas," where Reagan had the potential to extract "latent conservative support" from voters who "can be generated through effective utilization of key issues and organization to give the Governor a resounding victory." But Reagan first had to overcome Texans' suspicions toward Reagan's social security policy following the catastrophe of the $90 billion redistribution plan. The "misinterpretation" of Reagan's policy on social security was "continuing to erode his support among the generally conservative senior citizens, where his appeal could be the strongest." Reagan had to clarify his commitment to social security, but also draw attention to other issues affecting Texans and Americans nationwide. Among these were national defense. The report recommended that Reagan direct his tough defense posture toward workers in Houston, San Antonio, and Corpus Christi, people who had lost their jobs to base closures and military cuts. Moreover, a "major policy address on national defense posture/local base closures should be in San Antonio before as many retired officers as can be brought in and aired Statewide." The agency also suggested Reagan sell his opposition to the Panama Canal treaties in the Gulf Port, which presumably would suffer economically if the United States renounced its oversight of the canal.[87]

The subject of national defense—more than other policy issues—overcame Texans' anxieties that Reagan would eliminate federal programs like Social Security. Indeed, Reagan's national defense policy appealed to residents of a state who received 8 percent of total federal defense expenditures. Texans were a product of the Sunbelt South: a population who "generally opposes high federal spending on domestic programs and supports generous outlays for military and space spending."[88] Where Reagan began his speeches in the early primaries by focusing on government bureaucracy, he now made "the decline in U.S. military power" his opening concern in Texas.[89] Reagan continued to give half-hour televised addresses on national defense that were financed by individual donors who purchased airtime for the campaign. A sole donor, "Mr. McAllister," gave enough money to buy a "1/2 hour of TV time to show Reagan's stock 1/2 hour talk."[90]

Reagan's momentum in Texas resulted from the campaign's ability to resourcefully organize and collaborate with members of the Cold War coalition in ways he did not prior to North Carolina. The Reagan campaign established a reciprocal and symbiotic relationship with supporters in Texas, using their concerns on national defense as opportunities for building a broader constituency. Reagan framed foreign policy and national defense issues in Texas to appeal to the widest group of voters possible, forming associations and relationships between the sinking economy at home (particularly in Cold War communities) and the weakening of American military power abroad. Texans' distrust of détente had obviously predated the Reagan campaign in 1976, but Reagan managed to profit from public suspicion, if not outright antagonism toward détente, as an insurgent candidate willing to reverse the foreign policy consensus among Democrats and Republicans. Throughout the Texas primary, Reagan reminded voters that their decision on election day could alter America's Cold War foreign policy and its bearing on defense spending at home and bring new leadership—an outsider's perspective—into the White House.

Indeed, Reagan's national defense policies united voters throughout the state. In cities on the Gulf of Mexico, Reagan played up his message that the Panama Canal treaties were a giveaway to the communists, which ACU chairman M. Stanton Evans said was treated as a "local issue there."[91] Reagan criticized Kissinger's tour of Rhodesia in San Antonio, a city that had the "heaviest concentration of active & retired military," and confirmed his approval for the Byrd Amendment. In doing so, the *New York Times* noted that Reagan was addressing "George Wallace Democrats, whose support he has actively sought."[92] In April 1976, just as the contest between Reagan and Ford grew heated, Ford was accused of transferring military installations to Texas in order to win votes in the Lone Star State. Moreover, less than two weeks away from the primary, rumors also surfaced that Ford had decided to wait until after the Texas primary to decide on whether to announce a plan to increase the size of the navy by six hundred ships. If Reagan won Texas based upon his criticism of U.S. military weakness, the Department of Defense would then announce the rebuilding and expansion of the naval fleet.[93] Ford tried to refute Reagan's charges that he allowed the United States to fall into "a position of military inferiority." Ford called these accusations "preposterous" and said Reagan had zealously resorted to focusing on national defense "because a grab bag of other issues has been tried and failed." Ford's attempts to defend his record on foreign policy demonstrated to the *Times* "that Mr. Reagan had turned [national defense] into the focal point of the May 1 Republican primary in Texas." As Ford crisscrossed the state of Texas, "from Central to West Texas to the Panhandle," the president was met with voters' questions "about national defense, the Panama Canal, and détente."[94]

On May 1, Texas Republicans voted for Reagan over Ford nearly two to one. After Reagan won Texas, major media outlets reported on how foreign policy issues such as the arms race engendered success for right-wing Republicans like Reagan. The *New York Times* noted that the focus in the Republican primary after May 1976 was on "whether the United States is No. 1 in military power." The *Times* compared Reagan's comments on the supposed weakness of the United States to Kennedy's 1960 campaign where he blamed Eisenhower for a "missile gap" between the United States and the Soviet Union.[95] *Time* magazine also observed that "national security was one of Reagan's big winners" in Texas where "Reagan attacked Ford for cutting back on military bases . . . while continuing to subsidize the United Nations." Reagan's win on national defense issues, the magazine posited, would force Ford to modify his positions on U.S. foreign policy and possibly even "dump Kissinger."[96] That same month, Ford received returned donation letters with the words "I will not support you in any way until you get rid of Henry Kissenger [*sic*]" scrawled on them. Other critics of Ford asked the president to "kick Kissinger out on his Dead End." In response, Ford's campaign staff felt they were "in trouble," as Ford had lost "what has traditionally been the exclusive province of an incumbent president . . . foreign policy."[97] Barry Goldwater wrote to Ford on May 7, six days after his loss in Texas, advising him "to be more punchy" in his speeches but not to get into a sparring match with Reagan over the issues, telling him outright that he was "not going to get the Reagan vote. These are the same people who got me the nomination [in 1964] and they will never swerve." Rather than trying to convert Reagan voters, Ford should target "middle America." Goldwater concluded by telling Ford to "get off Panama" and focus on other issues.[98]

In post-Texas primaries, Reagan's attention to Cold War defense generated new public criticism of Ford's national defense policy. The campaign's victory in Texas reinforced public criticism of détente, but also made the electorate more attentive to foreign policy issues—and willing to vote for Reagan because of them. Rather than reacting to preexisting discontents over the direction of American foreign policy, Reagan's win in Texas allowed him to broaden his coalition. Reagan won the next three primaries: Georgia and Indiana on May 4 and Nebraska on May 11. In Indiana, where Reagan received a third of his votes from Democratic crossovers, the "questions of détente, defense spending, and above all, the role of the United States vis-à-vis the rest of the world were among Reagan's best levers."[99] By the time of the California primary in June, more voters admitted to be voting for—or against—Reagan because of his stance on national defense and foreign affairs. Anne Nixon, chairperson of the Monterey Citizens for Reagan chapter, solicited donations for Reagan by touting Reagan's stance on national defense and criticizing Ford's handling of U.S.-Soviet relations and American policy in Vietnam, Greece, and Angola. Nixon told Californians that while Ford was a "nice guy" who reduced the tide of Democratic spending in Washington, Reagan was the only man who "understands the national peril from without" and was an "articulate campaigner for Americanism."[100]

Reagan overwhelmingly won his home state, beating Ford by thirty percentage points and setting the stage for a showdown over Republican delegates at the Republican National Convention in Kansas City. In the days leading up to the convention, Reagan's base reiterated that the way to beat Ford was to maintain his attacks on the president's national defense and foreign policy. Voters sent Reagan their advice and checks for donations in small amounts of five, ten, or twenty-five dollars. William Haggerty from Canonsburg, Pennsylvania, was a "registered Democrat" and told Reagan that "the way to win the number of needed delegates" was to play up the threat of the Soviet Union. Grace and Lee Wooster were "retired registered Democrats" who found that claims that there was "no difference" between Ford and Reagan were untrue and enclosed an article from the conservative magazine the *Christian Crusade Weekly* that suggested Ford and Kissinger had allowed the Soviets to expand their military power. Florence Daige of Attleboro, Massachusetts, told Reagan that he "alone can save our country and Panama Canal. We need [a] leader who will build this country up to Number 1 and say no to the Russians, [and] open our defense plants to give our men work." One person wrote to Reagan's wife Nancy that Reagan should introduce into the Republican platform a demand for the resignation of Henry Kissinger, believing the secretary of state's conduct to "be enough to defeat Gerald Ford."[101]

While Reagan had the support of the Cold War coalition—at least a portion of it—at the outset of the convention, he lost members of his base after he chose Pennsylvania senator Richard Schweiker as his vice presidential nominee. Schweiker was a liberal Republican with strong ties to labor but fell in line with Reagan's positions on defense. Reagan felt Schweiker would lure Ford voters to Reagan. Reagan had captured the foreign policy hawks that disliked Ford for his defense of détente but thought the selection of Schweiker could attract moderate voters who preferred the president's economic policies but not his foreign policy. For many of Reagan's most dedicated supporters, however, men like Schweiker represented what was wrong with the Republican Party. One Reagan voter who professed to being an "independent-leaning-toward-Democrat" claimed Reagan "blew it" by picking Schweiker "just like Wallace did when he picked [General] Curtis LeMay" in 1968. He was contemplating donating "a few dollars to your campaign till this Schweiker came on" the ticket. Most of Reagan's top advisors and aides, including Helms and the representative from Ohio, John Ashbrook, privately disapproved of Reagan's choice, believing Schweiker to have failed the test of being a true conservative. But others favored the choice of Schweiker. Reverend Salvator Franco from New Hyde Park, New York, praised Reagan's pick for vice president as "Schweiker is for prayer in school, against busing and gun control, against abortion on demand and thinks détente has been a one-way street." Franco said the "people in Nassau County [are] anxious to support [the] Reagan Schweiker ticket."[102] Events on the convention floor also hurt Reagan. The Mississippi delegation made the surprise move of shifting delegates to Ford, despite the state voting for Reagan in its primary. The bleeding of Reagan supporters due to the falling out over Schweiker and the Mississippi delegation meant the end of Reagan's candidacy. After all the votes were counted, Ford had 1,187 delegates, while Reagan had 1,070. Reagan conceded to Ford, but not before his supporters inserted a "morality in foreign policy plank" into the Republican Party platform. While it did not call for Kissinger's resignation, it did criticize détente and the Helsinki Accords and praised Alexandr Solzhenitsyn. Furthermore, as historian John Lewis Gaddis argues, Reagan forced Ford "to disassociate himself symbolically, if not in substance, from the entire concept of détente" during the campaign.[103] After the Florida primary, Ford used the term "peace through strength," rather than détente, a slogan later used in alluding to Reagan's foreign policy.

Through his appeal to Republicans and crossover Democrats on détente and national defense, Reagan's 1976 campaign facilitated a broader process of political realignment in the 1970s. Reagan's campaign—and Reagan himself—represented a shifting political consensus in the 1970s, one that occurred for many reasons. First, structural forces aligned for Reagan at a convenient time. Economic anxiety, the end of the Vietnam War, public antipathy toward the political system, schisms among Democrats on the defense budget, and various international events aroused anger among voters, which shaped political constituencies in favor of higher military spending. National defense thus enabled Reagan to build a coalition that outweighed specific concerns about spending on government programs, the size of the federal state, or social issues. Indeed, Reagan's focus on national defense spending allowed him to reach into a grab bag of issues related to the subject: American internationalism, federal spending priorities, the role of the federal government, and the condition of the American economy, to name a few. Reagan's general message on the need for higher defense spending had currency among hard-line conservative Republicans and Sunbelt Democrats, and moderate anticommunist Republicans as well, allowing Reagan to elide his early reputation as an antigovernment zealot. Reagan's brazen support for the "remilitarization" of the Cold War also placed demands upon policy makers—Democrats and Republicans alike—to renew a foreign policy that refused concessions with communist powers and expanded American military power beyond 1976.

But Reagan still lost the election. Months later, Reagan attributed his defeat to Ford's influence in the northern states and the power moderate Republicans still held within the party. Reagan told former president Richard Nixon that the reason he was defeated in Kansas City was New York Republican Nelson Rockefeller's influence in a few "North East states where the party structure controlled the vote."[104] While Ford defeated Reagan in the primary election, he lost in the general election against Democrat Jimmy Carter. Americans wanted someone removed from the mainstream of American politics, and Carter delivered. A former governor of Georgia, Carter promoted his background as a Washington outsider on the campaign trail and vowed to change the culture of policy making in Washington, D.C., making it more transparent. Carter was unlike previous postwar Democratic candidates since the advent of the New Deal. In some ways, Carter sounded similar to Reagan, as Carter favored the deregulation of business and supply-side economics. Expanding government programs was not the solution to economic deprivation, Carter felt. In this sense, Carter was the first post–New Deal president.[105] In his first State of the Union Address, Carter told Congress and the American people that Americans "need to realize that there is a limit to the role and function of government. Government cannot solve our problems" as it was unable to "eliminate poverty or provide a bountiful economy."[106] In his foreign policy, Carter was dedicated to arms control and nuclear disarmament and talked about cutting the defense budget. Carter also made human rights an obligation of his foreign policy agenda. Carter had, in his words, "studied the record of abuses in different nations as reported by Amnesty International, the United Nations, and other organizations" and expected that human rights issues would "cut across our relations with the Soviet Union and other totalitarian governments." Carter aimed to combine his human rights agenda with détente with the Soviet Union, finally ending what he felt was the dispassionate realism that characterized Kissinger's diplomacy.[107]

Carter discovered, however, that by pursuing rapprochement with the Soviets, he would reunite the diverse factions within the Cold War coalition against his administration. The combination of changes to the international political system and the effects the Cold War coalition had on the political landscape after 1976 set in motion a conglomeration of forces that Carter was forced to confront at the outset of, and indeed throughout, his administration. Moreover, new groups and individuals emerged in the second half of the 1970s that questioned America's post-Vietnam foreign policy, ones that gravitated toward Reagan and who changed the politics of the Cold War coalition. After Reagan's campaign generated new political energy within the Cold War coalition, dislike and distrust toward détente lingered among the electorate. Carter had to deal with the consequences.

Carter's opponents on foreign policy came from both Cold War liberal and the Republican Right. Organizations such as the Committee on the Present Danger (CPD) consisted of Cold War hawks from both parties whose main "objective [was] to alert the nation to the growing threat posed by the Soviet drive for world domination."[108] The CPD was the product of the 1975 CIA report entitled Team B, which countered the Ford administration's official claim that détente created a lasting peace. In addition to these national security elites, Christian evangelicals like Pat Robertson, Tim LaHaye, and Jerry Falwell gave Carter greater problems. Evangelicals had largely backed Carter's election, believing his claim to be a "born-again" Christian meant he wanted to repeal abortion, mandate school prayer in public schools, and put a halt to the gay rights movement. Leading evangelicals soon discovered, however, that Carter's Christianity did not mean using the state to dictate human behavior. For Carter, religious worship was a private matter that should not be politicized in the public sphere.

Carter further antagonized the opponents of détente by spending his political capital on the ratification of the Panama Canal treaties. After Carter signed the treaties on September 7, 1977, evangelicals' honeymoon with Carter was over. Evangelical Christians were fiercely anticommunist and viewed a strong national defense as important as busing or abortion. In the eyes of evangelicals, Carter had a clear choice: he opposed the Panama Canal treaties or appeased communist dictators. Evangelicals decided that Carter's decision on the Panama Canal was evidence of the latter. In the following months, evangelicals led by the Reverend John Gimenez of Virginia Beach, held "Washington for Jesus" rallies at the capital to ban abortion and "double the defense budget."[109] Carter met with evangelical leaders such as Oral Roberts and Jerry Falwell only once, and the meeting did not go well.[110]

Those members of Congress who supported the Panama Canal treaties also faced trouble, as the 1978 midterm elections unseated Republicans and Democrats who voted for the treaties. Whereas the 1976 election saw the gradual emergence of PACs, by 1978 they came to dominate electoral politics. Among right-wing PACs, the National Conservative Political Action Committee (NCPAC) spent the largest amount of money during the 1978 election. NCPAC spent a total of $2,842,851 during the midterm elections, $200,000 of which went directly to antitreaty candidates.[111] Right-wing PACs also steered money and attention to key states that voted for Reagan in 1976, hoping to remove from office the Democrats and Republicans who voted for the Panama Canal treaties. NCPAC, Citizens for the Republic, and the Committee for the Survival of a Free Congress, also targeted candidates who in their view failed to possess the attributes that qualified them as "conservative."

The controversy over the Panama Canal treaties also ousted Sunbelt Democrats and Watergate babies from Congress. In states like Texas, 79 percent of the public were still opposed to the treaty, with little separation between Democrats and Republicans.[112] Little-known right-wing Republican Gordon Humphrey was successful in defeating Tom McIntyre for a Senate seat in New Hampshire in 1978 largely by stressing his opposition to turning over the Panama Canal to the Panamanians. In an editorial, the *Manchester Union Leader* said the fight over the canal "was a critical battle between the Liberal Establishment and the American people, and for that reason" it was the "pivotal issue of 1978, whose repercussions one way or the other will affect the lives of us all, not only here in the United States but, for that matter, on a worldwide scale."[113] NCPAC and the Conservative

Caucus also attacked McIntyre over his support of the Panama Canal treaties, claiming his voting record threatened the security of the United States.[114] In other Senate races between Democrat Dick Clark and Republican Roger Jepsen in Iowa and Democrat William Hathaway and Republican Bill Cohen in Maine, the canal issue played a secondary role in the defeat of the Democratic candidates. As historian Adam Clymer has written, the Panama Canal treaties "served as a lightning rod as conservatives tried to take over the Republican Party" in the 1970s.[115]

The Panama Canal was not the only contentious foreign policy issue that confronted the Carter administration. Carter also tried to quell opposition to the second round of SALT talks with the Soviets. Particularly discomforting was the opposition to SALT II from white ethnic Americans who Republicans actively courted in the 1970s. The debate over SALT II among American immigrants from the Soviet bloc took place in the midst of lingering concerns over the Helsinki Accords that affected "Eastern Europeans who come from countries totally dominated by the Soviet Union." Philip Crane, a Republican congressman from Illinois and chairman of the ACU, created a group called Alliance for Freedom that planned to defeat SALT II—and was "composed heavily of Eastern European ethnics."[116] Eastern European immigrants living in Pittsburgh, Pennsylvania (a key state for Carter in 1980), attended a breakfast with members of the Carter administration in 1979 who tried to convince them on the merits of the arms talks. The Carter administration walked away from the meeting dissatisfied with the results, noting that Eastern European immigrants' "deep distrust of the Soviet Union" will imperil public backing for SALT II.[117] In addition to the public unrest over SALT II, the Carter administration noted that Greek Americans were also upset over Carter's handling of American relations with Cyprus, and Polish Americans were concerned over the direction of U.S.-Soviet relations. Polish Americans' disaffection toward Carter troubled the campaign since one "major factor contributing to Ford's losing the 1976 election was his statement that Poland is a free country." In short, Carter was losing support from white ethnics over national defense issues.[118]

In addition to trying to woo ethnic groups, Carter's staff also tried to build a coalition of Republicans and Democrats around his proposal for a strong but leaner defense budget. Presidential assistant Anne Wexler believed that Carter's defense budget required the "involvement of the good government groups and conservative religious groups," which she said "have more influence with the Republicans and Southern Members." In addition to these groups, Wexler believed the defense budget needed support from the AFL-CIO and business if Carter wanted to avoid alienating two very large constituencies. But the AFL-CIO continued to fight the Cold War during the Carter administration. Carter had poor relations with labor during much of his presidency, but the AFL-CIO resisted large defense cuts and opposed the Transfer Amendment in 1979, which would reallocate a portion of defense spending to domestic programs. Referring to the California initiative that placed a cap on property taxes, the union said the Transfer Amendment was like "applying the Proposition 13 meat-ax" to defense at a time when there was a "consensus that the Soviet Union has been engaged in a massive military buildup."[119]

A bipartisan coalition on defense proved impossible considering the mounting critiques of Carter's leadership on foreign policy. Growing opposition to Carter among the Cold War coalition made the president adopt a new strategy toward national defense. From national security elites like Jeanne Kirkpatrick, who attacked the foundations of Carter's human rights policy—Carter "actively collaborated in the replacement of moderate autocrats friendly to American interests with less friendly autocrats of extremist persuasion," Kirkpatrick wrote—to the growing cadre of religious fundamentalists led by Falwell, Roberts, and Pat Robertson who believed Carter abandoned the world to communism, the president had little chance or opportunity to achieve a human rights–based foreign policy.[120] Moreover, the reluctance of labor, business, white southerners, and ethnic groups to support détente painted Carter into a corner on national defense policy. After 1978, and the Soviet invasion of Afghanistan, Carter shifted to the right on foreign policy and national defense. The president's talk of defense cuts changed to requests for defense increases, as Carter announced the building of the MX missile (which he earlier opposed) and increased funding for the Trident II nuclear submarine program.[121]

Carter's vacillation on détente and defense weakened his reelection campaign. When he ran against Carter in 1980, Reagan continued the campaign rhetoric he used against détente in 1976. Now the context had changed. Unrest over high oil prices, stagflation, the Iran hostage crisis, and the invasion of Afghanistan made Carter's reelection uncertain at best. While the 1980 campaign was mostly about economic issues, those Americans who were Reagan supporters in 1976 because of his foreign policy fell behind the candidate again in 1980 on his domestic policy. Reagan campaigned for president in 1980 on the basis that Carter's failures were symptomatic of the bankruptcy of liberalism. Reagan also linked domestic and foreign policy together, something he had done well in 1976. In touring states like Virginia, Reagan lured military workers in Norfolk, promising pay increases and a more muscular foreign policy.[122] Anne Wexler recommended that Carter focus his campaign against Reagan on similar grounds, writing that Carter should run on the theme of "Rebuilding America's Strength," which eerily echoed Reagan's "Peace through Strength" platform in 1976. Wexler said that Carter should point out to voters that he "reversed the decline in real defense spending to rebuild our military strength." The slogan "Rebuilding America's Strength" also encompassed Carter's policies toward the economy, employment, and energy, as the president was "rebuilding our country's strength in the world—both militarily and morally—and rebuilding our economic strength."[123]

Carter's new, tough foreign policy signaled the demise of the anti-militarist moment in the Democratic Party—and its fleeting popularity in the late 1960s and early 1970s. With his newfound support for the MX missile and increased defense spending after 1978, Carter lent credence to the muscular discourse and policies of Reagan, committing the Democratic Party to a hawkish foreign policy in the remaining months of the 1970s. For these reasons, Carter contributed to the structural and rhetorical reemergence of defense spending and the Cold War economy as *the* solution to foreign policy crises, one that would have domestic consequences for workers in the Cold War economy and members of the Cold War coalition. Carter's call for a buildup of military forces as a political solution—as a response to "rebuilding our country's strength"—was a return to the Cold War liberalism of his predecessors, but constructed in the context of the austerity politics of the 1970s, it furthered the policy agenda of the Right.

On November 4, 1980, Ronald Reagan defeated Jimmy Carter in the largest electoral landside since 1932—a victory that relied upon the Cold War coalition and the history of the 1976 Republican primary. While the economy was the major concern among most voters in 1980, members of the Cold War coalition continued to feel threatened by defense cutbacks, fearing further retrenchment in foreign policy would lead to plant and base closures, a loss of jobs, and a reduction of federal benefits provided by defense spending, voters turned to Reagan and right-wing politicians for answers. That Reagan would pick up the largest number of electoral votes (489) since Franklin D. Roosevelt was an interesting, if not surprising event. Indeed, Reagan succeeded in capturing the White House because of—not despite of—the legacy of New Deal liberalism and the New Deal state on matters of national defense. With the Democratic Party disjointed on foreign policy following the 1972 campaign, and increasingly headed toward muddled, moderate path on defense spending, Reagan offered a clear alternative that more Americans were willing to accept in the mid-1970s: increased defense spending to build up America's strength at home and abroad. This policy was right out of New Deal and Cold War liberals' playbooks—and it was the answer members of the Cold War coalition wanted, and expected, to hear. Because the Panama Canal Treaty, the civil war in Rhodesia, and the Helsinki Accords imperiled national morale and military superiority, and the job security of Americans who depended on the Cold War, the only mitigating response was increased military power. This is what Reagan offered the American people. And the Democratic Party in the 1970s had no consistent convincing alternatives to military

Keynesianism, save defense conversion, which had less appeal in a time of austerity—and because of the inchoate form it took among its supporters. The Cold War coalition that formed around Reagan—and which Reagan organized, cultivated, and strengthened—thus felt disillusioned by the party system and its ability to generate tangible economic gains for voters, and right-leaning figures like Reagan offered clear-eyed and reductive solutions, in and beyond the 1970s.

As we shall see in the next chapter, when the Cold War coalition rallied behind the warfare state—and a militaristic foreign policy—in the 1970s and 1980s, some of its members fared better than others—just as they did in the 1950s and '60s. In 1972, Lockheed workers in Burbank, California, exemplified the anxieties faced by the unionized, blue-collar workforce—which would shed more jobs in the 1980s than in the 1970s. With 58 percent of the defense workforce in blue-collar positions, and Rustbelt states averaging job losses in defense of over 20 percent after 1972, the working class took the brunt of the damage done by defense cuts after 1980. When Reagan therefore offered working-class Americans the opportunity "to return their money to them" in the 1980s—in the form of tax cuts and potential jobs in the defense economy—this message had great appeal among these members of the Cold War coalition; but the outcome of Reagan's policies, both foreign and domestic, would cause the working class more harm than good.[124]

CHAPTER FIVE
War and Peace in the "Age of Inequality"

Whereas in 1951 the future seemed bright for workers and executives at Electric Boat in Groton, Connecticut, only to have that future dashed by the mid-1950s, the company felt hope anew in the early 1980s. In 1981, newly elected Republican president Ronald Reagan announced a drastic increase in the defense budget to meet the Soviet threat following the invasion of Afghanistan. Electric Boat, and Groton, welcomed Reagan's announcement. Employees and executives alike ignored the previous thirty years of undulations in the defense budget, the turbulence of the late 1950s and early 1960s, and the drastic cuts in the 1970s after Vietnam and predicted Reagan would inject a long-term economic stimulus into the state, one that would keep defense manufacturing alive in the region—which was "still the tail that wags the dog around here," according to one economist for the Connecticut Bank and Trust Company. While Reagan's budget also called for concurrent cuts to domestic expenditures, Democratic officials in Connecticut felt the increases in defense spending were "going to soften the blow of some the [domestic] cuts," said representative Samuel Gejdenson. "That's probably the only good news from the President's message."[1]

The retrenchment and repurposing of domestic welfare spending was always contingent upon the expansion of the warfare state, but Reagan made this project more explicit than any Cold War president. After he was elected president—and at least during his first term—Reagan presumed the right-wing critique of American foreign policy since Vietnam was correct: the United States lagged in military capabilities in relation to the Soviet Union, wavered in dealing with communism abroad, and was too reluctant to exercise military predominance to threaten and defeat America's global enemies. In response to what he believed was a decade of neglect of America's military, Reagan raised defense spending by 35 percent during his time in office. No deficit was too large to Reagan if it prevented a Soviet attack.[2] Defense monies under Reagan's administration went toward a wide variety of programs. Much of defense spending under Reagan went to research and development in expensive projects like the Strategic Defense Initiative (SDI) and Cold War interventions in Central America and elsewhere in the developing world. Like presidents before him, Reagan relied on American military might to deter potential threats from communist countries. As a policy, "containment" was rejected, but not the means used by prior policy makers to deter communist expansion: exorbitant defense spending. New international threats from the Soviet Union and its allies seemingly demanded a return to the arms and technology race—communism once again appeared to be marching toward the West. Reagan responded to the new international context of the Cold War with a mission to "roll back" communism by placing the United States in a position of military dominance over the Soviet Union.

was communism the threat or just the S.U. who embodied it?

But the Reagan defense buildup was also an extension of the administration's domestic policy. Indeed, Reagan and his fellow Republicans saw the defense economy as an antidote to domestic economic pressures in a postindustrial age.[3] In allocating defense contracts, Republicans in Congress and the Reagan administration embraced a unique form of defense Keynesianism to ameliorate and stimulate employment. The economic contributions of the defense program were implied more than outright acknowledged by the Reagan administration, as few administration officials admitted being quasi-Keynesians. But Reagan knew SDI had an important role to play in the American economy. In the president's speeches on SDI and the defense buildup, Reagan promoted the missile defense system as a check to Soviet power, but also frequently touted the economic growth and good-paying jobs SDI brought to Americans.

Military Keynesianism under Reagan disproportionately enhanced the fortunes of the wealthy to the detriment of the working class and racial minorities in the defense workforce. As with previous administrations, including Franklin D. Roosevelt's, Reagan's defense and foreign policies shifted more military monies away from the Midwest and Northeast, and into the West and Sunbelt, continuing the trend that began during the Korean War. As the Reagan defense buildup divvied up contracts to companies dominated by nonunion, white-collar labor, it also meant declining union membership and greater racial and gender inequality in the defense workplace. High-tech areas in the western region of the country benefited the most from investment in SDI. The missile defense shield remained an experimental and untested program, which meant most of the jobs for SDI went to skilled engineers, mathematicians, and physicists. Rather than production of current defense products—which required a manufacturing base—Reagan's weapons systems were developmental and required no major investment in industry. With an eye toward defeating the Soviets in a race for military predominance, Reagan's defense policy meant investment in new programs, not preexisting weapons of war, which resulted in a loss of jobs for many unskilled Cold War workers. Reagan's economic policies thus promoted "nontradable sectors like real estate, financial services, and defense," which resulted in "hobbling tradable manufacturing and agriculture." The 1980s therefore marked a point of culmination for the military-industrial complex, as the political economy in the United States was now dominated by high-tech companies reliant upon knowledge workers rather than industrial production—a trend that the Cold War economy fostered. Reagan's defense policy thereby exacerbated the problems of deindustrialization, promoting the fortunes of the skilled workforce and the shift to what historian Judith Stein has called the "Age of Inequality."[4]

Reagan had little interest in the details of military contracting, but the economics of his foreign and defense policies had a decisive role in the remaking of American politics. Defense spending under Reagan offered temporary growth to some Cold War communities but did not benefit the entire defense economy. The unequal distribution of contracts and disproportionate investment in Cold War communities during the Reagan years meant military contractors that profited the least from the defense buildup merged with bigger defense companies, or drastically downsized. These policies all meant unemployment on some scale, and the numbers of unemployed were largest in the Northeast and Midwest.

The end of the Cold War intensified economic inequality and hardship across the country. When the Cold War ended, defense spending was reduced by over $100 billion, and further cutbacks in defense ensued. As a percentage of GDP, defense was cut by more than half from 1987 to 2000. And the defense jobs lost to peace were not replaced by better ones. Like other regions affected by plant closures, the service economy often replaced the defense economy in communities hardest hit by the end of the Cold War. The downturn in defense most affected working-class defense employees, as many found themselves displaced or underemployed after 1991—skilled workers had more mobility and better opportunities than their working-class counterparts. Antimilitarists on the Left (from within and outside of the Democratic Party) continued to sell defense conversion to ameliorate the situation in defense employment, but there were few buyers. Defense companies were resistant to conversion, and their workers feared being dislocated or unemployed in the transition to nondefense work—before being laid off.

With the inability of the Left to make inroads against the form of military Keynesianism propounded by the Reagan administration, the political rationales and economic consequences attached to the defense buildup reinforced American militarism—and impressions that the federal government had failed its citizens in some fashion. The twilight of the Cold War economy produced clear winners and losers that left a marked impact on American democracy in the 1980s, but the animosity felt by the Cold War coalition, from Northeast and Midwestern cities and suburbs toward newer sites of Cold War production in the South and West, produced fresh political tensions— ones revealed in Congress as legislators fought over which states and districts would receive which defense contracts. Yet these tensions made the Cold War coalition look not inward but outward to find the source of their problems. Inequality amidst the Cold War economy led to populist antagonism toward the federal government, as Americans requested the delivery of more defense monies to their communities while lambasting federal taxes and expenditures on items not explicitly related to defense. Members of the Cold War coalition did not turn against each other in the 1980s but continued to rail against an abstract federal government they felt no longer represented their interests—regardless of the administration in the executive branch or the composition of Congress.

* * *

Throughout his presidency, massive defense spending was the linchpin in Ronald Reagan's Cold War strategy. Reagan thought heightened defense spending would browbeat the Soviet Union into a position of strategic subservience. Accepting the popular opinion that détente had done near irreversible damage to American foreign policy, Reagan hoped to repair American might through defense increases larger even than those requested by military officials and defense corporations that profited from his policies. To some extent, massive defense spending unnerved the business community. Commerce Secretary Malcolm Baldridge, for example, reported meetings and "conversations with hundreds of businessmen, representing businesses of all sizes in finance and industry" in which the overwhelming consensus was that the resulting deficit was impeding economic growth. Anxiety over the deficit made "either continuing higher interest rates or inflation, or both, all too possible." Baldridge, however, declared cuts to defense spending off limits. Believing the deficit should only be tamed by cutting "the rest of government outside Defense as much as we can," he recommended increases in defense—though not to exceed 5 percent, as it was unclear whether the defense industry can "spend that large an increase efficiently." A rise of 8 percent would mean a backlog of defense orders since the United States defense industrial base had diminished since the 1960s and would not be able to handle the work requests from the Pentagon.[5]

David Stockman at the Office of Management and Budget (OMB) and "Cap" Weinberger at the Department of Defense, the two men and organizations that worked closely on Reagan's first defense budget, vied over the specifics. Stockman was an heir to the quasi-libertarian, Robert Taft wing of the Republican Party. Stockman was also an antigovernment ideologue who felt, as head of the OMB, that it was his job to begin "abruptly severing the umbilical cords of dependency that ran from Washington to every nook and cranny of the nation."[6] The "dependency" that Stockman referred to was the American welfare state, which Stockman believed drained the coffers of the federal government as Americans demanded more services from federal institutions. Defense, however (at least initially), did not enter into this paradigm. Stockman admitted being a "'big budget' proponent on defense," having been swayed by Jack Kemp and the journalist George Will (as well as the events of the Iranian hostage crisis from 1979 to 1981) on the need for a large defense budget. Stockman believed in higher defense budgets "with the zeal of the convert" and in the early days of a Reagan presidency hammered out an agreement with Weinberger for a real defense increase of 7 percent, equaling a defense budget of $1.46 trillion over five years.

But this figure surprised Stockman when he redid the calculations after meeting with Weinberger. Stockman favored large defense budgets, but a defense budget that high was excessive to the point that it would prevent the administration from considerably shrinking the size of the federal deficit. Stockman was suddenly distraught over Weinberger's indifference to the long-term costs of defense spending to the budget and the fate of the "Reagan Revolution." By then, however, it was too late. The proposed figures were released, and there was "squealing with delight throughout the military-industrial complex."[7]

Internal tensions over the specific figures aside, the consensus within the administration was that defense increases nearing hundreds of billions of dollars were needed to reverse the presumptive "weakness" of the United States' nuclear and conventional military arsenal relative to the Soviet Union.

Reagan received plentiful advice prior to the last significant meeting over the defense budget on September 9, 1981. Martin Anderson of the Office of Policy Development, classified in Stockman's memoirs as "a flinty anti-spender on everything," gave Reagan strident suggestions reminiscent of Cold War liberals in the 1950s. "National defense and economic policy are inseparable," Anderson said. The president must choose "between having a balanced budget, a strong economy, and significant, continuing increases in defense spending or having an unbalanced budget, a weak economy, and an eventual forced reduction in future defense spending." Murray Weidenbaum, Chairman of the Council of Economic Advisors concurred, stating that the president had the full support of the American public behind his defense policy, and that it too would serve the interests of America's domestic economy. "A strong national defense rests on two essential bases: a healthy national economy, and solid, widespread public support for defense expenditures." Reagan had both.[8] Reagan's advisors also told him to be mindful of his right-wing base that wanted more defense spending. Elizabeth Dole reminded him that "conservative organizations, as well as veterans and military groups" would demand defense expenditures at the present level and expect him to push for a balanced budget solely through cuts in social services.[9] It was Reagan's job to calibrate his defense policy between the hawks that supported him in the campaign and the broader public's vision.

Weinberger came prepared on September 9 to win over the president without Stockman getting in his way again. The OMB wanted to cut defense outlays by $30 billion for the remaining years of Reagan's first administration, but the defense secretary fought vigorously against cuts.[10] Weinberger warned that the OMB's proposal would "create the worst of all worlds" since it would undermine foreign policy by "caus[ing] us to fall further behind the Soviets" and not

This again ??

solve the deficit problem.[11] In loaded terms, Weinberger argued that the obsession over the deficit must be discounted when considering requests for defense increases. If the OMB budget went forward, the United States would have to suspend or cancel the use of Titan II rockets, eighteen naval ships, and two air force squadrons. Defense cuts would also mean the loss of 135,000 jobs in defense employment that would "spread through [the] economy," eventually leaving two hundred thousand Americans without work. And what if the president might "have to call on [the] military to protect national interests" in his first term? The United States could not carry out "the current foreign policy commitment" with its present defense capabilities. The results of the 1980 election spoke for themselves, Weinberger said. The American people wanted the United States to spend more on defense.[12]

The September 9 meeting determined how the Reagan administration would handle defense budget politics in the 1980s. Stockman tried to get Reagan to cut the projected 1982 budget by $20 billion, down from an original $30 billion. After Weinberger's presentation, however, Reagan felt it was impossible to go with Stockman's figure. He decided instead on a $13 billion cut over three years, a paltry sum. (Overall, defense would make up 7.5 percent of GDP.) Stockman's cuts "were based on pragmatism, not principle," he said, but in the end, "the President and Weinberger had decided to stick with principle."[13] Stockman was wounded by the defeat but publicly defended the increases he aimed to prevent behind closed doors. When, two years later, the Reagan administration asked for a defense budget of $247 billion for FY 1984, Stockman was one of the leading administration officials coaxing reticent senators to approve the increases.[14]

Reagan also faced opposition from Congress on his defense budget. Republicans and Democrats in Congress regularly rejected Reagan's defense budget when it was presented to them. By Reagan's second term, Congress was openly disturbed by the administration's hubris on defense spending—and Reagan's initial refusals to trim defense costs. When asked to reduce figures in the defense budget, Reagan officials eliminated projected pay increases for Department of Defense employees, rather than touch existing programs. This prompted Republican senator John Chafee from Rhode Island to comment that "defense has to bear its fair share" in budget cuts. Kansas Republican Bob Dole echoed Chafee, saying, "If the President wants budget restraint we've got to have defense included." The Reagan administration knew opposition to its yearly defense figures was forthcoming and often used large defense budgets as an advantage over Democratic opponents to cut social spending. When confronted with defense budget figures for the fiscal year 1985, house speaker and Massachusetts Democrat Tip O'Neill said that if Reagan "is willing to reduce the growth of defense spending then he will find that we will be helpful in nondefense areas."[15]

While congressional Republicans and Democrats scored victories in getting Reagan to prune the defense budget during his first term, they were modest accomplishments. Over Congress's objections, Reagan announced plans for building new missile and nuclear technologies, including the neutron bomb, the MX missile, and medium-range Pershing II missiles. The administration's strategy was to ask for astronomical increases and then rail against suggested, incremental cuts. This approach to defense spending had, in fact, been taken by every administration since Truman. The difference in each case was the international context. Now, in the 1980s, Reagan's defense increases inflamed tensions between the United States and the Soviet Union, igniting a "second Cold War" and erasing efforts at détente begun by Kennedy in 1963. With "peace through strength," the administration retriggered the arms race, even while discarding the premises behind mutual assured destruction.

Those who wanted to roll back communism through a massive defense buildup welcomed Reagan's early proposals on defense. The Committee on the Present Danger (CPD) was among the groups that searched for Reagan supporters among business elites and liberals disenchanted over the Democratic Party's antimilitarism in the 1970s. The CPD reached out to the U.S. Industrial Council (formerly the SSIC), the Council on Foreign Relations, the Chicago Committee, the Washington Institute of Foreign Affairs, and the National

Strategy Information Center, hoping they would open their wallets to help the CPD lobby Reagan and Congress on defense.[16] The working relationship between the CPD and Reagan came immediately. One month after Reagan's first speech on SDI, advisors Lyn Nofziger and Frank Carlucci wrote to the CPD under the auspices of the American Foundation, requesting "help in communicating the need for a strong national defense to the American people." Nofziger and Carlucci sought to embark upon "a nationwide communications campaign that will emphasize the necessity as well as the many rewards of a strong defense effort" to the public.[17] In addition to groups like the CPD, the Reagan administration also looked to capture support for its national defense policy among evangelicals. A National Association of Evangelicals Gallup poll conducted in 1983 revealed that 61 percent of evangelical respondents favored "Reagan's handling of the nuclear arms situation." Fifty-four percent of evangelicals agreed "that America's falling behind in the arms race would increase the danger of nuclear war more than a continuation of the arms race."[18]

If Reagan's defense buildup catalyzed his base, it also motivated opposition among the Left. Antinuclear activists concerned about the buildup of nuclear weapons coalesced in a nuclear freeze movement in response to Reagan's relaunching of the Cold War. Eventually becoming an international phenomenon, the nuclear freeze movement took to the streets to protest the escalation of nuclear weapons.[19] Americans mobilized by the thousands in favor of nuclear abolition. Collecting petitions outside supermarkets in New England, organizing profreeze workshops and seminars in the Midwest, filming commercials in favor of the freeze—including in the Sunbelt South—nuclear freeze activists expanded the movement to a global scale.[20] One grassroots supporter of the freeze campaign, E. B. Mullen from Schenectady, wrote Assistant Secretary of Defense Richard Allen in March 1981 to complain about his recent speech to the Conservative Political Action Committee that criticized the movement. Mullen noted that Allen could easily castigate liberals in favor of the freeze, but it would not detract from the push for disarmament, since many Americans were not "ready to accompany you to the nuclear incinerator."[21] An estimated five hundred thousand to one million Americans gathered in Central Park to demonstrate against the arms race the following summer. The freeze movement dominated headlines in the early years of Reagan's presidency, making nuclear diplomacy a constant household topic of debate. Even members of the evangelical right were skeptical about the use of nuclear weapons. Seventy-seven percent of evangelicals thought a "bilateral" freeze agreement was a good idea, provided there were equitable stipulations for a drawdown on both sides.[22]

With antinuclear fervor at levels not seen since the 1960s, a right-wing, antifreeze movement formed to counter its success. It too reached global dimensions. Students for Peace and Security (SPS), based in Boston and London, worked to dampen the success of the "freezniks" among the young through counterprotests "to the ban-the-bomb crowd." Melanie Sturm, an undergraduate at Tufts, explained part of the appeal. Strum joined SPS because she feared the freeze movement was "emboldening the Soviets to continue an aggressive foreign policy."[23] SPS was not the lone antifreeze organization. The London-based companion to SPS, the Coalition for Peace through Security, received $10,000 from the Heritage Foundation for making their "top priority" the defeat of the freeze movement. The Coalition for Peace through Security distributed pamphlets to coincide with antinuclear protests and enlisted members of the American military and national security elites, like Midge Decter of the CPD, to make statements against the freeze.[24] Such groups also gave important support to Reagan from the other side of the Atlantic. When the president planned to meet with the British prime minister in June 1982, the Campaign for Nuclear Disarmament planned a reception committee to show that British citizens "want[ed] peace, not nuclear holocaust" and to protest meddling in Central America, "Reagan's other red carpet."[25] Among a coalition of supporters, however, the local organization Peace with Freedom countered with the argument that "unilateral . . . disarmament by Britain or any Nuclear weapons/freeze . . . would give the Soviet Union a permanent built-in advantage over the United States." Not unlike American evangelicals later on, however, Peace with Freedom inevitably wanted to "see an end to the nuclear arms race"; disarmament was off the table so long as it was not multilateral.[26]

The broader public paid close attention to the freeze campaign as well. David Rawls, a high school teacher in Silverdale, Washington wrote to the CPD on November 8, 1982, asking to be placed on the organization's mailing list and for other information for a class he was teaching on nuclear age decisions. Rawls thought the CPD literature would stimulate debate on nuclear weapons, especially since "our community is home of the Trident missile system and the Puget Sound Naval Shipyard."[27] In Washington, Connecticut, locals clashed over a resolution to support the freeze, passed in April only to be voted down in June, after residents circulated antifreeze pamphlets portraying activists (including one local reverend) as Soviet spies. Michel Craig, who led the grassroots campaign, summed up his feelings by saying, "If you wish to vote for the Brezhnev, Kennedy freeze, I recommend you also vote to have Washington, Conn., renamed Marx, Moscow, or Misinformed."[28]

While the nuclear freeze movement muddied his assumptions that the public wanted more defense spending, Reagan continued to press on with peace through strength, feeling the activists did not represent the public sentiment at large. The nuclear freeze made the announcement of SDI more problematic than Reagan and his supporters wanted, however. SDI was the fulfillment of a decades-old dream to build a missile defense shield around the United States, using a system of satellites to deploy lasers intercepting Soviet missiles in the event of a nuclear war. A corollary to peace through strength, SDI emphasized the need for new weapons and technology to counter the Soviet Union. The program was grounded in more fantasy than science, and dubbed "Star Wars" by critics, after the popular 1977 movie. To its skeptics, SDI seemed just as implausible as the movie's plotline. Some members of the administration such as Assistant Secretary of Defense Richard Perle embraced the term; others thought it hindered the program even before its initial stages of research and development. John Lenczowski of the National Security Council recommended alternative nicknames for SDI, proposing substitutes for "Star Wars" such as "SHIELD" or "Sky Wall" or "Guardian System," any name that signaled "that the SDI is the functional equivalent of building a wall around your city to keep out the invaders."[29] Robert McFarlane like the idea, but other appellations failed to have the traction of the catchy "Star Wars."

SDI proved to be a useful tool in Reagan's diplomatic arsenal when it came time to negotiate treaties with the USSR in 1986. Reagan officials dismissed suggestions that SDI would be a bargaining chip, but the president privately hoped SDI would cajole the Soviets into supporting arms agreements favorable to the United States, as Nixon had tried to do with the anti–ballistic missile system.[30] When Reagan met with Gorbachev in Reykjavik to discuss the reduction of nuclear weapons, SDI was used to force the Soviets to accommodate American proposals for a nuclear arms treaty. Gorbachev refused. Before agreeing to universal cuts in nuclear weapons, he demanded Reagan relegate SDI to a research and development stage, not an active program. Reagan stonewalled, declaring SDI nonnegotiable.

The domestic politics surrounding SDI also shaped Reagan's argument that SDI was a defensive response to Soviet rearmament. SDI was a "deterrent" mechanism to counter Soviet expansionism, Reagan officials claimed; this was "the proper strategic context" for the public to understand the program. Despite the popularity of the freeze movement, local and national polls taken before the Reykjavik summit showed increased support for missile defense following the public relations campaign. Sixty-eight percent of Americans believed Reagan should not compromise over SDI; only 20 percent thought it was beneficial for the interests of nuclear disarmament.[31] In the defense-rich state of California, 70 percent of those polled "clearly supported the president's ballistic missile defense initiative." Indeed, public support for SDI was one of the reasons why the administration viewed the missile defense shield as "important" to American foreign policy.[32]

The Reagan administration convinced a swath of the public that SDI was vital to preventing a nuclear war, but in reality, SDI operated as an extension of military Keynesianism, as a boon to the military-industrial complex, more than it contributed to American national security interests. When Congress approved funding for SDI, upper-class suburban areas in the West, many that leaned toward conservative Republicans, benefited most. As the fortunes of SDI's contractors rose, defense monies went disproportionately to suburbs outside Denver and Washington, D.C., regions with high property values and high incomes. The chief contractor for SDI was Martin Marietta, located in Waterton (outside Littleton, Colorado), a Denver suburb. At the end of the third quarter in 1987, Martin Marietta had net sales of $4.75 billion, net earnings of $202 million, and capital assets of $535 million; it employed 11,397 in its Astronautics Group, 1,638 people in its Information and Communications Systems, and 1,700 in Data Systems—a total of 14,735 employees. Martin Marietta's headquarters in Denver also brought a large influx of revenue to the state. The company paid $20.6 million in Colorado taxes and $7.6 million in local property taxes.[33]

Martin Marietta's fantastic financial success was a direct product of Cold War spending. Before the federal government directed the aerospace and defense industry's expansion into Colorado, cities like Waterton were sparsely populated towns without a driving economic force. As with many defense communities, these were cities invented by the federal government. National regulations stipulated that defense factories be built in isolated regions away from population centers. This spurred suburban construction to accommodate the influx of defense employees, creating high-tech Cold War defense communities populated by wealthy engineers and scientists.[34] SDI also raised the stock prices of defense contractors. Investors bought up defense stocks in larger numbers during the first half of the 1980, as military stocks, the New York Times reported, were "in vogue."[35]

As a massive defense project, SDI was largely research based rather than production based. Unlike the manufacturing of Trident missiles or heavy aircraft carriers, large factories were not needed. With deindustrialization taking hold of American cities, even in Cold War communities, and SDI in a perpetual state of experimentation, there was little to manufacture. Political scientist Ann Markusen has argued that SDI represented the "tertiarization of the defense industries," the age of a "new trend—the development of pure research complexes."[36] SDI was indicative of how federal defense spending would function under a conservative president managing a postindustrial economy. SDI represented a high-tech and experimental model for defense contracting that was replicated by companies across the nation. In addition to Lockheed, other defense contactors, such as Rockwell, based in Southern California, transitioned to high-tech commercial electronics work after orders for its largest plane, the B-1 bomber, were canceled in 1987. Although the company earned $12.3 billion in revenues, over eighteen thousand people were laid off. Rockwell CEO Robert Anderson wanted the company to work toward diversification of its industry, the oft-stated but elusive goal of defense companies since the 1950s. But Rockwell struggled to make up its losses from the B-1 by bidding for future defense contracts. So did Lockheed when the C-5B plane was canceled.[37] The defense industry was just as dependent upon government contracts in the 1980s as it was in the 1950s.

The transformation in defense reflected Wall Street's capture of the economy in the 1980s. In addition to the expanding defense sector, Reagan provided federal assistance in the form of subsidies, tax cuts, and other "nontradable" changes to the law governing real estate and finance.[38] As Wall Street increasingly directed the course of economic events in the 1980s, the financial sector came to have greater input in other areas of the economy. As America's industrial economy deteriorated, investment markets did not respond well to undiversified defense corporations dependent upon federal procurement to manufacture large equipment.[39] After the slight boom in defense stocks faded, downsizing, hostile takeovers, and consolidated mergers and acquisitions threatened contractors who had not received an equal portion of funds from the defense buildup.

The decline in defense stocks most affected companies in the Northeast. Fearing job losses, Jack Kemp wrote to Reagan asking him to prevent the acquisition of Grumman aerospace by LTV Corporation. Kemp was afraid the buyout would "lead to the liquidation of

Grumman operations and the resultant loss of hundreds of jobs in New York." The full weight of federal regulations and laws, including antitrust laws and violations of federal statues regarding defense contracting, were impediments to any deal, Kemp implied. The preservation of Grumman would "insure the wellbeing of our national defense industrial base" and prevent disastrous "consequences for Grumman employees and shareholders, for New York aerospace workers and the state economy." LTV dropped its takeover of Grumman in November 1981, but Grumman struggled on until merging with Northrop in 1994. As major military electronics and defense companies were bought out or went bankrupt, Wall Street predicted the "takeover trend" would continue into the near future.[40]

SDI also mobilized members of the Cold War coalition to support right-leaning politicians in forthcoming elections. During the 1984 campaign, Reagan's science adviser Jay Keyworth thought it was a "good idea" to follow aide Mike Schwartz's suggestion to enlist local Republican voters to promote SDI. "We have, in the Republican Congressional candidates, a potentially effective grass-roots mechanism for making the case for SDI."[41] The Senate race between Representative Ken Kramer and Democrat Tim Wirth in Colorado put this strategy into action during the 1986 midterm elections. Kramer, an antigovernment conservative Republican, ran on his record of promoting SDI in the waning weeks of his campaign. He used SDI to further his image as a job creator, boasting to a newspaper reporter about his role in getting the National Test Facility to open in Colorado Springs, which was responsible for developing a large share of the necessary equipment for SDI. Kramer said that the National Test Facility's arrival was just one significant good to come out of SDI. He claimed SDI would bring eight thousand jobs to Colorado, at a time when the region suffered from persistent economic problems. The Democratic Wirth recognized the salience of SDI and did not want to center his campaign on his opposition to the missile defense system. As his campaign manager said, "There are a lot of livelihoods riding on S.D.I., and we don't want to seem anti-job."[42]

With election day nearing, Reagan appeared at a rally for Kramer, praising him for his stance on SDI. Kramer's supporters cheered while anti-SDI demonstrators confronted Reagan with signs: "Keep Star Wars in the Movie Theaters."[43] SDI was, Reagan said, "America's insurance policy to protect us from accidents or some madman who might come along, as a Hitler did or a Qadhafi, or just in case the Soviets don't keep their side of a bargain." Linking antigovernment rhetoric to the local and international context of the Cold War, Reagan went on to say that Kramer "has proven crucial in our efforts to cut your taxes and get big government off your backs," but was also "central in our efforts to rebuild the nation's defenses." Reagan continued on to a discussion of SDI, saying that Kramer was an early and "strong supporter of our Strategic Defense Initiative. And he helped convince the administration to put the major research center that will be the brains of SDI right here in Colorado." Kramer understood "our Strategic Defense Initiative will open the door to a new technological age. Just as America's space program created new jobs and industries, SDI could open whole new fields of technology and industry, providing jobs for thousands, as Ken said, right here in Colorado and improving the quality of life in America and around the world."[44]

But Kramer lost the election, even with Reagan's endorsement. The jobs SDI brought to Colorado could not make up for employment losses in other areas of the state. Considering Colorado voters' concerns over unemployment and Kramer's reputation as a right-wing radical, the election was quite close—Wirth won by only 16,455 votes. In the affluent Sixth Congressional District, home of Waterton/Littleton (and more than 95 percent white) and Martin Marietta, Kramer defeated Wirth by a near two to one margin, 104,359 to 53,384 votes.[45] After Kramer's loss, Reagan continued to turn to Coloradoans employed by SDI to promote his economic and defense policies. Approximately a year after Kramer's defeat, Reagan visited the Denver headquarters of Martin Marietta on November 24, 1987, to launch a public relations event for SDI. The National Security Council (NSC) prepared drafts of Reagan's speech to two thousand Martin Marietta employees, telling Reagan that he should make clear that SDI is "strengthening deterrence" and downplay arms control while emphasizing Soviet efforts to build their own version of SDI. American intelligence claimed the Soviets spent $200 billion of their budget "on strategic defense programs over the last 10 years, roughly what they've spent on offense," versus America's $10 billion. Reagan should emphasize this point to workers, the NSC suggested. After Reagan toured the Martin Marietta facility and received updates on the Zenith Star (the program developing chemical lasers to be emitted from space), he took the podium, telling the scientists and engineers, "You are laboring to develop a defensive system that will change history. Once you've completed your work, the world will never be the same."[46]

In the final analysis, SDI accomplished little for American foreign policy, and did more harm than good toward ending the Cold War. The weapons system reinvigorated Cold War militarism and temporarily derailed a rapprochement between the superpowers that could have begun earlier in the decade. SDI was created within the context of U.S. foreign policy, but it functioned to serve the domestic ends of an austerity agenda. SDI was an expansive jobs program: a public works agency more than a deterrent to nuclear war. SDI employed the highly educated and affluent to build a missile defense system that had no feasible application to the current foreign policy environment. Moreover, it reinforced class and regional tensions, steering federal benefits to an overwhelmingly white set of middle- and upper-class elites. Forty years earlier, Truman sought to put unemployed members of the New Deal coalition (union members and the working class) back to work through military Keynesianism. Reagan now sought to do the same for the Cold War coalition, to the benefit of its most privileged members. Containment was discarded in favor of rollback, but Reagan officials were governing within Cold War Democrats' parameters of how to fight the Cold War.

SDI also reflected transformations in the political economy of defense that benefitted affluent whites. Since the 1950s, defense had overwhelmingly enriched middle- and upper-class white Americans, but with the manufacturing base of the defense industry hollowed out, the Reagan administration provided a capstone to a thirty-year process of deindustrialization in defense. Industrial areas in the Northeast were largely left out of SDI contracts as specialized and specific localities in the West and Sunbelt took over. As a result, this new era for defense was felt with a force by members of the Cold War coalition suffering from unemployment. The continued reorientation of the Cold War economy toward post-industrialism, coupled with the decline of the Soviet Union in the 1980s, proved detrimental to many defense workers, and would be fateful in the remaking of the Cold War coalition, and American democracy, in the 1980s.

* * *

While Reagan continued his defense buildup in his second term, he also took steps to renew a détente with the Soviet Union. On December 8, 1987, Reagan met with Mikhail Gorbachev to sign the Intermediate-Range Nuclear Forces Treaty (INF), which eliminated the numbers of intercontinental ballistic missiles that carried nuclear warheads. Few of Reagan's right-wing supporters suspected the president would consider, let alone sign, a nuclear arms treaty with a Soviet head of state before 1987.

The road to the INF treaty started at the Reykjavik summit in 1986. Days before the summit, Republican congressional representatives encouraged Reagan to retain suspicion of the Soviet Union and not fall into a discussion of the Soviets' "arms control agenda" as the only "true cause of East-West tension is not armaments, but the totalitarian philosophy of the Soviet Union." Whereas ten years ago Reagan had made opposition to the Helsinki Accords part of his campaign message, now the president praised them, and his supporters told him to point out to Gorbachev that the Soviet Union "continues to violate the modest human rights guarantees embodied in Helsinki."[47] Reagan did bring up human rights issues at Reykjavik, but it had little effect on the outcome of the talks. The Reykjavik summit failed to produce a new shift in Soviet-U.S. relations, but the meeting allowed Gorbachev and Reagan to develop a bourgeoning friendship and recognition of each other's desire to reduce nuclear weapons, particularly after the Able Archer disaster. When it was announced that Gorbachev would visit Washington, D.C., to sign the INF treaty, the Right was in stunned disbelief, thinking the president had committed treason to their cause. After Reagan signed the INF treaty, columnist George Will wrote that the president revealed his true colors as a follower of détente. Will was puzzled by Reagan's foreign policy since it "produced much surprise but little delight" among the Right. As Reagan's presidency neared its end, the time was right "for conservatives to look back with bewilderment and ahead with trepidation," said Will.[48]

As Will's comments reveal, despite close association with Reagan, the Right was never consistently satisfied with the president's foreign policy, even before his personal diplomacy with Gorbachev. Disagreement first surfaced on a large scale in 1982, after the release of the Reagan budget and the president's request for tax increases to make up for revenue lost in the 1981 tax cut. After the first hundred days, conservatives mourned the Reagan of the campaign trail. They were satisfied with his rhetoric but upset with his policies. Reagan campaigned on an austerity platform, but he was forced to compromise with Congress on federal spending. The Heritage Foundation complained that in 1982 "Big Government continue[d] to grow." Budget cuts were not enough to shrink government; "the big games in town—the Department of Energy and the Department of Education—still are operating full tilt, and success in other areas is primarily limited to cutting back on the size of budget increases."[49] Direct-mail strategist Richard Viguerie warned members of the administration that if the Right did not get its way, "Our efforts on these cuts will make our Panama Canal treaty fight look small by comparison."[50]

That same year, members of right-wing organizations—including the American Conservative Union, the Conservative Caucus, and National Defense Council—complained that Reagan had not done enough to provide aid and diplomatic recognition to America's allies, breaking his campaign promises for a more anticommunist foreign policy.[51] The Conservative Caucus, the Eagle Forum, the Moral Majority, and the High Frontier urged Reagan to send needed arms so that Taiwan could prevent capitulation to China.[52] As activist conservatives found the president modulating his foreign policy to political pressures, his luster wore. Richard D. Sellers from Montgomery, Alabama, a member of the Council on National Policy who contemplated running for Senate in 1984, told *National Review* publisher William Rusher that "conservatives must start working even harder on these very important national survival issues, since we are losing: the nuclear freeze passed the House, the President's proposed defense budget increase has been cut in half, and two House committees have voted to cut off covert aid intended to stop Communist expansion in Central America." Sellers formed the National Security Association in Montgomery with the hope of raising $250,000 to make sure that no further steps were taken to counter conservatives' foreign policy. Sellers wanted to enlist Rusher's "financial help to reverse the national security defeats we are now suffering."[53]

Cold Warriors had reservations about Reagan's foreign policy throughout his two terms. Democratic and Republican hawks particularly questioned Reagan's fortitude in dealing with the nuclear freeze and his commitment to overtaking the Soviet Union in military might, even before his second term. A March 1982 pamphlet published by the CPD asked, "Is the Reagan Defense Program Adequate?" It was not. "The administration's defense program is a minimal one. It will not halt the unfavorable trends in the U.S.-Soviet military balance, let alone reverse them."[54] The organization's members fought over its analysis of the Soviet threat, as disagreements mounted between those members in the administration and those outside of it. Responding to a June 20, 1984, pamphlet critical of Reagan's defense modernization, Richard Perle told Charls Walker of the CPD that "the draft gives the Administration too little credit for some of the strategic force improvements we have inaugurated, even granting the fact that some of those forces will not enter the inventory for another few years."[55] The CPD also suffered from self-inflicted wounds in the mid-1980s, as disagreements between the left and right wings of the organization made it difficult for the movement to press forward on defense. According to historian Justin Vaïsse, the main controversy was over "guns and butter" with the "Democrats and trade unionists among them" unwilling "to reduce other public spending (which Reagan had already cut drastically)."[56] The American Security Council (ASC) jumped at the chance "to capitalize on the strong defense and foreign affairs mandate of this administration," encouraging Reagan to update America's defense capabilities by building new technological defense projects instead of competing with the Soviet Union through outdated military equipment. Members of the ASC, Veterans of Foreign Wars, College Republicans, and the Reserve Officers Association also recommended the president meet with foreign anticommunist leaders too, such as the Angola UNITA leader Jonas Savimbi. Savimbi was treated to lunch by the ASC in December 1981 and was a guest of honor at a Heritage Foundation reception. The events were meant to illustrate the lengths Reagan would go to "resisting the expansion of Soviet influence" during his presidency.[57]

Cold Warriors' fears aside, diplomatic negotiations between Reagan and Gorbachev did not translate to a complete "reversal" of Reagan's approach to American foreign policy. Reagan did not think the INF treaty and the subsequent reduction of nuclear weapons were opportunities to reduce the defense budget. On the contrary, Reagan still wanted increases in the size of the defense budget to be paid for by cutting social programs—and he did not reject Cold War anticommunism and peace through strength as his critics claimed. In budget negotiations on November 30, 1987, one week before the signing of the INF treaty, Reagan said that "our team [went] back to the bargaining table twice for better deals, one time to get a billion dollars more from entitlement spending, another to get revenue increases down to the kind I called for in the budget" that he had outlined earlier in the year. The federal deficit, Reagan insisted, was not due to the decline in revenue taken in by federal coffers, as the "cuts in tax rates aren't part of the deficit problem. They're part of the solution. Our tax rate cuts haven't lowered revenues one bit; in fact, just as we predicted, cutting tax rates produced a healthy, expanding, vibrant economy that enlarged tax revenues." The new budget projections left even more for defense "with about $3.5 billion more in defense outlays than last year," as Reagan touted the new defense programs that would lead to advances in military weaponry. Just because there was talk of arms agreements between the United States and Soviet Union, it was no time to be cutting defense programs that "have given us bargaining leverage." And on top of that, "with negotiated missile reductions coming, we will need even more urgently a strong conventional force to deter the Soviet Union's massive conventional force."[58] Reagan (and a Democratic-controlled Congress) approved a defense budget of $304 billion for the fiscal year 1989, a more than $50 billion increase over the past four years.[59]

Reagan's defense and foreign policies invigorated the military-industrial complex and Cold War internationalism after his reelection in 1984—and after the Cold War ended. With the fall of the Berlin Wall in 1989, defense contractors and workers and residents in Cold War defense communities were thrown into a state of panic, concerned for their economic future. Leslie Gelb of the *New York Times* wrote that "with the demise of the Soviet Union, a battle is shaping up for the soul of the nation, and the defense budget now more than ever will be at the center."[60] And as the Cold War coalition decried further cuts to the defense budget, it soon became apparent that Reagan's defense buildup—like the military buildup for Korea and Vietnam before it—renewed Americans' faith in military Keynesianism and liberal internationalism to solve their problems; and once again, the Cold War coalition traded opulence for misfortune in a matter of months.

Given their economic concerns, advocates for the defense industry worked overtime on Capitol Hill to protect Cold War defense programs from the chopping block. A coalition of Democrats, Republicans, labor unions, and business interests colluded to stop defense cuts, aiming to preserve the military-industrial complex for their economic and political gain. This coalition revealed its power in Congress, as Republicans joined forces with Democrats to preserve military contracts in an era of drastic cuts. For instance, right-leaning Republican Curt Weldon from Pennsylvania defended the V-22 Osprey helicopter program that employed six hundred workers at a Boeing plant under his jurisdiction. Weldon, along with his then-Democratic colleague in the Senate Arlen Specter worried there was "a predisposition against the V-22 and a rather conclusive one on the part of the Department of Defense."[61] To Weldon, the Osprey was "not a pork program. I believe in the technology." In defending the Osprey, Weldon found company with the United Auto Workers who feared that its eight thousand members would be out of work if the Osprey were defunded. When the union's close association with Boeing and other contractors for the Osprey was pointed out to the United Auto Workers Dirk Warden, he admitted that the two groups made strange bedfellows. Warden said he did not "want to leave the impression that we're in lockstep with [Boeing management]. But they can talk to some people we can't talk to and vice versa."[62]

While Weldon and Specter saved the Osprey from cuts, other members of the Cold War coalition were not as lucky. Indeed, the decline in military spending after the Cold War revealed how Reagan's defense policies proved inadequate in boosting the fortunes of the entire Cold War coalition. Economic areas in the Northeast and Midwest were hit hardest by the fall of the Soviet Union. Job losses in defense at the end of Reagan's presidency culminated a process of layoffs in the Northeast and Midwest that began in the 1970s. In southern Connecticut, workers prepared for job losses after 1989. President of UNC Naval Products (based in Montville, Connecticut), Bruce Andrews, told the House Committee on Economic Stabilization that federal help must be provided for his employees who were "veterans of the cold war."[63] Republican representative (and later governor) of Connecticut, John G. Rowland, worked with UNC employees to get them another contract after they lost one building a Navy reactor to Babcock & Wilcox, based in Lynchburg, Virginia. Rowland appeared to be weary of the impact global peace had on workers in his state as unemployment was "the other side of the peace dividend." Workers at UNC organized the S.O.S. (Save Our State) Committee that coordinated with "federal officials to help find Government contracts to replace the defense work at UNC and other Connecticut companies."[64]

Defense workers throughout the country, not just in Connecticut, were also affected by the "peace dividend." The end of the Cold War ultimately gave defense companies based in the Midwest the opportunity to lay off employees. Hundreds of employees were laid off at McDonnell Douglas's headquarters in St. Louis, as the company reduced its nationwide ranks by nine thousand employees. And while the St. Louis economy seemed to rebound quickly—due to the city's ability to entice medical research and technology companies—some workers were "at the end of their employment benefits and they're beginning to grasp at things." As St. Louis rapidly worked to make up for the losses in defense, workers were resentful about the lack of government help. Former employees of McDonnell Douglas in St. Louis drew comparisons between unemployed autoworkers with strong unions and themselves, who saw their benefits packages run out after six months. McDonnell Douglas employee Frank Hutson was angry that the government did nothing for defense workers. "If you have car makers that give their employees one, two, three years at 85 percent of their salaries, then I feel that McDonnell Douglas should have done the same thing." But if the company couldn't provide comparable packages alone, "then the Government should have stepped in and helped."[65] The governor of Ohio too lamented "the dark side of the peace dividend" as détente meant layoff notices for thousands of Ohioans. Like their colleagues in St. Louis, defense workers in Ohio were worried about how a transition to a peacetime economy would occur without disrupting their livelihoods. Some defense workers were also skeptical of federal programs that employed them on non-defense projects to build mass transit systems. While "beating swords into plowshares" after the Berlin Wall was "a nice theory" it was "not so easily translated into reality."[66]

While the Sunbelt also suffered from the "peace dividend," the downturn was incomparable to what defense industries in the Northeast and Midwest experienced. Thousands of layoffs occurred among military contractors in the Sunbelt, but no major companies went out of business. And while Lockheed Aircraft laid off seven thousand employees in southern California, Northeastern defense contractors went under—and saw massive job losses. For instance, defense companies like Fairchild Industries in Nassau County, Long Island, went bankrupt. By the end of the 1980s, Fairchild's financial portfolio was so poor that when the company did not win a contract for the T-46A jet, executives made the decision to lay off 2,500 employees. The competition for the T-46A contract went to Cessna Manufacturing Company in Wichita, Kansas (because of the lobbying efforts of Republican senator Bob Dole), and took the fate of Fairchild with it. By the end of the year, Fairchild closed its doors. Once again, the failure to diversify left the company dependent upon the Cold War. Without it, the company could not thrive. The loss of Fairchild was a loss for all of Nassau County. It meant declining profits for the various subcontractors to Fairchild, the suppliers of Fairchild's equipment, and even the closing of restaurants who supplied the workers with their lunches and coffees.[67]

Democrat Thomas Downey, who represented Suffolk County in the House of Representatives since 1975, felt compelled to save Fairchild. Elected among the class of Watergate babies in 1974, Downey was a leading voice against SDI and Reagan's foreign policy in Central America in the House of Representatives (as well as a supporter of arms control and the nuclear freeze movement). While opposed to the Reagan defense buildup, Downey nevertheless felt bound to the Cold War interests in his district and rushed to protect Fairchild and the jobs the company provided. Downey pronounced Fairchild's collapse "a human tragedy of the first order." Downey went on to say that Long Island was not just losing "manufacturing jobs—jewels in any economy—but we also stand to lose the jobs of all the contractors, vendors, and others who have depended on the factory." The answer for Downey, was therefore, more defense spending. Again, Downey, like his Democratic colleagues who represented Cold War communities, felt that defense funds needed to ensure the survival of his district, even while arguing that the foreign policy that created them was wrong.[68]

Fairchild was not the only defense contractor in Nassau County that endured cutbacks. During the early years of the Cold War, Grumman (a defense contractor on Long Island since 1936) employed 36,000 employees; by 1991, it had only 13,000. Shortly before merging with Northrop, Grumman executives touted their diversification efforts, saying that the company's losses were "not a result of what has happened with perestroika" and predicted no need for mass layoffs down the road. They were wrong. One year after their prediction, Grumman laid off 1,400 workers on Long Island and 1,900 throughout its workforce. The defense economy on Long Island, once employing more than 50 percent of the area's work force, by 1988 was responsible for only 25 percent of the jobs in the region. This number would only drop further by the end of the twentieth century.[69]

Suburban Long Island's crippling reliance on the Cold War economy led its residents to search for solutions to the downsizing of defense, with few answers. Economists thought a variety of other high-tech areas such as biotechnology would replace the defense economy in places like Long Island. But the introduction of the high-tech industry merely widened the income gap in the region. High-tech supplanted the Cold War defense economy, as did the low-wage service industry. The lack of high-paying, stable jobs in areas such as Long Island made tax rates, public school spending, and other areas of local government a growing concern to its residents. A drop in defense, combined with the downturn in the stock market after it crashed in 1988 following the savings and loan scandals, made Long Island residents search to make up for lost revenue. The inability to find "affordable housing" and cutting "the cost of public education" were now high on the list of concerns among business leaders and residents of the area.[70]

While the defense cuts led to unemployment across class lines, defense workers of color were hurt the most by the downturn in defense production. Since World War II, defense jobs had served as tickets to the middle class for African Americans. While Long Island defense contractors were notorious for discriminating against African Americans in their hiring practices, the jobs that were available to blacks (mostly in manufacturing) paid more than the national hourly average. Blacks also utilized employment in the defense industry to access social mobility, and by 1992, 20.6 percent of the men and women employed by defense industries were black. But cuts of over 160,000 people in the military workforce, and the elimination of government contracts in the 1960s, reduced the numbers of blacks employed by the defense industry. As defense contractors sent manufacturing jobs to Mid-Atlantic states like Pennsylvania, or to the South chasing cheaper labor and overhead costs, black communities saw more layoffs and increased segregation within suburban white communities in places like Long Island.[71]

As white Long Islanders decried the Berlin Wall's collapse and the diminution of the defense industry, black civil rights leaders on the island responded with mixed reactions. Black businessman and local entrepreneur Bruce Llewellyn ruffled feathers when he accused the Cold War economy of enfranchising whites over blacks. In criticizing America's inattention to "schools, health care and physical plants" to serve a larger defense budget, Llewellyn said, "Defense spending is the white people's welfare program." The military allowed whites on the island to accept the federal government without claiming dependency on a welfare state. "It's nice to be able to say that instead of going to the welfare office to get my check, I go to Grumman to get my check."[72] Llewellyn had sufficient evidence to make his point. Again, while the defense industry offered blacks access to good-paying jobs, blacks made up only a fraction of the defense workforce since World War II. For twenty-five years after 1941, the defense industry employed one out of every ten workers on Long Island, yet blacks made up less than 4 percent of the workforce for the first eighteen of those years. Out of fifty thousand workers, black employees numbered at approximately 1,900 up until 1960. Of those blacks that found work in the defense industry, many commuted to work as they were unable to find housing accessible to them, having been redlined for decades.[73] Housing segregation was rampant on Long Island and barred blacks from the suburbs, compounding troubles for blacks seeking employment at any one of the defense contractors in the area.

Llewellyn implicitly invoked this history while questioning the international and strategic need for massive warfare state, one that increased class and racial disparities in the United States. But white Grumman workers had none of it. Llewellyn's comments provoked an angry response from Grumman employee A. Roger Yackel from Huntington who said that "Grumman has a fully integrated work force." The diversity and democracy in the workforce made sure that "Grumman is nonunion" since its workers "are rated on a merit system, not on longevity." Yackel finished his comments by rhetorically questioning whether Llewellyn "has seen a welfare program that produced a lunar module, a first line of defense aircraft or postal trucks."[74] For Yackel, Grumman sustained economic growth on Long Island and throughout the country—while preserving national security.

But while Grumman employees like Yackel were quick to defend Grumman, they were critical of government involvement in their lives. The lack of high-paying, stable jobs in areas such as Long Island made tax rates, public school spending, and other areas of local government a growing concern to its residents. Suburban Long Island's crippling reliance on the Cold War economy led its residents to search for solutions to the downsizing of defense, with few answers. Frustrated and angry, Long Islanders felt government had burdened them with high taxes and the increased costs of living after the defense industry downsized. While dependent on the federal government for employment, they also felt abandoned by it.

The antigovernment discontent inspired a tax revolt on Long Island by the late 1980s. The Long Island tax revolt manifested itself in a variety of curious ways, many of which were similar to tax revolts across the country, including ones in states like California. By the late 1980s and early 1990s, county politicians—both Democrats and Republicans— riffed off of President George H. W. Bush's 1988 pledge to "read my lips" and not raise taxes. Local primary elections grew heated as the fate of school budgets lay in the balance; bills were introduced to enact property tax caps. The tax revolt also spread antigovernment messages that belied the reality behind the antigovernment rhetoric. President of the Long Island Association, James L. Larocca, argued that one out of every ten residents of Long Island worked for the government and it is now "the biggest employer." Larocca said the time of Long Island governments "operating like big urban machines rather than as conservative suburban bodies" is over.[76]

Thomas Downey's defeat in 1992 at the hands of Republican Rick Lazio revealed Long Islanders' unhappiness with the fate of the defense economy following the Cold War. Downey lost in a close election where only six percentage points separated the candidates. Unemployment in Suffolk County was one of the major issues in the campaign, as well as Downey's liberalism, characterized by what Lazio said was Downey's tax and spend policies and his detachment from local issues. Despite defending his record of supporting the defense economy on Long Island, which included obtaining federal funds for the F-14 bomber built by Grumman, Downey had difficulty escaping blame for the region's downturn. Downey also promoted his work to achieve defense conversion on the island, but voters saw his willingness to "spend money to diversify our defense industry" as a liability more than a service.[77]

With Republicans like Lazio now in charge, the prime solution to financial problems in former defense communities was reducing the government's burden on their regions while building up the military. Poor economic conditions made (now former) Cold War communities like Nassau and Suffolk Counties favor proposals for reducing taxes and eliminating the size of government. Indeed, the cuts in the defense brought local Long Island politicians like Republican county executive Thomas Gulotta of Nassau County to plea with state officials to alleviate the county's spending obligations, asking New York Governor Mario Cuomo to not "shift more of the burden onto the shoulders of local government, our taxpayers, and our home owners." State and federal officials had seemingly abandoned employees of the defense industry—and Long Island businesses that depended on the industry—after the Cold War, leaving its residents at the mercy of the unemployment line without substantial government assistance.[78]

Cutbacks in defense once again made defense workers and their political representatives into citizen lobbyists for the military-industrial complex, as the new era of international relations after 1989 created a crisis in the economic and political fortunes of many Americans. The local constituents of the Cold War aligned with national forces to keep the military-industrial complex afloat, as both "wings" of the Cold War coalition argued that the federal government had a commitment to the financial well-being of Americans and the national security of the United States. Having made them dependent upon the military-industrial complex, the federal government could not discard them and their communities when the international environment of the Cold War did not align with the interests of Cold War workers.

Grassroots activists on the Left hoped to channel this discontent into support for economic conversion. After the nuclear freeze campaign was defeated (or, arguably, abandoned) in the Senate, activists regrouped and refocused on the impact of the military-industrial complex in their local communities. Instead of protesting in the streets of New York City or Washington, D.C., the nuclear freeze movement aimed to sever the cord between defense monies and local communities, believing conversion was the way to disarmament and that congressional representatives should not be "held hostage to continue the arms race as a condition of supplying jobs and money to their constituencies."[79] Nuclear freeze activists and antimilitarist liberals worked together to create conversion programs to reemploy workers in the name of peace, but with little success. Kevin Bean, chairman of the Economic Conversion Task Force of the Connecticut Campaign for a U.S.-USSR Nuclear Arms Freeze, rightly stated that once skilled defense workers were laid off, their high-skilled jobs were replaced by low-wage service sector jobs. "Low-paying service jobs are the only alternatives for many laid-off defense workers whose skills are mismatched with the limited number of civilian jobs that would pay comparable to their previous jobs in defense facilities," said Bean. Jobs in defense were inherently unstable, and companies needed to stop going from contract to contract to survive, he suggested. The "permanent war economy" he said, cost the nation increases in productivity, interfered in the market economy, and was inefficient in creating jobs compared with the private sector. Globalization and outsourcing contributed to the problem too as defense dollars that went to Connecticut "go right back out to out-of-state-subsidiaries, vendors in the Sun Belt or the third world and coproduction setups overseas in order to cash in on cheaper labor, tax breaks, and to widen Congressional influence."[80]

But the Reagan administration resisted conversion to civilian work. With the Cold War coalition again confronted with the question of what the federal government's responsibility was in helping Americans put out of work by defense cuts, the overwhelming response by the Reagan administration was to do nothing, that the defense buildup would solve all problems. The Reagan administration seemed to think conversion was unimportant, as it slashed federal funds to the Economic Development Administration, one of the federal organizations responsible for conversion plans.[81] Under Reagan, moreover, the Office of Economic Adjustment—the main federal agency responsible for aiding defense communities affected by cuts to military programs—was reconfigured to provide assistance to localities that benefited from the Reagan defense buildup rather than those areas reeling from unemployment.[82]

Given this context, the program of defense conversion offered by activists like Bean proved less appealing to the Cold War coalition than military Keynesianism. Lack of enthusiasm for defense conversion derived from a climate of economic austerity in the United States. In criticizing the defense economy's hold over the lives of Connecticut's residents, Bean's logic elevated the primacy of the market over the state. Bean suggested that if the market did not have to compete with the federally subsidized defense sector, there would be more jobs available for Connecticut's residents; the state could not provide effective remedies to economic problems. This was a departure from earlier conversion efforts like George McGovern's National

Economic Conversion Commission, which relied on the state to oversee mandates on conversion. Moreover, conversion implied that there would be a period of transition from defense to civilian work—a period of joblessness. The Republican Right offered a more immediate, and attractive, political plan than conversion: direct job creation through defense, tax cuts to alleviate the cost of living, and an aggressive foreign policy to keep military contractors afloat—an agenda that seemed to be a better solution to chronic unemployment than conversion and one that more members of the Cold War coalition were willing to support. Reagan's defense policies therefore essentially left defense communities like Long Island and Connecticut more inclined to favor right-leaning Democrats and Republicans who critiqued government inefficiency while promoting more government spending on defense.

Once again, as it did in the 1960s and 1970s, the absence of defense conversion spelled collective disaster for working-class defense workers and defense workers of color. In 1986, Grumman was awarded $1.1 billion to make nearly one hundred thousand vans for the United States Postal Service, its largest contract ever. Many on Long Island boasted that it would bring jobs to the region and would contribute to growth to "industries flourishing on the Island . . . including electronics, defense, aerospace, financial services, real estate, manufacturing and tourism." But the vans were scheduled to be produced at a Grumman plant in Pennsylvania, hastening the downturn in production. This meant that working-class blacks were being "left out" of any potential boon, while wealthier blacks were flocking to the island if they had the skills and advantages to obtain available jobs. The *New York Times* reported that African Americans were "actually moving to the suburbs at a faster rate than whites," while noting that "those blacks do tend to be fairly well off." But those poor or out-of-work African Americans that "are already living in the suburbs," they were more likely "to be suffering."[83]

As blue-collar labor and defense workers of color suffered the most from a shrinking defense budget, Republican elites also used the Cold War's end as an opportunity to renew attacks on the federal state—on "big government." As members of Congress, defense executives, and Cold War workers demanded federal bailouts for the defense industry, activist conservatives saw opportunities for remaking tax and social welfare policy. The Heritage Foundation, for instance, argued in 1990 that it was time for the government to reroute taxpayer dollars that would have been used on defense to fund school vouchers or marriage tax credits. The end of the Cold War was another means to restore the market as a solution to what ails the country, for "a peace dividend could fund innovative market solutions to pressing social and economic problems." After close to fifty years, the Right recognized that "today's Big Government is the result not so much of the New Deal as of the massive power assembled in Washington to wage World War II and the cold war"—which was now able to focus on domestic issues. The Right should welcome the new era in U.S. foreign relations, said Heritage Foundation member Burton Yale Pines, as the "peace dividend" can be important "to conservatives for what it can do for their movement." The end of the Cold War provided a chance for the Right to "demand a dollar-for-dollar domestic cut for every Pentagon dollar cut" by Democrats and liberals.[84]

Pines's comments on the "peace dividend," combined with the fate of working-class defense workers, demonstrated how a political project of positioning warfare against welfare continued apace in the post–Cold War era—an era marked by unprecedented austerity and government retrenchment. Indeed, the Reagan years codified the national security state as an agent of inequality, as increased defense spending and tax cuts for the wealthy meant economic and political gains for those members of the Cold War coalition inclined to favor Republicans, or at the very least, right-wing politics. While Reagan confronted detractors and opponents on the Left (and sometimes the Right), they failed in their attempt to offer a political program that could curtail the financial and political rewards offered by the military-industrial complex. As the context of international affairs favored a return to "peace through strength" to alleviate global problems in the 1980s, antimilitarists waged a good fight, but they could not transform the political economy of American defense spending:

a political economy that had made the Cold War coalition a durable presence in American politics since the 1950s.

The history of Reagan's defense policies and their effects on the Cold War coalition therefore demonstrate that when confronted with the remains of Cold War liberalism and the institutions of the military economy, the Cold War coalition sought to preserve both. As they did in the past, members of the Cold War coalition eschewed antimilitarism in favor of military Keynesianism—or, expected economic growth through increased military spending. Democrats and Republicans in office caved to, accommodated, or welcomed the politics of the Cold War coalition in the 1980s—and by proxy, Reagan's foreign policy of peace through strength that protected the military programs that benefited the coalition. When antimilitarists were therefore presented with the advantageous moment to drastically abate the growth of the Cold War state after 1989, they fell victim to the same pressures they had been faced with for over forty years, leaving the Cold War coalition in a position to continue to influence (and react) to American politics after the Cold War's demise.

The end of the Cold War also renewed the Cold War coalition's disenchantment with the federal government in amorphous terms— and made politicians who expounded an antistatist discourse more appealing to voters in the coalition. Feeling burdened with high taxes and the increased costs of living once the defense industry downsized at the end of the Cold War, defense communities, particularly in the Northeast, believed once again they had been deserted by the federal government. Nassau and Suffolk Counties on Long Island never fully recovered from the peace dividend. The area became a haven for wealthy vacationers and commuters to Manhattan, but the local economy was typical of many postindustrial towns. While the region was touted by the *Wall Street Journal* as an "unlikely jobs engine," after the Great Recession of 2008, the paper acknowledged that half of the over thirty thousand jobs created on Long Island "were in low-wage industries like retail and restaurants" that catered to tourists. The high-paying "manufacturing and defense industry jobs that once defined the island aren't likely to return after being trimmed during the most recent recession." Northrop Grumman's workforce on Long Island went from 22,550 workers in the 1980s to 550 in 2013.[85]

In such a time of austerity, the Cold War coalition thought defense spending remained insufficient, that the government could always do more in the name of national security. Poor economic conditions (unemployment, low wages) made Cold War communities like Nassau and Suffolk Counties favor proposals for reducing taxes and eliminating the size of government on nondefense matters—even though residents of defense communities still requested more government involvement to subsidize their livelihoods. The remaining years of the 1980s offered the Cold War coalition pessimism about the role of the federal government and its ability to come to the aid of Americans in times of economic crisis, a politics that aligned with the GOP's rhetoric against the evils of big government and the need for an aggressive, expansive military posture.[86] This politics served the Right well in terms of attracting members of the Cold War coalition who either benefited from, or were harmed, by Reagan's defense policies.

During the Reagan administration, austerity and militarism ultimately became curious, if not necessarily unusual, bedfellows, working in tandem with each other—but mainly to the interests of elite members of the Cold War coalition. The end of the Cold War made the interaction between these two forces acute. As defense manufacturing declined dramatically, it forced sites of aerospace production like St. Louis, Missouri, and Long Island, New York, to adapt to the new service economy that replaced manufacturing and blue-collar jobs—making such residents campaign more for defense work. While the Cold War economy thrived in states like Colorado, it did so in areas with concentrations in white-collar labor, workers who were predisposed and now more inclined to favor mostly Republican and "new" Democrat proposals to end big government: lowering taxes, cutting social welfare, and limiting government spending on domestic programs. After the 1980s, austerity, militarism, and internationalism coincided in the policies of both Republicans and Democrats—and thrived in the larger political culture of the United States.

CONCLUSION

In his 1995 elegy and ode to Philadelphia mayor Ed Rendell *A Prayer for a City*, author Buzz Bizzinger praised the Democrat for trying to save ten thousand defense jobs at the city's naval shipyard in 1993. While not the home of major defense contractors, Philadelphia was a provider of shipyard work to residents of the city since World War II, and most of the defense jobs in Philadelphia were in manufacturing. As was the case with defense jobs in cities throughout the Rust Belt and Northeast, these jobs had dwindled in numbers since the Korean War. Dedicated to the economic future of the city—and concerned about his reelection—Rendell vowed to save the Philadelphia Naval Shipyard despite efforts by the United States Navy and the Bill Clinton administration to close it. While the shipyard had been threatened with the chopping block since the presidency of Lyndon Johnson, the end of the Cold War convinced the Department of Defense of its obsolescence.

Faced with the prospect of thousands of job losses, Rendell lobbied Clinton to prevent the shipyard's closure. Rendell won what were ultimately temporary gains. In 1993, the federal government ruled that the 8,400 jobs created from the shipyard would not be cut. Unrelenting panic turned to instant jubilation in Philadelphia. In celebrating Rendell's accomplishment, Bizzinger painted the mayor as a savior to the American working class, including workers like Jim Mangan—a longtime welder. With his job at the shipyard, Mangan could provide for his six children on his annual salary of $45,000—not much, but enough to get by in tough economic times for workers in defense manufacturing. Mangan told Bizzinger that politicians had always made lofty promises about keeping the shipyard open, but most of the previous promises went unfulfilled. Until Rendell. While Mangan was just happy to have a job, Rendell saw the victory as a triumph for local interests over federal elites, who had little interest in subsidizing urban areas and the jobs within them. In saving the shipyard, Rendell said, "Fuck the federal government. Fuck those bureaucrats whose contempt for cities could barely be concealed."[1]

But two years later, the Clinton administration reversed its decision, and Rendell and the city of Philadelphia lost their fight. The Philadelphia shipyard closed in 1995, leaving workers reeling and wondering where to go for work. In responding to the news, state representative Bill Keller told Secretary of Labor Robert Reich, "The workers are going to go out, and they'll never reenter the workforce. They'll have side jobs as bartenders and plumbers and carpenters, and they'll send their wives to work. Is that the economy you want?"[2] Keller's problematic notions of the male-breadwinner model aside, his concerns spoke to pervading economic anxieties among workers in the defense industry. One of these workers was Eric Legge. Legge had been employed for a quarter century at the shipyard and was angry that his career was gone overnight. "I think there's a lot of guys who feel betrayed," Legge said. "Guys counted on this place to send their kids to college, to get a retirement," he added.[3] But these concerns were irrelevant to the Department of Defense. In fact, Pentagon officials told workers they should welcome the shipyard's demise, for it represented a victory in the Cold War. Rear Admiral William A. Retz asked Philadelphians—as he presided over the ceremonies closing the shipyard—to "invite you to join me in a celebration . . . A celebration of the cold war, a victory that allowed us to begin to do more with less."[4]

Now in 1995, in terms of the naval shipyard, Rendell seemed resigned to the fate he fought so hard to prevent. For even as Rendell struggled to keep the shipyard open, he also sought to weaken the power of union workers and revitalize the city with a flood of capital from luxury real estate developers to replace the jobs created by the shipyard. Indeed, before leaving the mayor's office to serve as governor of Pennsylvania, Rendell revealed himself to be more of a "New Democrat" than a New Dealer. While fighting for the shipyard to remain open, Rendell imposed a four-year contract on the city's unions that entailed cuts to health care benefits and limited wage increases for public employees. Rendell also aimed to limit the autonomy of the unions to hire and fire workers. Rendell was candid in expressing his goal to achieve a balanced budget and "*to increase our tax base*" for the city.[5] The pensions of public employees and the power of the unions were an obstacle to this goal. After winning the fight with the unions, Rendell turned to private investors to bring new jobs to the city after the shipyard closed. Rendell turned to tourism and entertainment, to "a city workplace increasingly made up of waiters, ushers, tour guides, busboys, bellboys, sales clerks and interactive cyberhelpers." In short, nonunion jobs. As it did on Long Island, tourism spawned jobs "of both low skill and low self-esteem," and left the rebuilding of the shipyard to the retail industry rather than a new industrial workforce.[6]

Rendell's tenure as mayor of Philadelphia therefore reveals more than the economic fate of one city: it offers a microcosm of how the military economy operated in the post–Cold War era. As the new defense economy pushed more working-class and unionized workers out of its ranks, the Cold War coalition increasingly failed to represent their interests. With blue-collar jobs declining in Rust Belt states and states without right-to-work laws since the 1950s, the working class had less of a collective voice to advocate for their personal well-being. When the percentage of unemployed machinists and job setters in defense had decreased six-fold since 1964, while demand for white-collar jobs like computer specialists nearly doubled after the same year, the consequences were felt in the policy proposals made by Democrats and Republicans from the 1970s onward.[7] Moreover, the growing marginalization of working-class defense workers after the Cold War was a product of the overall decline of unions in the United States and the accompanying stagnation in workers' wages.

After 2011, union workers made up 11.9 percent of the total work-force, less than half of what they were at their height of 35 percent in the 1950s.

Moreover, in the post–Cold War period, military Keynesianism had less influence on blue-collar defense workers (even as they clung to those jobs), as the employment it once generated now failed to provide them with widespread employment. For Americans without an education or trained skills, both parties' promotion of the defense economy relegated them to low-wage work without job security and stable benefits—while still holding out the prospect that a few might benefit from the military economy. Changes to the political economy of defense increasingly meant that upwardly mobile, white Americans in the Cold War coalition received the largest gains from the military-industrial complex, even more so than they did in the 1960s and 1970s.

The transformation of the Cold War economy—and American democracy—in such terms was not an accident. Embedded within the origins and purpose of the national security state was the seedbed of large-scale economic inequality that came to characterize American political culture in the late twentieth and early twenty-first century. In shifting defense employment away from manufacturing and toward research and development, the Cold War provided the basis for high-tech development that made the postindustrial economy. Beginning in 1964, Congress was told that the Cold War was a boon to white-collar professionals (many of them white) and advocated policies to promote such jobs. Thus, defense workers of color and "blue-collar workers are fewer; while scientists, engineers, and technicians have gained in numbers in establishments serving defense and space procurement needs." The Cold War economy thus allowed a massive reallocation of wealth in spatial, class, and racial terms.[8]

But the creation of the Cold War defense economy in the 1940s and 1950s did not ipso facto determine the "Age of Inequality." The politics of a permanent war economy—one that formed out of the private-public partnerships fostered by the New Deal—also laid the foundation for austerity politics to take shape during and after the

1970s. As the political economy of the Cold War evolved within a broader context of postindustrialism and demilitarization, political opportunities opened for the conservative Right and neoliberal Left to promote and enact antistatist politics. The political climate had to be right for such changes to occur, and the climate proved increasingly favorable after the 1960s. Indeed, the aftermath of the Vietnam War proved advantageous for the Right—and the moderate Left— allowing them to champion policies that rolled back the New Deal state within the guise of national security. As a postindustrial economy developed alongside an antigovernment political culture, the combination proved vital to ensure continued political support for the military-industrial complex—and American militarism.

How Americans experienced, benefited from, and confronted the Cold War economy was therefore a political problem, one that saw austerity and militarism as answers to economic setbacks faced by Americans. This became evident in how the defense industry remained a source of good-paying jobs after the Cold War (despite the decline of jobs overall), an industry where Republican and Democratic politicians alike sought to score political points by attracting defense companies into their states and districts through government-backed loans, low taxes, and right-to-work laws. In 2011, for instance, Boeing moved some of its production facilities from Seattle to South Carolina (a right-to-work state), enticed by Governor Mark Sanford's promise of $170 million in state-backed loans for the company, along with South Carolina's history of antiunionism. But in 2015, Boeing encountered efforts by the International Association of Machinists (IAM) to unionize the workers. Sanford's replacement, South Carolina governor Nicki Haley, a staunch antiunion conservative, was openly hostile to the IAM and even participated in radio advertisements discouraging workers from joining the union, claiming it would "steal the success of the workers." In the end, Haley did Boeing's bidding, as the IAM canceled the proposed vote in 2015. In the words of historian Nelson Lichtenstein, the IAM's decision proved, "You don't need the National Guard anymore to beat up picketers.

You can use the power of the purse to persuade workers that it's not in their best interest to vote union."[9]

The anti–Cold War Left tried to stop the Cold War coalition from relying on the defense economy for jobs, but a long-term redress to military Keynesianism was especially difficult after the 1940s. While the anti–Cold War Left waged several attempts to downsize the Cold War economy after 1945, to enact programs of defense conversion, it could not retain a sizeable coalition behind their agenda. This was because the Democrats' economic and political commitments to the warfare state, alongside the anticommunist fervor of the early postwar period, purged leftist critics of American foreign policy from the party system. Without an active anticapitalist, anti–Cold War Left—one that rejected the warfare state—in elected positions of power, the militarization of the economy faced few democratic obstacles, or political checks on its influence.

Indeed, postwar liberals proved unable and unwilling to reject the Cold War economy to any significant degree. Quite the contrary. Cold War liberals argued that the economy and defense structure were capable of handling economic militarization without lasting consequences to American democracy. When Cold War Democrats formulated a grand strategy to confront communism through military and economic containment, few imagined the national security state becoming a problem for American liberalism. Cold War Democrats envisioned no distinct boundaries to the warfare state—increased defense spending was only a positive good for the economic health and national security of the United States.

Massive defense spending therefore put Cold War liberals in an increasingly difficult spot after the 1950s. If they sought to repudiate the military-industrial complex, they alienated themselves from their anticommunist policies that legitimated full employment through the warfare state and opened themselves up to Republican attacks that they coddled communists, imperiled national security, and disregarded the plight of the defense worker. However, Democrats increasingly felt propelled to rhetorically distance themselves from the military-industrial complex in the 1960s. Public criticism of the Vietnam War, excessive defense budgets, and wastefulness among the defense industry made Democrats believe that military Keynesianism was inadequate, that the defense budget needed to be trimmed; only then did Democrats turn away from the warfare state in large numbers. But Democrats' rejection of the warfare state often occurred in name only, as Democrats who represented constituents from Cold War communities remained committed to the military-industrial complex as a provider of jobs and regional growth. Moreover, antimilitarist Democrats repudiated military Keynesianism without providing an alternative to it. Various proposals for defense conversion were offered in the 1960s and 1970s, but as austerity ravaged the American economy in the 1970s, militarism supplanted antimilitarism— defense conversion retained less appeal as its proponents left office or failed to gained traction in the political climate. Even when defense conversion became a serious policy proposal once again in the 1980s, it was offered in a market-based form, as mainstream liberals and activists turned to the private sector to create jobs to replace defense work without providing any oversight in the federal state's ability to say what jobs would be created.

Moreover, as corporate mergers, downsizing, and layoffs in manufacturing and production dominated the defense industry in the 1980s, they were met by Democrats with a strange mixture of resistance and apathy. For Democrats within, or who represented members of, the Cold War coalition, the short-term response was to ask for the Pentagon to bail out localities through more defense spending. As wages declined, productivity fell, prices rose, and job security proved elusive, liberal Democrats' efforts to preserve and create defense jobs—to recapture their earlier support for military Keynesianism— was smart politics, but bad for the long-term health of American democracy. Military spending offered a way to lower the unemployment rate, modernize municipal infrastructure, and portray liberals as patriotic, progrowth, and promilitary Americans.[10] Democrats could not completely disavow the Cold War national security state— and the public's support for it altogether—even if they wanted to do so. But as Mayor Rendell's policies demonstrated, Democrats' long-term economic proposals envisioned that the technology, finance, and service sectors would stimulate employment when defense jobs went elsewhere. The result was that educated, well-paid workers had easier times keeping or finding jobs, while blue-collar workers were dispensed to low-wage occupations. The Democratic Party therefore partly deserves blame for the perpetuation of economic inequality in the United States within the past forty years, as it has left working-class defense workers (and the overall working class) in the lurch.[11]

But the responsibility for rampant inequality and unyielding militarism in American politics after the Cold War does not fall solely with Democrats. Never satisfied with "enough" military spending, Republicans used the national security state as a rhetorical weapon against those who aimed to cut the defense budget, even while embracing aspects of the New Deal, military Keynesianism, and Cold War liberalism. As the era of superpower détente fell apart in the mid-1970s, conservatives and Republicans conflated Cold War politics with anti-statism, using national defense to sell (or disguise) austerity politics to the American public. Americans' economic insecurities, the right-wing argued, could be resolved by growing the defense budget while reducing taxes and deregulating the private market. Members of the now post–Cold War coalition were attracted to this message—and sought the attention and help of national figures and political actors to realize this vision for America. Republicans thus found new constituencies among the working class, ethnic groups, and single-issue voters in defense communities by framing Cold War politics and foreign policy within a discussion of Americans' antipathy toward "big government" and military weakness. In turn, Republicans created a "discursive fiction," in the words of historian Matthew Lassiter, that they were the party of smaller government.[12]

But the entire Cold War coalition was predicated on this discursive fiction—on its constituents' beliefs that they were casualties of a faceless, bureaucratic federal government, resigned to dismiss their interests while at the same promoting (and profiting from) policies that expanded the federal government they so claimed to despise.

Whether anticommunist zealots, Cold War intellectuals, right-wing activists, tool-and-dye makers at Lockheed, labor organizers for the AFL-CIO, local councilpersons, military generals, corporate executives at Electric Boat, or aerospace engineers, these constitutive parts of the Cold War coalition collaborated on behalf of each other, often without explicit knowledge of doing so. These various actors moved in and out of the Cold War coalition at different times, mobilizing to protect their personal and political stakes in the Cold War, finding allies wherever they were found, and often falling short of their political goals and expectations—even in victory. In the end, the whole of the Cold War coalition became greater than the sum of its parts, its politics a product of the lowest ideological common denominator: the conviction that the federal government did not do enough on national defense and that the federal state betrayed the concerns of American workers and American citizens. And whether it was the goal of specific individuals within the Cold War coalition or not, this politics legitimized an ideological consensus that the state worked against the interests of the individual; that the national security of the United States remained at risk no matter the size of the defense budget; and that because the government had failed on these fronts, greater power must be given to the private sector for government to divest its control in managing the economy and providing federal benefits to the Cold War coalition—benefits that many of its members needed given the absence of a peacetime welfare state.

Since Americans relied on defense spending for employment and regional development well after the Cold War, it is no surprise that a similar coalition shaped the domestic politics of American foreign policy in the 2000s. The showdown over the budget "sequester" in early 2013 proved this point. The result of failed "supercommittee" negotiations to achieve a compromise in the debt-ceiling crisis in 2011, the "sequester" of $500 billion in defense spending threatened defense jobs from Alaska to New Hampshire. Like many Americans, defense workers were angered by the intransigence of conservative ideologues and placed considerable blame on the Right's failure to prevent possible defense cuts. But the Democrats did not emerge unscathed. In Maine, near the Portsmouth Naval Yard, defense workers did not "care which side caused Washington's latest crisis," they worried how to feed their families. Feeling alienated from government, shipyard worker "Butch" Huntley worried about how he was going to pay the costly medical bills for his ailing wife if he lost his job. "Both sides put us here," complained Huntley, believing that "Congress doesn't look at the individual. They just look at the bottom line." One of his coworkers said he and his family "basically put the American dream on hold" because of the poor economy.[13]

Opposition to the sequester among members of the Cold War coalition forced elected officials to (once more) confront the maxim that all politics are local. When it came to the Pentagon, conservative mantras of the free market and the evils of government intervention went to the wayside when lawmakers were pressured by constituents at home and their allies in Washington, D.C., Representative Scott Rigell (R-Virginia), had an 80 percent lifetime voting record from the American Conservative Union but also had the Newport News Shipyard in his district. When the sequester threatened to lay off a portion of the twenty-one thousand employees at the Newport News (which made aircraft carriers), Rigell broke with the antitax, antistatist wings of his party to try to compromise with Democrats and spare the shipyard from cuts. Any budget without revenue increases was not "a wise position and I don't hold that value," Rigell said.[14]

The scarcity of good jobs, continued inequality within the American political economy, and concerns over the strength of American military power kept the Cold War coalition alive and active. But the existence of the Cold War coalition and the Cold War economy (in its present size) after 1991 was not foreordained. When the Berlin Wall fell and the threat of global war dissipated, the national security state was questioned with fresh insights and faced the possibility of severe cuts by the Clinton administration. Defense spending dropped to 3.5 percent of GDP, its lowest point since World War II. But the emergence of the War on Terror made it once again increasingly difficult to conceive of dismantling the Cold War economy to any significant degree. The terrorist attacks of 9/11, and the wars in Afghanistan and

Iraq, fortuitously justified the domestic commitment to defense but in ways that now shape what historian Andrew Bacevich has called the "new American militarism": an era where the military-industrial complex seems necessary to secure the fate of American democracy.[15]

Such uncritical and reflexive patriotism fueled by America's "forever wars" disguises the otherwise conspicuous fact that the national security state continues to serve as an engine of employment while at the same time contributing to long-term inequality. Indeed, the United States' War on Terror proved that the Cold War provided a precedent for the national security state to stimulate jobs during the presidencies of George W. Bush and Barack Obama, even while wages stagnated and overall inequality worsened. In responding to the 9/11 attacks, Bush outspent Clinton on defense (with an average growth rate of 5.7 percent each year of his presidency) and expanded the network of federal agencies dealing with foreign policy matters such as the Department of Homeland Security, whose responsibilities included securing America's borders and warning Americans of impending terrorist attacks. Under Bush, like presidents before him, defense did not just serve a military or international purpose, but also a social one. In signing the 2002 National Defense Authorization Act, Bush lauded the legislation for establishing a "substantial and well-deserved increase in basic [military] pay" that also provided "improved educational opportunities as an incentive to reenlist, and more resources to improve military housing." Moreover, the legislation enhanced "job training and education opportunities for military spouses and access for home-schooled children of military families to facilities and programs of Department of Defense dependent schools."[16] Earmarking these programs as "defense" gave Bush and Republicans the leeway to continue their deficit spending without attention to the ongoing costs to the federal budget and offered defense spending as a proxy for economic growth—although it did not serve these ends.

Obama did not dramatically alter Bush's defense policy. As a senator and candidate for national office, Obama opposed the Iraq War and argued that the nation should redirect its attention to domestic issues after fighting protracted wars in the Middle East. As president, however, Obama followed the path of his predecessor on American foreign policy. Obama too promoted defense spending to create jobs during his presidency, even though the jobs that he worked to save were predominantly held by white-collar elites at this point. Obama also vigorously defended the national security state, arguing against defense cuts, claiming they would weaken American economic and international security. In a 2013 rally to save Virginia shipyard workers' jobs from budget cuts, Obama said that their "work, along with hundreds of thousands of jobs, are currently in jeopardy because of politics in Washington" and must be preserved.[17]

By expanding the warfare state to provide social benefits and simultaneously further the interests of American foreign policy on the global stage, Bush and Obama depended upon the institutional legacy of the Cold War state to enfranchise an increasingly select group of Americans. As New Deal and Cold War liberals did in building the national security state in the 1940s, Bush and Obama demanded more defense monies and the enhancement of America's military to defeat another abstract yet imminent threat to the United States. The ominous threat of terrorism informed the run-up to the Iraq War. Couched as another battle within the war against Al Qaeda, Bush faced little dissension from antistatist Republicans when he sent the United States into war against Saddam Hussein. Democrats and Republicans in Congress also authorized tax cuts along with military spending increases during the years of the Iraq War, enlarging the federal deficit even further. Once again, austerity and militarism reinforced each other in ways that kept the Cold War coalition alive and well.

Understanding the relationship between the political economy of the Cold War and American political culture after 1945 offers new insight into how massive defense spending has shaped the health of postwar American democracy. To see these effects fully, the Cold War must be viewed within an "intermestic" context. Rather than a global competition between communism and capitalism, or democracy and totalitarianism, it is important to view the global Cold War as an arbiter of social welfare policy and a distributer of economic benefits in forms that realigned American politics after 1945. Once we recognize the Cold War in these terms, we can begin to explain why Americans participate (or choose not to participate) in electoral politics—and why the country still lives with the economic progeny of America's fifty-year crusade against communism. The ultimate legacy of the Cold War therefore lies in its ability to transfigure American politics in ways that created new coalitions of Americans to keep the United States fighting the Cold War after 1991—to align militarism and austerity with the interests of American democracy. But seeing how the United States remains beholden to the Cold War should also give Americans hope, that in recognizing its political and economic legacy, we can move beyond it.

NOTES

Introduction

1. "At Defense Plant, No Peace if Jobs Are Lost," *New York Times*, February 4, 1990; "Dynamics Set to Trim 27,000 Jobs," *New York Times*, May 2, 1991.

2. "Dynamics Set to Trim 27,000 Jobs."

3. Michael Barone, Grant Ujifusa, and Douglas Matthews, *The Almanac of American Politics: 1992* (Washington, D.C: National Journal, 1991), 218.

4. "Political Rarity: 2 Lawmakers Bask in Thanks," *New York Times*, May 9, 1992.

5. "Political Rarity: 2 Lawmakers Bask in Thanks," *New York Times*, May 9, 1992; "House Votes Overwhelmingly to Restore Seawolf Submarine Funds," *New York Times*, May 8, 1992; "In Battle of Budget, Democrats Defend Military Hardware," *New York Times*, May 17, 1992.

6. On Cold War defense spending and American political culture, see Michael Sherry, *In the Shadow of War: The United States since the 1930s* (New Haven, CT: Yale University Press, 1995); Laura McEnaney, *Civil Defense Begins at Home: Militarization Meets Everyday Life in the Fifties* (Princeton, NJ: Princeton University Press, 2000); Alex Roland, *The Military-Industrial Complex* (Washington, DC: American Historical Association, 2001); Aaron Friedberg, *In the Shadow of the Garrison State: American Anti-Statism and Its Cold War Grand Strategy* (Princeton, NJ: Princeton University Press, 2000); Benjamin O. Fordham, *Building the Cold War Consensus: The Political Economy of U.S. National Security Policy, 1949–1951* (Ann Arbor: University of Michigan Press, 1998); Paul C. Koistinen, *State of War: The Political Economy of American Warfare, 1945–2011* (Lawrence: University Press of Kansas, 2012).

7. For the military as provider of welfare and rights-based protections, see James Sparrow, *Warfare State: Americans in the Age of Big-Government* (New

York: Oxford University Press, 2011); Jennifer Mittelstadt, *The Rise of the Military Welfare State* (Cambridge, MA: Harvard University Press, 2015).

8. The social impact of defense spending is explored in Ann Markusen, Peter Hall, Scott Campbell, and Sabina Deitrick, *The Rise of the Gunbelt: The Military Remapping of Industrial America* (New York: Oxford University Press, 1991); Bruce Schulman, *From Cotton Belt to Sunbelt: Federal Policy, Economic Development, and the Transformation of the South, 1938–1980* (Durham, NC: Duke University Press, 1994); Roger W. Lotchin, *Fortress California, 1910–1961: From Warfare to Welfare* (New York: Oxford University Press, 1992); Ann Markusen and Joel Yudken, *Dismantling the Cold War Economy* (New York: Basic Books, 1992); Margaret Pugh O'Mara, *Cities of Knowledge: Cold War Science and the Search for the Next Silicon Valley* (Princeton, NJ: Princeton University Press, 2004); Kari Fredrickson, *Cold War Dixie: Militarization and Modernization in the American South* (Athens: University of Georgia Press, 2014).

9. John Accordino, *Captives of the Cold War Economy: The Struggle for Defense Conversion in American Communities* (Westport, CT: Praeger, 2000). This book also draws connections between international events and local politics, or what some scholars have called the "local Cold War." Scholarship on the local Cold War is limited but growing. See Jeffrey Engel, editor, *Local Consequences of the Global Cold War* (Stanford, CA: Stanford University Press, 2008); Gretchen Heefner, *The Missile Next Door: The Minuteman in the American Heartland* (Cambridge, MA: Harvard University Press, 2012); Kate Brown, *Plutopia: Nuclear Families, Atomic Cities, and the Great Soviet and American Plutonium Disasters* (New York: Oxford University Press, 2013).

10. By looking at the political contradictions within the Cold War coalition, this book demonstrates that not all defense workers were conservatives but rather occupied what historian Matthew D. Lassiter has termed the "volatile center" of American politics. Matthew D. Lassiter, "Suburban Strategies: The Volatile Center in Postwar American Politics," in *The Democratic Experiment: New Directions in American Political History,* ed. Meg Jacobs, William J. Novak, and Julian E. Zelizer (Princeton, NJ: Princeton University Press, 2003), 327–49.

11. On the rise of American conservatism after 1945, see Lisa McGirr, *Suburban Warriors: The Origins of the New American Right* (Princeton, NJ: Princeton University Press, 2000); Joseph Crespino, *In Search of Another Country: Mississippi and the Conservative Counterrevolution* (Princeton, NJ: Princeton University Press, 2009); Kim Phillips-Fein, *Invisible Hands: The Making of the Conservative Movement from the New Deal to Reagan* (New York: W.W. Norton, 2009); Kevin Kruse, *White Flight: Atlanta and the Making of Modern Conservatism* (Princeton, NJ: Princeton University Press, 2005); Joseph E. Lowndes, *From the New Deal to the New Right: Race and the Southern Origins of Modern Conservatism* (New Haven:

Yale University Press, 2008); Rick Perlstein, *Before the Storm: Barry Goldwater and the Unmaking of the American Consensus* (New York: Nation Books, 2009).

12. For these figures, see Markusen and Yudken, *Dismantling the Cold War Economy*, 175. Markusen and Yudken calculate not the total amount of funds rewarded to each region of the country, but the individual contracts per capita. The Sunbelt South remained the largest beneficiary of total defense funds during the Cold War.

13. Ira Katznelson, *Fear Itself: The New Deal and the Origins of Our Time* (New York: Liveright, 2013).

14. On the New Deal order, see Gary Gerstle and Steve Fraser, eds., *The Rise and Fall of the New Deal Order: 1930–1980* (Princeton, NJ: Princeton University Press, 1989). On how the New Deal benefited Americans across class and racial divides—despite the New Deal reinforcing the racial caste system of the Jim Crow South—see Harvard Sitkoff, *A New Deal for Blacks: The Emergence of Civil Rights as a National Issue* (New York: Oxford University Press, 1978); Gavin Wright, *Sharing the Prize: The Economics of the Civil Rights Revolution in the American South* (Cambridge, MA: Harvard University Press, 2013). On the contradictory aspects of the New Deal coalition, see William E. Leuchtenburg, *Franklin D. Roosevelt and the New Deal: 1932–1940* (New York: Harper, 2009).

15. See also Daniel Bessner, *Democracy in Exile: Hans Speier and the Rise of the Defense Intellectual* (Ithaca: Cornell University Press, 2018).

16. For more on this point, see Julian E. Zelizer, "Rethinking the History of American Conservatism," *Reviews in American History* 38, no. 2 (2010): 367–92; Kim Phillips-Fein, "Conservatism: A Round Table," *Journal of American History* 98, no. 3 (2011): 723–43; Lily Geismer, *Don't Blame Us: Suburban Liberals and the Transformation of the Democratic Party* (Princeton, NJ: Princeton University Press, 2015).

17. Alan Brinkley, *The End of Reform: New Deal Liberalism in Recession and War* (New York: Alfred K. Knopf, 1995); Laura McEnaney, *Postwar: Waging Peace in Chicago* (Philadelphia: University of Pennsylvania Press, 2018). For a different view, see Sparrow, *Warfare State*.

18. McGirr, *Suburban Warriors*; Darren Dochuk, *From Bible Belt to Sunbelt: Plain Folk Religion, Grassroots Politics, and the Rise of Evangelical Conservatism* (New York, W.W. Norton, 2010); Michelle Nickerson, *Mothers of Conservatism: Women and the Postwar Right* (Princeton, NJ: Princeton University Press, 2012).

19. Markusen and Yudken, *Dismantling the Cold War Economy*, 168.

20. Josh Sides, *L.A. City Limits: African American Los Angeles from the Great Depression to the Present* (Berkeley, University of California Press, 2003); Timothy G. Keogh, "Suburbs in Black and White: Race, the Decline of Industry, and Suburban Social Policy in Long Island, New York" (PhD diss., City University of New York, 2016). For a counterargument, see Jennifer Delton, *Racial Integration in Corporate America, 1940–1990* (New York: Cambridge University Press, 2009).

Delton argues that defense contractors were ahead of their time in promoting racial integration, but her cases are few, and many efforts by defense contractors to integrate the workplace resulted in racial tokenism.

21. Mark R. Wilson, "The New Deal Order and the Military-Industrial Complex: A Reassessment," unpublished paper (in author's possession); Mark Wilson, "Farewell to Progressivism: The Second World War and the Privatization of the 'Military-Industrial Complex,'" in *Capital Gains: Business and Politics in Twentieth-Century America,* ed. Richard R. John and Kim Phillips-Fein (Philadelphia: University of Pennsylvania Press, 2016), 80–94; Mark Wilson, *Destructive Creation: American Business and the Winning of World War II* (Philadelphia: University of Pennsylvania Press, 2016).

22. On the 1970s and international politics, see Niall Ferguson, Charles S. Maier, Erez Manela, and Daniel J. Sargent, eds., *The Shock of the Global: The 1970s in Perspective* (Cambridge, MA: Harvard University Press, 2010). On the interrelationship between domestic and international affairs during the 1970s, see Campbell Craig and Fredrik Logevall, *America's Cold War: The Politics of Insecurity* (Cambridge, MA: Belknap Press of Harvard University Press, 2009).

23. Michael J. Hogan, *A Cross of Iron: Harry S. Truman and the Origins of the National Security State, 1945–1954* (New York: Cambridge University Press, 1998); Douglas Stuart, *Creating the National Security State: A History of the Law That Transformed America* (Princeton, NJ: Princeton University Press, 2008); Jason Scott Smith, *Building New Deal Liberalism: The Political Economy of Public Works, 1933–1956* (New York: Cambridge University Press, 2009).

24. Kim Phillips-Fein has aptly written that while conservatives experienced a "deeply felt sense of themselves as outsiders on the defensive, they were never the excluded figures they believed themselves to be." Kim Phillips-Fein, "Conservatism: A Round Table," 739. See William Rusher, *The Rise of the Right* (New York: William Morrow, 1984); Richard A. Viguerie, *The New Right: We're Ready to Lead* (Falls Church, VA: Viguerie Company, 1980). Such works that highlight the narrative of exclusion are Donald T. Critchlow, *The Conservative Ascendency: How the G.O.P. Right Made Political History* (Cambridge, MA: Harvard University Press, 2007); Laura Jane Gifford, *The Center Cannot Hold: The 1960 Presidential Election and the Rise of Modern Conservatism* (Dekalb: Northern Illinois University Press, 2009).

25. On the limits of left/right partisan binaries to define American politics, see Brent Cebul, Lily Geismer, and Mason Williams, eds., *Shaped by the State: Toward a New Political History of the Twentieth Century* (Chicago: University of Chicago Press, 2019).

26. See "Antimilitarism Can Be Too Much of a Good Thing," *New York Times,* October 19, 1969.

27. Mittelstadt, *The Rise of the Military Welfare State*. On Americans' attitudes toward welfare see Michael Katz, *The Underserving Poor: From the War on Poverty to the War on Welfare* (New York: Pantheon, 1989); Martin Gilens, *Why Americans Hate Welfare Race, Media, and the Politics of Antipoverty Policy* (Chicago: University of Chicago Press, 2000); Francis Fox Piven and Richard Cloward, *Regulating the Poor: The Functions of Public Welfare* (New York: Vintage, 1971).

Chapter One:
Where the Global Meets the Parochial

1. "50-Year-Old Electric Boat Co. Stronger Now than Ever, Hopkins, Its President, Reports," *New York Times*, May 19, 1949; "Electric Boat Company Earns $3,872,293,177% Gain—Sales Up 98% to 82,638,055," *New York Times*, April 1, 1952; "New Supercarrier to Be Built Here," *New York Times*, July 20, 1952.

2. Telegram to Harry Truman from Walter Reuther, October 9, 1951, 1951 Miscellaneous A to Z, OF 264 folder, White House Central Files, Office Files, Harry S. Truman Library, Independence, Missouri (hereafter HTL).

3. Memorandum from John R. Steelman, September 2, 1949, box 30, September 1949 (unemployment) [1 of 2, September 1–12] folder, Papers of John R. Steelman, HTL; Nelson Lichtenstein, *Walter Reuther: The Most Dangerous Man in Detroit* (New York: Basic Books, 1995), 176.

4. Laura McEnaney, *Civil Defense Begins at Home: Militarization Meets Everyday Life in the Fifties* (Princeton, NJ: Princeton University Press, 2000).

5. Mary Dudziak, *War Time: An Idea, Its History, and Its Consequences* (New York: Oxford University Press, 2012), 91; Jennifer Mittelstadt, *The Rise of the Military Welfare State* (Cambridge, MA: Harvard University Press, 2015).

6. Jason Scott Smith, *Building New Deal Liberalism: The Political Economy of Public Works, 1933–1956* (New York: Cambridge University Press, 2009), 206–7.

7. Smith, *Building New Deal Liberalism*, 208.

8. Smith, *Building New Deal Liberalism*, 47.

9. Alan Brinkley, *The End of Reform: New Deal Liberalism in Recession and War* (New York: Vintage, 1996), 240–41.

10. James Sparrow, *Warfare State: World War II Americans and the Age of Big Government* (New York: Oxford University Press, 2011), 249.

11. Robert Collins, *More: The Politics of Economic Growth in Postwar America* (New York: Oxford University Press, 2000); Speech by Harry Truman to Annual Convention of the American Legion, August 27, 1949, box 39, 1949, August 27, Philadelphia, PA, Annual Convention of the American Legion folder, Clark Clifford Papers, HTL.

12. Judith Stein, *Pivotal Decade: How the United States Traded Factories for Finance in the 1970s* (New Haven CT: Yale University Press, 2010), 4; Daniel J. Sargent, "Pax Americana: Sketches for an Undiplomatic History," *Diplomatic History* 42, no. 3 (June 2018): 357–76.

13. Ernest R. May, *Lessons of the Past: The Use and Misuse of History in American Foreign Policy* (New York: Oxford University Press, 1975); Melvyn P. Leffler, *A Preponderance of Power: National Security, The Truman Administration, and the Cold War* (Stanford, CA: Stanford University Press, 1992).

14. Mark Wilson, "The Advantages of Obscurity: World War II Tax Carry-back Provisions and the Normalization of Corporate Welfare," in *What's Good for Business: Business and American Politics since World War II*, ed. Kim Phillips-Fein and Julian E. Zelizer (New York: Oxford University Press, 2012), 16–44; Bruce Schulman, *From Cotton Belt to Sunbelt: Federal Policy, Economic Development, and the Transformation of the South, 1938–1980* (Durham, NC: Duke University Press, 1994), 146; Heefner, *The Missile Next Door*, 65–67.

15. Leffler, *Preponderance of Power*, 229; Ira Katznelson, *Fear Itself: The New Deal and the Origins of Our Time* (New York: Liveright, 2013), 423.

16. The passage of the 1946 Employment Act was largely ineffective in working toward full employment since it prevented the federal government from creating jobs to lower the unemployment rate. Republicans and southern Democrats worked together to take federal enforcement out of the bill. However, the Council of Economic Advisers (which was formed by the act) led by Leon Keyserling, a Keynesian, continued to promote full employment policies into 1949. Jonathan Bell, *The Liberal State on Trial: The Cold War and American Politics in the Truman Years* (New York: Columbia University Press, 2004), 178–79. For the fate of full employment, see Margaret Weir, *Politics and Jobs: The Boundaries of Employment Policy in the United* States (Princeton, NJ: Princeton University Press, 1992).

17. Bell, *The Liberal State on Trial*, 28.

18. "Revolutionary Radicalism," address by John B. Trevor, April 17, 1940, box 1, Communism, info folder, John B. Trevor Jr. Papers (hereafter JBTP), Bentley Historical Library, University of Michigan (hereafter BHL).

19. Ellen Shrecker, *Many Are the Crimes: McCarthyism in America* (New York: Little Brown and Company, 1998).

20. Quoted in David K. Johnson, *The Lavender Scare: The Cold War Persecution of Gays and Lesbians in the Federal Government* (Chicago: University of Chicago Press, 2004), 90.

21. Schrecker, *Many Are the Crimes*, 377.

22. Bell, *Liberal State on Trial*, 25–33, 44.

23. "Senate G.O.P. Seeks Non-Defense Cuts," *New York Times*, May 11, 1961.

24. Letter to Clarence O. Madsen from Hubert Humphrey, mayor's political files, box 25, Democratic-Farmer-Labor correspondence, Hubert H. Humphrey Papers, Minnesota Historical Society, St. Paul, Minnesota; Bell, *The Liberal State on Trial*, chap. 2, esp. 14; Jennifer A. Delton, *Making Minnesota Liberal: Civil Rights and the Transformation of the Democratic Party* (Minneapolis: University of Minnesota Press, 2002), 135–42.

25. Arthur Schlesinger Jr., *The Vital Center: The Politics of Freedom* (Boston: Houghton Mifflin, 1949), 171.

26. For more on this point, see Manfred Berg, "Black Civil Rights and Liberal Anticommunism: The NAACP in the Early Cold War," *Journal of American History* 94, no. 1 (June 2007): 75–96. For a counterpoint, see Schrecker, *Many Are the Crimes*. As Donna Haverty-Stacke points out, New Deal liberals—including President Franklin Roosevelt—targeted socialists, Trotskyists, and communists for subversion under the 1941 Smith Act well before the Cold War. Anticommunism was a feature, not a bug, of the Democratic Party. See Donna Haverty-Stacke, *Trotskyists on Trial: Free Speech and Political Persecution since the Age of FDR* (New York: New York University Press, 2016).

27. See Bell, *Liberal State on Trial*, 273–74.

28. Mary Dudziak, *Cold War Civil Rights: Race and the Image of American Democracy* (Princeton, NJ: Princeton University Press, 2011).

29. President Harry S. Truman's Address before a Joint Session of Congress, March 12, 1947, Yale Avalon Project, http://avalon.law.yale.edu/20th_century/trudoc.asp.

30. "Hoover Supports $5,300,000,000 ERP; Opposition Fading," *New York Times*, March 25, 1948.

31. Vinson quoted in Julian Zelizer, *Arsenal of Democracy: The Politics of National Security—from World War II to the War on Terrorism* (New York: Basic Books, 2010), 69.

32. F. A. Hayek, *The Road to Serfdom* (Chicago: University of Chicago Press, 2007), 80–81.

33. See Jennifer Burns, *Goddess of the Market: Ayn Rand and the American Right* (New York: Oxford University Press, 2009).

34. Katznelson, *Fear Itself*, 423.

35. Hogan, *Cross of Iron*, 100.

36. Speech by Robert A. Taft at Dayton, Ohio, September 13, 1950, box 309, 1950 Campaign Miscellany National Defense Program, 1949 folder, Robert A. Taft papers, Library of Congress, Washington, DC (hereafter LOC). For America's

reliance on air power prior to, during, and following World War II, see Michael Sherry, *The Rise of American Airpower: The Creation of Armageddon* (New Haven, CT: Yale University Press, 1989).

37. On the distinction, see Aaron Friedberg, *In the Shadow of the Garrison State: America's Anti-Statism and Its Cold War Grand Strategy* (Princeton, NJ: Princeton University Press, 2001).

38. Hogan, *Cross of Iron*, 99–100; Phil Williams, "Isolationism or Discerning Internationalism: Robert Taft, Mike Mansfield and US Troops in Europe," *Review of International Studies* 8, no. 1 (January 1982): 27–38.

39. *Congressional Record*, 1948, vol. 94, 4445; 5400; Hogan, *Cross of Iron*, 113.

40. For the various strands of conservative thought toward American foreign policy, see Colin Dueck, *Hard Line: The Republican Party and U.S. Foreign Policy since World War II* (Princeton, NJ: Princeton University Press, 2010).

41. Quoted in John Milton Cooper, *Breaking the Heart of the World: Woodrow Wilson and the Fight for the League of Nations* (New York: Cambridge University Press, 2001), 103.

42. Letter from Ms. Ja Reindel to Clare Hoffman, April 14, 1947, box 10, Hoffman Radio Talks, April 14, 1948 folder, Clare Hoffman papers, BHL; Letter to Clare Hoffman from Mrs. Grant Ballantine, March 9, 1947, box 10, Hoffman Radio Talks, March 11, 1947 (aid to Greece) folder, Clare E. Hoffman papers, BHL.

43. Letter to Clare Hoffman from George Sefcik, January 2, 1951, box 35, Foreign Policy folder, Clare Hoffman Papers, BHL.

44. Letter to Arthur Vandenberg from L. E. Osmer, March 15, 1947, reel 4, Arthur Vandenberg Papers (hereafter AVP), BHL.

45. Letter to Arthur Vandenberg from Ralph M. Shaw, reel 4, AVP, BHL.

46. Arthur Vandenberg, "Internationalism—Good and Bad," April 16, 1925, speech made before the Eighteenth District Conference of "International Rotary" at London, Ontario, reel 6, AVP, BHL.

47. Historian Lawrence S. Kaplan covers Vandenberg's "conversion experience" in *The Conversion of Senator Arthur H. Vandenberg: From Isolation to International Engagement* (Lexington: University of Kentucky Press, 2015), chap. 6.

48. Letter to Ralph M. Shaw from Arthur Vandenberg, March 19, 1947, reel 4, AVP, BHL; Letter to Arthur Vandenberg from Jones Luther Risk, May 4, 1947, reel 4, AVP, BHL; Letter to Malcolm Bingay from Arthur Vandenberg, December 29, 1947, reel 4, AVP BHL.

49. For Rand's isolationism, see Burns, *Goddess of the Market*, 58; "The Plan as Prepared by Postwar Recover Commission (PRC)," page 4, box 16, 1945 Postwar Recovery Commission folder, Gerald L. K. Smith papers, BHL; *Nationalist News*

Service, November 30, 1945, box 16, 1945 Nationalist News Service (newsletters) folder, Gerald L. K. Smith papers (hereafter GLKSP), BHL.

50. *Nationalist News Service*, November 30, 1945, box 16, 1945 Nationalist News Service (newsletters) folder, GLKSP, BHL. For the geographical dimensions of Smith's and AFP's supporters, see the return addresses of checks and money orders sent to the AFP in box 20, America First Party, record of checks and money orders received (1) folder, GLKSP, BHL.

51. "Notes—Re: Dinner," box 1, Allied Patriotic Societies-Lit. folder, JBTP, BHL.

52. Henry A. Wallace, "The Way to Peace," *Vital Speeches of the Day*, October 1, 1946; Henry A. Wallace, "The Path to Peace with Russia," *New Republic* 115 (1946): 401–6.

53. J. Samuel Walker, *Henry A. Wallace and American Foreign Policy* (Westport, CT: Greenwood Press, 1976), chap. 9.

54. Thomas W. Devine, *Henry Wallace's 1948 Presidential Campaign and the Future of American Liberalism* (Chapel Hill: University of North Carolina Press, 2013), 41.

55. Devine, *Henry Wallace's 1948 Presidential Campaign*, 116.

56. "Wisconsin PAC Ousts 7 as Wallace Aides," *New York Times*, August 3, 1948; "48,000 Hear Wallace Assert Prejudice Will Fail in South," *New York Times*, September 11, 1948; "AFL Bars Support of Wallace; Calls Him Front for Communists," *New York Times*, February 3, 1948; "Wallace Assailed by Green, Reuther," *New York Times*, February 28, 1948.

57. Michael Kazin, *American Dreamers: How the Left Changed a Nation* (New York: Penguin, 2011), 203.

58. Wallace quoted in Devine, *Henry Wallace's 1948 Presidential Campaign*, 270.

59. Frank Kofsky, *Harry S. Truman and the War Scare of 1948* (New York: Basic Books, 1993), 89 and 147.

60. See the text of NSC-68 in Ernest R. May, ed., *American Cold War Strategy: Interpreting NSC-68* (Boston: Bedford St. Martin's, 1993), 28. For NSC-68 and growth politics, see Collins, *More*, 24.

61. Tim Barker, "It Doesn't Have to Be a War," *Dissent Magazine*, March 20, 2020, https://www.dissentmagazine.org/online_articles/coronavirus-defense -production-act-industrial policy.

62. Hogan, *Cross of Iron*, 353.

63. *Congressional Record*, 1950, vol. 96, First Congress, Second Session, 1950, 12500. For the roll call votes on the DPA, see *Congressional Record*, 1950, 12910 and 12224–25.

64. "Report of the Chairman National Security Resources Board," NSRB General [2 of 2] folder, White House Press Secretary Files, HTL; Memorandum for Mr. Symington, September 8, 1950, NSRB Memorandum to Stuart Symington, box 127, September 8, 1950 folder, President's Secretary Files, HTL.

65. Edmund F. Wehrle, "'Aid Where It Is Needed Most': American Labor's Military-Industrial Complex," *Enterprise and Society* 12, no. 1 (March 2011): 96–119.

66. Letter to John T. Connor from John Steelman, May 16, 1952, box 40, May 1952 (Office of Defense Mobilization) [2 of 2, May 15–29] folder, Papers of John R. Steelman, HTL.

67. Memo to the Council of Economic Advisors from J. L. Fisher, September 29, 1952, box 6, Leon H. Keyserling Papers, HTL.

68. Brinkley, *The End of Reform.*

69. Letter to Stuart Symington from Leon Keyserling on July 31, 1953, box 20, Leon H. Keyserling papers, HTL.

70. "Republic Engineers Produced Korean 'Workhorse,'" *Long Island Daily Press*, January 17, 1955, 23A; Keogh, "Suburbs in Black and White," 204. Many thanks to Tim Keogh for providing me with the Levittown statistic.

71. See Ann Markusen, Peter Hall, Scott Campbell, and Sabina Deitrick, *The Rise of the Gunbelt: The Military Remapping of Industrial America* (New York: Oxford University Press, 1991), 16–17; Ann Markusen and Joel Yudken, *Dismantling the Cold War Economy* (New York: Basic Books, 1992), 175.

72. Markusen et al., *Rise of the Gunbelt*, 14–16; Ann Markusen and Virginia Carlson, "Deindustrialization in the Midwest: Causes and Responses," in *Deindustrialization and Regional Economic Transformation,* ed. Lloyd Rodwin and Hidehiko Sazanami (Boston: Unwin Hyman, 1989), 29–59.

73. Thomas Sugrue, *The Origins of the Urban Crisis: Race and Inequality in Postwar Detroit* (Princeton, NJ: Princeton University Press, 1995), chap. 5. Letter to Clare Hoffman from John Sonnenberg, December 20, 1954, box 20, Unemployment folder, Clare E. Hoffman papers, BHL; Letter to Clare Hoffman from William Zizzi, May 1956, box 20, Unemployment folder, Clare E. Hoffman papers, BHL.

74. Letter from Edward Wren to President Truman, May 27, 1950, box 1034, OF 24 Miscellaneous (1950) folder, White House Central Files, HTL.

75. Letter to the President from Denver M. Christy, April 3, 1951, White House Official Files, White House Central Files, box 1034, file 264, HTL.

76. Letter from John C. Wolf to Truman, September 14, 1950, White House Official Files, White House Central Files, box 1034, file 264, HTL; Letter from J. Willard Washington to President, undated, White House Official Files, White House Central Files, box 1034, file 264, HTL.

77. Letter to Henry Jackson, June 9, 1951, box 9, folder 37, accession 3560–002, Henry Jackson papers (hereafter HJP), Special Collections, University of Washington, Seattle; Letter from Henry Jackson, June 13, 1951, box 9, folder 37, accession 3560–002, HJP, Special Collections, University of Washington, Seattle.

78. Letter to Henry Jackson, September 27, 1951, accession 3560–002, box 52, folder 2, HJP.

79. Keogh, "Suburbs in Black and White," 210; Thomas Sugrue, *The Origins of the Urban Crisis: Race and Inequality in Postwar Detroit* (Princeton, NJ: Princeton University Press, 1995), 144.

80. Kari Frederickson, *Cold War Dixie: Militarization and Modernization in the American South* (Athens: University of Georgia Press, 2013), 103–4.

81. Keough, "Suburbs in Black and White," 59, 208.

82. Letter from Daniel Flood to Matthew J. Connelly, August 24, 1951, box 1034, OF 264 Miscellaneous (1950) X-Y-Z folder, White House Central Files, HTL.

83. "Isolationist Test Looms in Suffolk," *New York Times*, September 12, 1954; "Plane Contract Clarified by U.S.," *New York Times*, January 17, 1966. See the website for the Office of the Clerk for the House of Representatives to view pdf files of House election results in the midterm elections of the 1950s, http://clerk.house.gov/member_info/electionInfo/index.aspx.

84. Conversations with Chris Foss have helped to flesh this point out better. His project on the Pacific Northwest in the Cold War argues that Jackson's attachment to Boeing—and large defense budgets—was born from reluctant political expedience. See Christopher Foss, "Facing the World: The Politics of National Defense and Trade in Washington and Oregon Since World War II" (PhD diss., University of Colorado, Boulder, 2016).

85. Schulman, *From Cotton Belt to Sunbelt*, 139–46; "House Group Asks Marines Be Tripled to Corps of 325,000," *New York Times*, October 5, 1950; "'Rivers Delivers': The Powerful Armed Services Chairman from Hell Hole Swamp Comes Up with Plums for G.I.'s and the Home Folks," *New York Times*, August 29, 1965.

86. Kari Fredrickson, *The Dixiecrat Revolt and the End of the Solid South, 1932–1968* (Durham: University of North Carolina Press, 2001), 230–31; Fredrickson, *Cold War Dixie.*

87. "Look Who's Talking," OF 267-D file, box 1035, White House Central Files, HTL, "Death of Decency," box 1035, OF 267-D file, White House Central Files, HTL.

88. Andrew Highsmith, *Demolition Means Progress: Flint, Michigan and the Fate of the American Metropolis* (Chicago: University of Chicago Press, 2015), 328; Markusen and Carlson, "Deindustrialization in the Midwest," 29–59.

89. "Defense Cuts Have Slight Economic Impact," *New York Times*, September 8, 1957; "Defense Cutbacks Start Job Debates," *New York Times*, July 10, 1953; "Defense Cutback Hit by Auto Union," *New York Times*, October 13, 1957.

90. Donald T. Critchlow, *Phyllis Schlafly and Grassroots Conservatism: A Woman's Crusade* (Princeton, NJ: Princeton University Press, 2005), 55.

91. Frank Chodorov, "Politics as Usual," *Human Events*, August 16, 1950.

92. "Why I Oppose Truman's Foreign Policy," box 453, 1952 Campaign Foreign Policy folder, Robert A. Taft papers, LOC.

93. Quoted in Bell, *The Liberal State on Trial*, 216.

94. Letter to Donald S. Dawson from Robert L. Holliday, March 13, 1952, box 1742, file 2950, White House Central Files, HTL.

95. On the problem with the term "isolationist," see Brooke Blower, "From Isolationism to Neutrality: A New Framework for Understanding American Political Culture, 1919–1941," *Diplomatic History* 38 (2014): 345–76.

96. Speech by Robert A. Taft at Dayton, Ohio, September 13, 1950, 1950 Campaign Miscellany National Defense Program, box 309, 1949 folder, Robert A. Taft papers, LOC.

97. "Why I Oppose Truman's Foreign Policy."

98. John T. Flynn, *Militarism: The New Slavery for America*, 1955, , box 1, America's Future—John T. Flynn folder, JBTP, BHL.

99. "Sacrificing for Communism," Dan Smoot Report, April 8, 1957, box 8, Foreign Policy folder, JBTP, BHL.

100. Buckley quoted in Zelizer, *Arsenal of Democracy*, 89.

101. Joan Robinson, "The Second Crisis of Economic Theory," *American Economic Review* 62, no. 1/2 (March 1, 1972): 1–10.

102. Robinson, "The Second Crisis of Economic Theory."

Chapter Two:
The National Politics of International Stability

1. "News Conference of Honorable Robert S. McNamara, December 12, 1963," RG18–003, series 1, box 36, folder 01, AFL-CIO Department of Legislation, 1906–1978, George S. Meany Memorial Archives, Silver Spring, Maryland (hereafter GMMA); Thomas J. Knock, "'Come Home America': The Story of George McGovern," in *Vietnam and the American Political Tradition, ed.* Randall B. Woods (New York: Cambridge University Press, 2003), 82–120.

2. For more on the Cold War seminars, see *Lori L. Bogle, The Pentagon's Battle for the American Mind: The Early Cold War* (College Station: Texas A&M University Press, 2004).

3. Campbell Craig, *Destroying the Village: Eisenhower and Thermonuclear War* (New York: Columbia University Press, 1998); Aaron Friedberg, *In the Shadow of the Garrison State: America's Anti-Statism and Its Cold War Grand Strategy* (Princeton, NJ: Princeton University Press, 2001), 138–39; John Lewis Gaddis, *Strategies of Containment: A Critical Appraisal of American National Security Policy during the Cold War* (New York: Oxford University Press, 2005).

4. Dwight D. Eisenhower, "The Chance for Peace," April 16, 1953, https://millercenter.org/the-presidency/presidential-speeches/april-16-1953-chance-peace.

5. Craig, *Destroying the Village*.

6. Bulletin No. 13, July 18, 1956, GO-GR, series XII, box 194 (Vada Horsch Subject Files), National Association of Manufacturers Papers (hereafter NAM papers), Hagley Museum and Library, Wilmington, Delaware (hereafter HML).

7. "L.I. Group Scores U.S. on Layoffs," *New York Times*, October 10, 1957.

8. "Grumman Drops 500 Workers," *Bayport News*, October 3, 1957; "GOP Unite in Fight for Grumman Subcontract Work," *Bethpage Tribune*," August 3, 1972.

9. On the decline of the Rust Belt in the 1950s, see Ann Markusen, Peter Hall, Scott Campbell, and Sabina Deitrick, *The Rise of the Gunbelt: The Military Remapping of Industrial America* (New York: Oxford University Press, 1991), chap. 1.

10. "Upsurge Is Seen in L.I. Economy," *New York Times*, February 2, 1958; Gaddis, *Strategies of Containment*, 145.

11. Gaddis, *Strategies of Containment*, 145.

12. Jonathan Schoenwald, *A Time for Choosing: The Rise of Modern American Conservatism* (New York: Oxford University Press, 2001), 102; Joseph Crespino, "Strom Thurmond's Sunbelt: Rethinking Regional Politics and the Rise of the Right," in *Sunbelt Rising: The Politics of Space, Place, and Region*, ed. Michelle Nickerson and Joseph Crespino (Philadelphia: University of Pennsylvania Press, 2011), 82–102; Memo from James S. Russell, Vice Chief of Naval Operations to All Ships and Stations, November 14, 1958, Group Research Records, Inc., box 381, Military—Anti-Communist Propaganda for Public folder, Columbia University, Rare Book and Manuscript Library, New York (hereafter GRR).

13. Sample Form—Initial Release in National Security Seminar Publicity folder, box 385, National Security Seminar folder GRR; Blank Form: National Security Seminar: Radio and TV Spot Announcements, box 385, National Security Seminar folder, GRR.

14. "Faubus and the Clergy," *Arkansas Gazette*, March 27, 1960, box 385, National Security Seminar folder, GRR; "Preliminaries Set for Armed Forces Conference Here," *Vallejo Times-Herald*, June 30, 1961, box 385, National Security Seminar folder, GRR.

15. "Chamber of Commerce Sets National Security Seminar," *El Paso Times*, July 2, 1961, box 385, National Security Seminar Publicity folder, GRR; "Record—Smashing Seminar Opens," *El Paso Today*, November 1, 1961, box 385, National Security Seminar Publicity folder, GRR; "Successful Seminar Completed," *El Paso Times*, November 11, 1961, box 385, National Security Seminar Publicity folder, GRR.

16. Letter from John McKnight to Marsh Wattson, April 27, 1961, announcement attached to letter, box 381, Military—Anti Communist Propaganda for Public folder, GRR; "What Others Have Said," box 385, National Security Seminar Publicity folder, GRR; "Seminar Praised," *Herald Review*, box 385, National Security Seminar Publicity folder, GRR.

17. Zoom Memorandum January 16, 1961, box 381, Military—Anti-Communist Propaganda for Public folder, GRR; Pacific Missile Range Officer's Wives' Luncheon announcement, box 381, Military—Anti-Communist Propaganda for Public folder, GRR; Open Letter from Ventura County Democratic Control Committee, box 381, Military—Anti-Communist Propaganda for Public folder, GRR.

18. For the Walker case and conservatives' uproar over "military muzzlings," see Crespino, "Strom Thurmond's Sunbelt"; Schoenwald, *A Time for Choosing*, chap. 4; Rick Perlstein, *Before the Storm: Barry Goldwater and the Unmaking of the American Consensus* (New York: Nation Books, 2009), 147–48. The Indiana woman is quoted in Schoenwald, *A Time for Choosing*, 119.

19. Letter from John McKnight to Marsh Wattson, April 27, 1961, box 381, Military—Anti-Communist Propaganda for Public folder, GRR; "Cold War Seminars Aim to Alert Americans to Communist Danger," *Washington Post*, August 6, 1961, box 381, Military—Anti-Communist Propaganda for Public folder, GRR; The Fulbright Memo," August 9, 1961, box 381, Military—Anti-Communist Propaganda for Public folder, GRR.

20. *Congressional Record*—Senate, August 2, 1961, 14433–38. For the impact of Fulbright's memo on the DOD, see Crespino, "Strom Thurmond's Sunbelt," 70.

21. "Letter to the Editor," *Record News*, Gillette, Wyoming, October 25, 1962, box 302, Southern Lunacy folder, GRR; "California Republican, a Member of the Far-Right Group, Cites Removal of General Walker from His Command," *New York Times*, April 20, 1961; Perlstein, *Before the Storm*, 148–49; "Right-Wing Groups Multiplying Appeals in Southern California," *New York Times*, October 29, 1961; Randall B. Woods, *Fulbright: A Biography* (New York: Cambridge University Press, 1995), 286.

22. "Speech by Senator J.W. Fulbright, "Public Policy and Military Responsibility," August 21, 1961, box 385, Military and Politics folder, GRR.

23. "Puzzle of the Military Mind," *New York Times*, November 18, 1962.

24. "Cold War Education Conference Meets in Tampa," box 425, Group Research Report, June 21, 1963, vol. 2, no. 12 folder, GRR.

25. Letter to Frank Barnett from M. G. Bayne, July 3, 1974, Frank Barnett File, Hoover Institution on War, Revolution, and Peace, Stanford University, Stanford, California.

26. Historian Joseph Crespino makes a similar point. In exploring the career of Strom Thurmond, Crespino argues that Thurmond's involvement in the Walker scandal and his support for a more expansive foreign policy allowed the South Carolina senator to transform his reputation from Dixiecrat segregationist to acceptable Sunbelt politician. See Crespino, "Strom Thurmond's Sunbelt."

27. On the popularity of the "missile gap" in Cold War defense communities, see Christopher Preble, *John F. Kennedy and the Missile Gap* (Dekalb: Northern Illinois University Press, 2004). Campbell Craig and Fredrik Logevall, *America's Cold War: The Politics of Insecurity* (Cambridge, MA: Belknap University Press of Harvard, 2009), 192; "Special Message to the Congress on Urgent National Needs," May 25, 1961, *John F. Kennedy Library*, https://www.jfklibrary.org/archives /other-resources/john-f-kennedy-speeches/united-states-congress-special -message-19610525. See also Walter MacDougall, *The Heavens and the Earth: A Political History of the Space Age* (New York: Basic Books, 1985).

28. "SANE, Public Petition, 1961," in *American Foreign Relations Since 1898: A Documentary Reader*, ed. Jeremi Suri (Hoboken, NJ: Wiley Publishing, 2010), 112–13; Lawrence Wittner, *Resisting the Bomb: A History of the World Nuclear Disarmament Movement, 1954–1970* (Stanford, CA: Stanford University Press, 1997); "World Congress for General Disarmament and Peace Appeal by J. D. Bernal, January 29 1962," RG18–003, 1944–1973 series I, box 65, folder 21, Jay Lovestone Files, GMMA.

29. John Lewis Gaddis, *The Long Peace: Inquiries into the History of the Cold War* (New York: Oxford University Press, 1989).

30. Group Research Report December 4, 1962, I-5, box 425, 12-4-62 folder, GRR; Letter to Susan Ballentine from Charles Edison, March 26, 1965, box 84, Committee for the Monroe Doctrine folder (1 of 2), GRR; "Those Missiles Are Still in Cuba," box 506, "Q-Z" folder, GRR. See also the online exhibit on Group Research, Inc., https://exhibitions.library.columbia.edu/exhibits/show /group_research/enemies/institutional.

31. See attached petition to letter from John Franklin Hendon to Homer Thornberry, March 25, 1963, box 84, Committee for the Monroe Doctrine folder (1 of 2), GRR; Letter from Helen Conover to George Cheesley, August 6, 1963, box 9, C folder, Marvin Liebman Papers, Hoover Institution on War, Revolution, and Peace, Stanford University, Stanford, California.

32. "Letter to the Editor," *Record News*, Gillette, Wyoming, October 25, 1962, box 302, Southern Lunacy folder, GRR; "A Critical Analysis and a Constructive Answer," National Association of Americans for Goldwater, box 155, folder 5, William A. Rusher Papers, LOC (hereafter WRP).

33. Minutes of the Meeting of the NAM Government Economy Committee, December 1, 1964. Govt. Economy Committee Minutes, series I, box 24, 1964 folder, NAM Papers, HML.

34. Memorandum of Conversation, August 26, 1962, U.S. Department of State, *Foreign Relations of the United States*, 1961–1963, vol. 11, pp. 857–58; David Coleman, "The Missiles of November, December, January, February . . . : The Problem of Acceptable Risk in the Cuban Missile Crisis Settlement," *Journal of Cold War Studies* 9 (2007): 5–48; Alexandr Fursenko and Timothy Naftali, *"One Hell of a Gamble": Khrushchev, Castro, and Kennedy, 1958–1964* (New York: W.W. Norton, 1997), 327–28.

35. Fursenko and Naftali, *"One Hell of a Gamble,"* 337–38; Francis J. Gavin, "Blasts from the Past: Proliferation Lessons from the 1960s," *International Security* 29, no. 3 (winter 2004–5): 100–35.

36. Friedberg, *In the Shadow of the Garrison State,* 235–36. For McNamara's approach toward nuclear strategy following the Cuban Missile Crisis, see Lawrence Freedman, *The Evolution of Nuclear Strategy,* 3rd ed. (New York: Palgrave MacMillan, 2003), 230–42; McGeorge Bundy, *Danger and Survival: Choices about the Bomb in the First Fifty Years* (New York: Vintage, 1990), 543–48; Shane J. Maddock, *Nuclear Apartheid: The Quest for American Atomic Supremacy from World War II to the Present* (Chapel Hill: University of North Carolina Press, 2010), chap. 8.

37. Wittner, *Resisting the Bomb,* 406.

38. Richard Franklin Bensel, *The Political Economy of American Industrialization, 1877–1900* (New York: Cambridge University Press, 2000), 39–40; Bruce Schulman, *From Cotton Belt to Sunbelt: Federal Policy, Economic Development, and the Transformation of the South, 1938–1980* (Durham, NC: Duke University Press, 1994), 139.

39. See Markusen et al., *The Rise of the Gunbelt,* 3. For more on this point, see Matthew D. Lassiter, "Big Government and Family Values: Political Culture in the Metropolitan Sunbelt," *Sunbelt Rising,* 83–109; Darren Dochuk, *From Bible Belt to Sunbelt: Plain Folk Religion, Grassroots Politics, and the Rise of Evangelical Conservatism* (New York, W.W. Norton, 2010).

40. Barry Goldwater, "The G.O.P. Invades the South," box 155, folder 2, WRP; "Goldwater Declares 1964 Could Well Be GOP Year," box 154, folder 7, WRP. While race was not the only issue that led to the rise of postwar conservatism, it certainly

was a significant factor. See Dan T. Carter, *The Politics of Rage: George Wallace, the Origins of the New Conservatism, and the Transformation of American Politics* (Baton Rouge: Louisiana State University Press, 2000). Schulman, *From Cotton Belt to Sunbelt*, 138.

41. "Address by Senator Strom Thurmond (R-SC) at a Luncheon of the NAM, Plaza Hotel, New York City, 12:30 p.m., November 16, 1967," series IV, box 39, NAM papers; "Disarmament—Wishful Thinking," *Militant Truth*, May 1963, box 220, Militant Truth (Sherman A. Patterson ed.) folder, GRR; "Some Highlights of Presidential Politics: A Summary with Attachments, October 10, 1963," box 154, folder 7, WRP; Strom Thurmond, *The Faith We Have Not Kept* (San Diego: Viewpoint Books, 1968); Donald T. Critchlow, *Phyllis Schlafly and Grassroots Conservatism: A Woman's Crusade* (Princeton, NJ: Princeton University Press, 2005), 166; "Senator Says Soviet Leads in Defense Against Missiles," *New York Times*, March 25, 1963; Joseph Crespino, *Strom Thurmond's America* (New York: Hill and Wang, 2012), 160.

42. Letter to Southern States Industrial Council Members from Thurman Sensing, July 15, 1963, attached speech "Cuba," box 302, Southern States Industrial Council folder, GRR.

43. Luther J. Carter, "A 'Voice' Guides Conservative South," *Norfolk Virginian Pilot*, August 2, 1964, box 302, Southern States Industrial Council folder, GRR; Kim Phillips-Fein, *Invisible Hands: The Making of the Conservative Movement from the New Deal to Reagan* (New York: W.W. Norton, 2009), 12–23.

44. "A Declaration of Policy: Adopted by the Board of Directors of the Southern States Industrial Council," May 21-22-23, 1962," box 302, Notes on Southern States Industrial Council on Tyre Taylor from New York Times references folder, GRR. For more on the SSIC, see Katherine Rye Jewell, *Dollars for Dixie: Business and the Transformation of Conservatism in the Twentieth Century* (New York: Cambridge University Press, 2017).

45. "Ex-Officers Listed in Defense Jobs by House Group," *New York Times*, January 18, 1960; "Senator Fulbright vs. Pentagon 'Educators'" August 12, 1961, *Post Dispatch*, box 381, Military—Anti-Communist Propaganda for Public folder, GRR; Letter from Frank R. Burnett to William F. Buckley, November 16, 1966, box 40, General Correspondence, 1966, William F. Buckley Papers, Yale University, Sterling Memorial Library, New Haven, CT.

46. United States Senate, Committee on Foreign Relations, *Hearings, Nuclear Test Ban Treaty*, Eighty-Eighth Congress, First Session, August 12–27, 1963, p. 749; Sara Diamond, *Roads to Dominion: Right-Wing Movements and Political Power in the United States* (New York: Guilford Press, 1995), 152; Group Research Reports, vol. 2, no. 3, box 425, January 12, 1963 folder, GRR; Robert David Johnson, *Congress*

and the Cold War (New York: Cambridge University Press, 2005), 90–91; Marc Trachtenberg, *A Constructed Peace: The Making of the European Settlement, 1945–1963* (Princeton, NJ: Princeton University Press, 1999), 383–87; Vojtech Mastny, "The 1963 Limited Test Ban Treaty: A Missed Opportunity for Détente?," *Journal of Cold War Studies* 10, no. 1 (winter 2008): 3–25. The results of a Harris Poll conducted in September 1963 showed that 81 percent of those interviewed supported the LTBT. See Bernard J. Firestone, "Kennedy and the Test Ban: Presidential Leadership and Arms Control," in *John F. Kennedy and Europe*, ed. Douglas Brinkley and Richard T. Griffiths (Baton Rouge: Louisiana State University Press, 1999), 91.

47. "Urge Senate Restore Cuts in Arms Fund," *Chicago Tribune*, August 21, 1963; "Sharp Debates Shaping Up on Test Ban," *New York Times*, August 4, 1963; "The TFX Plane, Its Economic Overtones," *Chicago Daily Tribune*, November 25, 1962.

48. Carter, "A 'Voice' Guides Conservative South." Katherine Rye Jewell, *Dollars for Dixie: Business and the Transformation of Conservatism in the Twentieth-Century* (New York: Cambridge University Press, 2017), 279–81.

49. "Goldwater fans get more active," box 425, no. 5, Mar 13 folder, GRR; F. Clifton White and William J. Gill, *Suite 3505: The Story of the Draft Goldwater Movement* (Ashland, OH: Ashbrook Press, 1992), 177; Letter to Ralph J. Bachenheimer from David E. Stalter, November 8, 1962, box 155, folder 5, WRP; Frank Cullen Brophy, "Must Goldwater Be Destroyed," box 155, folder 2, WRP. In 1962, the F. Clifton White Committee was the official face of the Draft Goldwater movement.

50. Perlstein, *Before the Storm*, 126; Lisa McGirr, *Suburban Warriors: The Origins of the New American Right* (Princeton, NJ: Princeton University Press, 2000); Dochuk, *From Bible Belt to Sunbelt*, 237–39.

51. "Goldwater Lays War Aim to Reds," *New York Times*, October 2, 1964.

52. "Box Score for '64: Can Anybody Beat Kennedy," *Time*, October 4, 1963, box 154, folder 7, WRP; "Goldwater's Desperate Battle," *Saturday Evening Post*, October 24, 1964.

53. For the 1964 election results in these counties, see the website, http://uselectionatlas.org/RESULTS/national.php?year=1964. See also *Statistics of the Presidential and Congressional Election, 1964* (Washington, DC: Government Printing Office, 1965), 30.

54. For more on this point, see Elizabeth Tandy Shermer, "Origins of the Conservative Ascendancy: Barry Goldwater's Early Senate Career and De-Legitimization of Organized Labor," *Journal of American History* 95, no. 3 (December 2008): 678–709.

55. "Two Big Unions Aim to Organize Grumman Plant," *Long Island Daily Press*, September 17, 1961; "Union Cites Aims in Campaign to 'Take' Grumman,"

Long Island Daily Press, January 14, 1962; "UAW Comes Out in the Open in Organization of Grumman," *Long Island Daily Press*, January 7, 1962; "Grumman Workers Accepting Layoffs without Worry," *New York Times*, March 8, 1970.

56. "Where the Cutback Cuts Deep," *Saturday Evening Post*, September 12, 1964.

57. Schulman, *From Cotton Belt to Sunbelt*, 139.

58. "Where the Cutback Cuts Deep." In 1962, there were 32,800 total workers employed in the aircraft and parts industry located in Nassau and Suffolk Counties. Republic Aviation alone employed 18,000 workers. I thank Tim Keogh for pointing me toward this statistical information. See William K. Kaiser, Charles E. Stonier, and Raymond V. DiScala, *The Development of the Aerospace Industry on Long Island* (Hempstead, NY: Hofstra University, 1968); "An Open Letter to President Kennedy," *Newsday*, February 8, 1962. On Republic's dependence on the federal government, see Timothy G. Keogh, "Suburbs in Black and White: Race, the Decline of Industry, and Suburban Social Policy in Long Island, New York" (PhD diss., City University of New York, 2016), 216.

59. Thomas J. Knock, *The Rise of a Prairie Statesman: The Life and Times of George McGovern* (Princeton, NJ: Princeton University Press, 2016), 292; United States Senate, Committee on Commerce, *Hearings, National Economic Conversion Commission*, Eighty-Eighth Congress, Second Session, May 25 and June 22, 1964, 1; "Where the Cutback Cuts Deep."

60. Michael Brenes, "Here's What Happened to the Last Green New Deal," *Politico*, December 19, 2018.

61. Stephen R. Patnode, "Labor's Lost Love: The Influence of Gender, Race, and Class on the Workplace in Postwar America" (PhD diss., SUNY Stonybrook, 2008), 49. At Grumman, for instance, only 1.1 percent of the workforce (187 workers) was black in 1962. Out of 187 workers, 157 worked in production or manufacturing. Only two were managers. See Keogh, "Suburbs in Black and White," 225.

62. *McDonnell Douglas Corp. v. Green*, 411 U.S. 792 (1973); "CORE Says It Will Stop Talking, Start Acting in Grumman Case," *Newsday*, November 1, 1965; Keogh, "Suburbs in Black and White," 225–66.

63. "Where the Cutback Cuts Deep"; "F-111B Trouble Cuts Grumman Payroll by 800," *Newsday*, April 18, 1967; "Pike Says Pentagon Cuts Back on Ordering Jets for Vietnam," *Newsday*, October 4, 1967; Keogh, "Suburbs in Black and White," 239.

64. Keogh, "Suburbs in Black and White," 221–22.

65. "Where the Cutback Cuts Deep."

66. "Budget Expert Says Defense Spending Too Low," *Human Events*, November 21, 1970.

Chapter Three:
Vietnam and Antimilitarism in the 1960s

1. William R. Wilson, "How to Get Rid of a Complex," NAM Reports, February 16, 1970, box 37, Military Industrial Complex folder, NAM papers.

2. "Gallup Poll Reports 49% Believe Involvement in Vietnam an Error," *New York Times*, March 10, 1968; "61% in Poll Assert Entry into the War Was U.S. 'Mistake,'" *New York Times*, June 6, 1971; Andrew Johns, *Vietnam's Second Front: Domestic Politics, the War, and the Republican Party* (Lawrence: University of Kansas, 2010), 190.

3. "A Time to Break Silence," speech delivered by Martin Luther King Jr., April 4, 1967, Riverside Church, New York, NY, in *A Testament of Hope: The Essential Writings and Speeches of Martin Luther King, Jr.*, ed. James A. Washington (New York: Harper Collins, 1986), 232–33; Peniel Joseph, *Waiting 'til the Midnight Hour: A Narrative History of Black Power in America* (New York: Henry Holt & Company), 181.

4. Throughout this chapter, I refer to the group of individuals who sought to reduce or eliminate the national security state and defense expenditures as "antimilitarists." I define this term in the introduction, but to reiterate, I apply the term antimilitarist to a range of individuals. These include members of Congress as diverse as George S. McGovern, John Sherman Cooper, and Stuart Symington (after 1968). The term "antimilitarists" also denotes members of the New Left, peace activists, and the broader antiwar movement. While antimilitarists in Congress and the New Left cannot be compared in terms of tactics, strategy, and political ideology, they shared a desire for reorganizing America's military commitments abroad and cutting the defense budget.

5. For conservatives' often contentious relationship with the Nixon administration and its foreign policy, see Sarah Katherine Mergel, *Conservative Intellectuals and Richard Nixon: Rethinking the Rise of the Right* (New York: Palgrave Macmillan, 2010); Sandra Scanlon, "The Conservative Lobby and Nixon's 'Peace with Honor' in Vietnam," *Journal of American Studies* 43 (2009): 255–76; Seth Offenbach, *The Conservative Movement and the Vietnam War: The Other Side of Vietnam* (Philadelphia: Routledge, 2019); Jeremi Suri, "Détente and Its Discontents" in *Rightward Bound: Making American Conservative in the 1970s*, ed. Bruce J. Schulman and Julian E. Zelizer (Cambridge, MA: Harvard University Press, 2008), 227–45; Julian Zelizer, "Détente and Domestic Politics," *Diplomatic History* 33, no. 4 (September 2009): 653–70.

6. President Johnson and Richard Russell, 12:05 p.m., March 6, 1965, tape WH6503.04, citation no. 7207, Lyndon B. Johnson Recordings. For Johnson's

decision-making in the months leading up to the Americanization of the war, see Fredrik Logevall, *Choosing War: The Lost Chance for Peace and the Escalation of War in Vietnam* (Berkeley: University of California Press, 1999). Logevall claims that as early as June 1964, if Johnson was given the choice "between withdrawal and escalation, he would choose escalation" (161).

7. Van Gosse, *The New Left: A Brief History with Documents, 1950–1975* (Boston: Bedford St. Martin's, 2005), 4–7.

8. Thomas J. Knock, "'Come Home America': The Story of George McGovern," in *Vietnam and the American Political Tradition*, ed. Randall B. Woods (New York: Cambridge University Press, 2003), 113.

9. Michael S. Foley, *Confronting the War Machine: Draft Resistance during the Vietnam War* (Chapel Hill: University of North Carolina Press, 2003), 234.

10. Maurice Isserman and Michael Kazin, *America Divided: The Civil War of the 1960s*, 3rd ed. (New York: Oxford University Press, 2008), 192–94; Hoopes quoted in Foley, *Confronting the War Machine*, 258.

11. Allen Matusow, *The Unraveling of America: A History of Liberalism in the 1960s* (New York: Harper and Row), 308–10; Tom Hayden, *The Port Huron Statement: The Visionary Call of the 1960s Revolution* (New York: Avalon, 2005), 87–88.

12. C. Wright Mills, *The Power Elite* (New York: Oxford University Press, 1956), 222. For more on Mills, see Daniel Geary, "'Becoming International Again': C. Wright Mills and the Emergence of a Global New Left, 1956–1962," *Journal of American History* 95, no. 3 (December 2008), 710–36; Michael Sherry, *In the Shadow of War: The United States since the 1930s* (New Haven, CT: Yale University Press, 1997), 141.

13. "Excerpts from Remarks of George Cline Smith before the Conference on Industry Leadership for National Defense, Sponsored by the National Association of Manufacturers, September 24, 1965," box 39, Meeting—September 24, 1965—-N.Y.C. Industry Leadership for National Defense folder, NAM papers.

14. "$12-Million Jet Contract to LI Firm," *Newsday*, August 10, 1966; "Grumman Sets Record in 9-Month Earnings," *Newsday*, November 11, 1966; "Millions for Grumman for A-6A Aircraft," *Long Island Daily Press*, June 7, 1966.

15. Peter B. Levy, *The New Left and Labor in the 1960s* (Dekalb: University of Illinois Press, 1994), 150; Isserman and Kazin, *America Divided*, 239.

16. Richard J. Barnet, *The Economy of Death* (New York: Atheneum, 1969); George Thayer, *The War Business: The International Trade in Armaments* (New York: Simon and Schuster, 1969). See also, Seymour Melman, *Pentagon Capitalism: The Political Economy of War* (New York: McGraw Hill, 1970); Sidney Lens, *The Military-Industrial Complex* (Philadelphia: Pilgrim Press, 1970).

17. Christopher Lehmann-Haupt, "The Military-Industrial Complex," *New York Times*, June 6, 1969; David Shoup, "The New American Militarism," *Atlantic*

Monthly, April 1969; "What Is the Military Industrial Complex?," *Time*, April 9, 1969.

18. For more on the controversy over the film, see Beth Bailey, *America's Army: Making the All-Volunteer Force* (Cambridge, MA: Belknap Press of Harvard University Press, 2009), 84–85. For conservative criticism of *The Selling of the Pentagon* and *Arms and Security: How Much Is Enough?* see "TV Special: ABC Touts Disarmament," *Washington Report*, August 25, 1972, box 40, American Security Council Report folder, NAM papers.

19. Robert Dallek, *Nixon and Kissinger: Partners in Power* (New York: Harper Collins, 2007), 137.

20. Miller quoted in Robert David Johnson, *Congress and the Cold War* (New York: Cambridge University Press), 148.

21. David S. Meyer, *A Winter of Discontent: The Nuclear Freeze and American Politics* (New York: Cambridge University Press, 1990), 142.

22. American Security Council, *The ABM and the Changed Strategic Military Balance: A Study by a Special American Security Council Committee of 31 Experts* (Washington, DC: Acropolis Books, 1969), 70–71.

23. Charles Benson, "Deterrence through Defense," *National Review*, March 9, 1971, 251–59.

24. Benson, "Deterrence through Defense."

25. Letter from Daniel J. Fink to Dean Acheson, June 20, 1969, box 74, folder 10, LOC, Paul H. Nitze Papers (hereafter PHNP); Letter from Daniel J. Fink to John C. Stennis, May 5, 1969, PHNP.

26. Memo from Richard Pearle and Paul Wolfowitz to Dorothy Fosdick, Re: Remarks on Senator Muskie's Speech to the Senate, Friday August 1, August 4, 1969, box 74, folder 10, PHNP.

27. Johnson, *Congress and the Cold War*, 148–57.

28. "The SST Prototype Program and Near Term Inflationary Pressure, box 1, Boeing 1969–1970 folder, Crawford H. Greenewalt papers (hereafter CHG), HML. For the Nixon administration's concerns over balance of payments in the early 1970s, see Judith Stein, *Pivotal Decade: How the United States Traded Factories for Finance in the Seventies* (New Haven, CT: Yale University Press, 2010), 43–47.

29. Memorandum to George S. Moore from Robert E. Lewis, "Re: Economic Advantages of the SST," box 1, Boeing 1969–1970 folder, CHG, HML.

30. *Congressional Record*, June 10, 1971, box 38, Soviet Threat 1971 folder, NAM papers.

31. An excellent discussion of the C5-A scandal is in William Hartung, *Prophets of War: Lockheed Martin and the Making of the Military-Industrial Complex* (New York: Nation Books, 2011), chap. 4. See also Berkeley Rice, *The C5-A*

Scandal: An Inside Story of the Military-Industrial Complex (Boston: Houghton Mifflin, 1971).

32. "52% in Poll Cite War as Top Issue," *New York Times*, August 4, 1968.

33. Nixon quoted in Johns, *Vietnam's Second Front*, 191.

34. Nixon often employed "color-blind" language to sway southern suburbanites to his campaign. See Matthew Lassiter, *The Silent Majority: Suburban Politics in the Sunbelt South* (Princeton, NJ: Princeton University Press, 2005), 245.

35. Kissinger quoted in Mario Del Pero, *The Eccentric Realist: Henry Kissinger and the Shaping of American Foreign Policy* (Ithaca, NY: Cornell University Press, 2010), 102.

36. Henry Kissinger, *White House Years* (New York: Simon and Schuster, 2011), 199.

37. "How Should Business Respond to Its Critics?," box 39, Speeches 1971 folder, Charles B. McCoy papers (hereafter CBM), HML.

38. "Farewell Radio and Television Address to the American People, January 17, 1961," *Public Papers of the Presidents, Dwight D. Eisenhower, 1953–1961,* https://www.presidency.ucsb.edu/documents/farewell-radio-and-television -address-the-american-people.

39. "What Eisenhower Really Said About the Military-Industrial Complex," box 37, Military-Industrial Complex folder, NAM papers. See also Jonathan M. Soffer, "The National Association of Manufacturers and the Militarization of American Conservatism," *Business History Review* 75 (winter 2001): 775–805.

40. Michael Brenes, "Disarming the Devil: The Conservative Campaign against a Nuclear Détente in the 1960s," in *The Right Side of the Sixties: Reexamining Conservatism's Decade of Transformation,* ed. Daniel K. Williams and Laura Jane Gifford (New York: Palgrave MacMillan, 2012).

41. On the defense lobby during World War II, see Mark R. Wilson, *Destructive Creation: American Business and the Winning of World War II* (Philadelphia: University of Pennsylvania Press, 2016).

42. Letter to Robert Walsh from Werner Gullander, March 27, 1970, series I, box 98, NAM-CODSIA Memorandum folder, NAM papers; Letter to John Stuart from T. T. Arden, President of Robertshaw Controls Company, December 15, 1969, series I, box 98, NAM-CODSIA Memorandum folder, NAM papers; Memo from John A. Stuart, April 15, 1969, series I, box 98, NAM-CODSIA Memorandum folder, NAM papers.

43. Dale Van Atta, *With Honor: Melvin Laird in War, Peace, and Politics* (Madison: University of Wisconsin Press, 2008), 308.

44. Letter to Melvin Laird, September 25, 1970, series IV, box 36, Profit Policy (1972) folder, NAM papers; Speech by Daniel Z. Henkin at the NAM National

Defense Committee Fall Conference, November 17, 1969, box 37, Daniel Z. Henkin folder, NAM papers; Speech by Melvin Laird before Electronics Industries Association Conference, March 11, 1970, accession 3560–006, box 54, folder 8, Henry M. Jackson Papers, University of Washington, Seattle, Washington (hereafter HMJP).

45. "An Address by Hon. Barry Goldwater before the 75th Congress of American Industry, December 4, 1970," series IV, box 38, Goldwater, November 1970 folder, NAM papers.

46. "Introductory Remarks—Senator Thurmond," Spring Conference, May 11, 1967, series IV, box 39, Speeches folder, NAM papers.

47. Frank L. Barnett, Commencement Address at University of South Carolina, June 6, 1970, box 66, folder 3, William Rusher Papers (hereafter WRP), LOC.

48. "An Interview with NAM's Defense Chairman," series IV, box 36, National Defense folder, NAM papers.

49. "Preview for the Chemical Industry," address by Charles B. McCoy at Ninety-Eighth Annual Business Meeting Manufacturing Chemists Association, June 4, 1970, box 30, Speeches 1970 folder, CBM, HML; Letter to Sanford Josephson from Samuel Lenher June 12, 1970, box 30, Speeches 1970 folder, CBM, HML; Remarks by Charles B. McCoy to DuPont Veterans Association, box 30, Speeches 1970 folder, CBM, HML.

50. Jeremi Suri, *Power and Protest: Global Revolution and the Rise of Détente* (Cambridge, MA: Harvard University Press, 2003); Robert S. Litwack, *Détente and the Nixon Doctrine: American Foreign Relations and the Pursuit of Stability, 1969–1976* (New York: Cambridge University Press, 1984), 123.

51. Lewis Sorley, *Arms Transfers under Nixon: A Policy Analysis* (Lexington: University Press of Kentucky, 1983).

52. For more on Kissinger, Nixon, and détente, see Del Pero, *The Eccentric Realist*; Dallek, *Nixon and Kissinger*; Jussi Hanhimaki, *The Flawed Architect: Henry Kissinger and American Foreign Policy* (New York: Oxford University Press, 2005); Litwack, *Détente and the Nixon Doctrine*; Jeremi Suri, *Henry Kissinger and the American Century* (Cambridge, MA: Belknap Press, 2007). The definitive work on the years of détente is by Raymond L. Garthoff, *Détente and Confrontation: American-Soviet Relations from Nixon to Reagan* (Washington, DC: Brookings Institution, 1994).

53. Hanhimaki, *The Flawed Architect*, 32–38.

54. Mergel, *Conservative Intellectuals and Richard Nixon*, 72–81.

55. H. R. Haldeman, *The Haldeman Diaries: Inside the Nixon White House* (New York: G.P. Putnam's Sons, 1994), 332.

56. William F. Buckley, "Say It Isn't So, Mr. President," *New York Times Magazine*, August 1, 1971, p. SM8.

57. Memorandum of Conversation, August 12, 1971, box 1025, folder 32, Presidential/HAK Memcons, Richard M. Nixon Presidential Library, Yorba Linda, California (hereafter RMNPL).

58. Memorandum of Conversation, August 12, 1971, box 1025, folder 32, Presidential/HAK Memcons, RMNPL. Despite exclusively blaming Congress for defense cuts, Nixon did take some measures to reduce the defense budget, but in the words of H. R. Haldeman, "in the right ways." In a meeting between Nixon, Henry Kissinger, and Haldeman on July 23, 1971, Nixon lobbed "violent blasts at officers' clubs, Air Force excesses, and so forth," and urged Kissinger to "really shake the trees" of the military because "never has a country spent more for less on defense than does America." Nixon went on to say he wanted a 5 percent cut in the defense budget and a 25 percent cut in the intelligence budget for the coming fiscal year. See Haldeman, *Haldeman Diaries*, 330.

59. Richard Nixon and H. R. Haldeman, September 24, 1971, Tape rmn_e578a, Nixon Recordings, Miller Center for Public Affairs.

60. Haldeman, *Haldeman Diaries*, 332; Richard Nixon and H. R. Haldeman, July 28, 1971, tape 549b, Nixon Recordings, Miller Center for Public Affairs.

61. Jefferson Cowie, *Stayin' Alive: The 1970s and the Last Days of the Working Class* (New York: New Press, 2010), 125–26.

62. "The Outlook for Employment in Today's Economy," an address by F. Ritter Shumway before the Association of Personnel Agencies of New York, April 3, 1971, series I, box 27, F. Ritter Shumway President COCUSA 1970–1971 Speeches Statements Articles Vol. I folder, Papers of the Chamber of Commerce of the United States of America, HML.

63. "Nixon's Former SST Promoter Turns to the Job of Solving Society's Woes through Technology," December 14, 1971, *Wall Street Journal*, series IV, box 36, National Defense folder, NAM papers.

64. "Grumman to Cut Aerospace Corp. Staff 3,000 in '71," *Long Island Daily Press*, January 20, 1971.

65. Memo on Telephone Call to Ronald Reagan, June 22, 1970, box 830, NSC Names Files, Gov. Reagan [Jun 69–Nov 73] folder, RMNPL.

66. Letter to Henry Kissinger from Ronald Reagan, undated, box 830, NSC Names Files, Gov. Reagan [Jun 69–Nov 73] folder, RMNPL.

67. Hartung, *Prophets of War*, 104–5.

68. The President's News Conference, May 1, 1971, *Public Papers of the President of the United States, Richard Nixon*, https://www.presidency.ucsb.edu /documents/the-presidents-news-conference-134. For the economic context of the Lockheed loan debate, see Stein, *Pivotal Decade*, chap. 2.

69. Peter D. H. Stockton, "Lockheed Threatens to Die," *Nation*, April 6, 1970.

70. Statement on Lockheed, August 2, 1971, box 13, Public Relations folder, James L. Buckley papers (JLBP); Memorandum for John D. Ehrlichman, June 21, 1971, White House Central Files—Subject Files—Business/Economics, box 36 Ex B E 4–1 Aerospace [1971–1974] folder 2 of 3, RMNPL.

71. "The Lockheed Bailout Battle," *Time*, August 9, 1971; Hartung, *Prophets of War*, 109.

72. Resolution No. 3145, White House Central Files—Subject Files—Business/Economics, box 36 Ex B E 4–1 Aerospace [1971–1974] folder 2 of 3, RMNPL.

73. United States Senate, Senate Committee on Banking, Housing, and Urban Affairs, *Hearings, Emergency Loan Guarantee Legislation, Part 2*, Ninety-Second Congress, First Session, July 7–9, 1971 (Washington, DC: U.S. Government Printing Office, 1971), 1193–94. For more on Lockheed's connection to Cobb County, see Matthew D. Lassiter, "Big Government and Family Values: Political Culture in the Metropolitan Sunbelt," in *Sunbelt Rising: The Politics of Space, Place, and Region*, ed. Michelle Nickerson and Joseph Crespino (Philadelphia: University of Pennsylvania Press, 2011), 83–109.

74. Letter to Edward Reinecke from Dwight L. Chapin, July 15, 1971, White House Central Files—Subject Files—Business/Economics, box 36, Ex B E 4–1 Aerospace [1971–1974] folder, RMNPL; Memorandum for Dwight Chapin from Stephen Bull, July 12, 1971, White House Central Files—Subject Files—Business/Economics, box 36, Ex B E 4–1 Aerospace [1971–1974] folder, RMNPL.

75. Memorandum for H. R. Haldeman from Dwight L. Chapin, July 7, 1971, White House Central Files—Subject Files—Business/Economics, box 36, Ex B E 4–1 Aerospace [1971–1974] folder, RMNPL. For Nixon's "southern strategy" and efforts toward building a New Majority, see Kevin Phillips, *The Emerging Republican Majority* (New Rochelle, NY: Arlington House, 1969).

76. Hartung, *Prophets of War*, 108–113.

77. "2 Union Men Differ on Lockheed Loan," *Chicago Tribune*, July 20, 1971.

78. Richard Nixon and Carl Curtis, August 2, 1971, tape 007–045, Nixon Recordings, Miller Center for Public Affairs; Richard Nixon and Barry Goldwater, August 2, 1971, tape 007–046, Nixon Recordings, Miller Center for Public Affairs; Hartung, *Prophets of War*, 112; Richard Nixon and George Aiken, tape 007–050, Nixon Recordings, Miller Center for Public Affairs; Richard Nixon and Caleb Boggs, August 2, 1971, tape 007–054, Nixon Recordings, Miller Center for Public Affairs; Haldeman, *Haldeman Diaries*, 335.

79. Letter to James Buckley from William Proxmire, August 3, 1971, box 4, James L. Buckley papers.

80. Haldeman, *Haldeman Diaries*, 344.

81. Letter to Clark MacGregor from Barry M. Goldwater Jr., March 30, 1972, White House Central Files—Subject Files—Business/Economics, box 36, Ex B E 4–1 Aerospace [1971–1974] folder 3 of 3, RMNPL.

82. Letter and Informational Survey to Barry Goldwater from Ted Antonich, February 1972, White House Central Files—Subject Files—Business/Economics, box 36, Ex B E 4–1 Aerospace [1971–1974] folder 3 of 3, RMNPL.

83. Memorandum for Peter M. Flanigan, June 21, 1971, White House Central Files—Subject Files—Business/Economics, box 36, Ex B E 4–1 Aerospace [1971–1974] folder, RMNPL.

84. "Pay Unit Provides for the Recovery of Frozen Raises," *New York Times*, January 1972; "Among Lockheed Workers, a Nixon Backer Is Rare," *New York Times*, September 16, 1972. For more on the background of the Pay Board, see Benjamin Waterhouse, "Mobilizing for the Market: Organized Business, Wage-Price Controls, and the Politics of Inflation, 1971–1974," *Journal of American History* 100, no. 2 (September 2013): 454–78.

85. "Jobs for Whom?" *Chicago Tribune*, August 3, 1971; "Dangerous Precedent," *Chicago Tribune*, August 11, 1971.

86. "Job Losses at Grumman Send Shivers through Long Island," *New York Times*, October 21, 1971; "The Economic Blues," *Time*, August 16, 1971; "Feeding the Hungry," *Chicago Tribune*, December 14, 1971.

Chapter Four:
The Cold War Returns

1. For the public "discontents" toward détente, see Jeremi Suri, "Détente and Its Discontents," in Bruce J. Schulman and Julian E. Zelizer, *Rightward Bound: Making American Conservative in the 1970s* (Cambridge: Harvard University Press, 2008), 227–45; Julian Zelizer, "Détente and Domestic Politics," *Diplomatic History* 33, no. 4 (September 2009), 653–70.

2. Letter to Clarke Reed from Ronald Reagan, June 28, 1976, box 4, folder 5, Jaquelin H. Hume Papers, Hoover Institution on War, Peace, and Revolution, Stanford University, Stanford, California (hereafter JHH papers). Letter to Jaquelin H. Hume from Ronald Reagan, July 9, 1976, JHH papers.

3. See Schulman and Zelizer, eds. *Rightward Bound*; Bruce J. Schulman, *The Seventies: The Great Shift in American Culture, Society, and Politics* (Cambridge, MA: Da Capo Press, 2002); Laura Klarman, *Right Star Rising: A New Politics, 1974–1980* (New York: W.W. Norton, 2010); Dominic Sandbrook, *Mad as Hell: The Crisis of the 1970s and the Rise of the Populist Right* (New York: Knopf, 2011).

4. Adam Clymer, *Drawing the Line at the Big Ditch: The Panama Canal Treaties and the Rise of the Right* (Lawrence: University Press of Kansas, 2008), 26; Klarman, *Right Star Rising*, 167.

5. Meg Jacobs and Julian Zelizer, *Conservatives in Power: The Reagan Years, 1981–1989; A Brief History with Documents* (Boston: Bedford St. Martin, 2010).

6. For the odds in Las Vegas against McGovern, see Jefferson Cowie, *Stayin' Alive: The 1970s and the Last Days of the Working Class* (New York: New Press, 2010), 96.

7. Theodore H. White, *The Making of the President, 1972* (New York: Atheneum Publishers, 1973), 117.

8. White, *The Making of the President, 1972*, 117; Memorandum for H. R. Haldeman from Robert M. Teeter, August 8, 1972, box 65, August 8, 1972—H. R. Haldeman—Richard Nixon/George McGovern Strong/Weak Issues folder, Robert Teeter Papers (hereafter RTP), Gerald R. Ford Presidential Library (hereafter GRFL), Ann Arbor, Michigan; Memorandum for Clark MacGregor from Robert M. Teeter, September 28, 1972, box 65, September 28, 1972—Clark MacGregor—the President's Trip to New York and California folder, RTP, GRFL.

9. Letter to Henry Jackson, December 21, 1965, accession 3560–4, box 161, folder 17, Henry M. Jackson Papers, Special Collections Library, University of Washington, Seattle, Washington; Letter to Henry Jackson, October 15, 1969, accession 3560–4, box 184, folder 1, HMJP.

10. Lily Geismer, *Don't Blame Us: Suburban Liberals and the Transformation of the Democratic Party* (Princeton, NJ: Princeton University Press, 2015), 154.

11. For the impact of the McGovern-Fraser reforms, see Bruce Miroff, *The Liberals' Moment: The McGovern Insurgency and the Identity Crisis of the Democratic Party* (Lawrence: University Press of Kansas, 2009), 19–23.

12. Hunter S. Thompson, *Fear and Loathing on the Campaign Trail '72* (New York: Simon and Schuster, 1973), 185; Letter to Henry Jackson, October 10, 1972, accession 3560–12, box 33, folder 30, HMJP.

13. Edmund F. Wehrle, "Welfare and Warfare: American Organized Labor Approaches the Military-Industrial Complex, 1949–1964," *Armed Forces and Society* 29, no. 4 (summer 2003): 525–46.

14. United States Senate, Committee on Commerce, *Hearings, National Economic Conversion Commission*, Eighty-Eighth Congress, Second Session, May 25 and June 22 1964, 43.

15. United States Senate, Committee on Commerce, *Hearings, National Economic Conversion Commission*, Eighty-Eighth Congress, Second Session, May 25 and June 22 1964, 39.

16. "Among Lockheed Workers, a Nixon Backer Is Rare," *New York Times*, September 16, 1972.

17. Transcript of Television Advertisement, "Defense Spending," McGovern, 1972, http://www.livingroomcandidate.org/commercials/1972/defense-spending.

18. William Schneider Jr., "Abolish Defense," *National Review*, May 26, 1972.

19. "Jobs and Other Issues Stir Conflict in Coast Primary," *New York Times*, May 28, 1972.

20. For the ad, see "The McGovern Defense," https://www.youtube.com /watch?v=ag-FF03VvNo; "Connolly Sees More Democrats Supporting Nixon," *New York Times*, September 21, 1972.

21. "Jobs and Other Issues Memorandum for the President from James T. Lynn, November 4, 1975, box 19, Ronald Reagan folder, Richard Cheney Files, GRFL; Thompson, *Fear and Loathing on the Campaign Trail '72*, 65–66.

22. Geismer, *Don't Blame Us*, 154.

23. "Among Lockheed Workers, a Nixon Backer Is Rare."

24. Geismer, *Don't Blame Us*, 154. See also Judith Stein, *Pivotal Decade: How the United States Traded Factories for Finance in the 1970s* (New Haven, CT: Yale University Press, 2010).

25. Miroff, *The Liberals' Moment*, chap. 3.

26. "Among Lockheed Workers, a Nixon Backer Is Rare."

27. Michael L. Wachter, "The Wage Process: An Analysis of the Early 1970s," *Brookings Papers on Economic Activity* 2 (1974): 507–25.

28. Industry Wage Survey, Nonferrous Foundries, June 1970, *Bulletin of the United States Bureau of Labor Statistics* (Washington, DC: U.S. Government Printing Office, 1972), 11.

29. "Among Lockheed Workers, a Nixon Backer Is Rare."

30. "Peace Will Bring Joblessness to Bomb Plant," *New York Times*, December 8, 1972.

31. For more on this point, see Sam Rosenfeld, "Parties in the Age of Fracture: The 1970s Origins of Modern Polarization," paper presented at the Fourth Annual Boston University American Political History Graduate Conference, March 24, 2012 (paper in author's possession).

32. Doug Rossinow, *The Politics of Authenticity: Liberalism, Christianity, and the New Left in America* (New York: Columbia University Press, 1998), 219.

33. Nelson Lichtenstein, *State of the Union: A Century of American Labor* (Princeton, NJ: Princeton University Press, 2005), chap. 3.

34. Geismer, *Don't Blame Us*, 152.

35. Cowie, *Stayin' Alive*, 122.

36. Julian Zelizer, *On Capitol Hill: The Struggle to Reform Congress and its Consequences* (New York: Oxford University Press, 2004), 156; Hart quoted in Cowie, *Stayin' Alive*, 123.

37. Quoted in Cowie, *Stayin' Alive*, 236.

38. For the upper-class backgrounds of the 1974 Democrats, See Cowie, *Stayin' Alive*, 235–36; Hayes quoted in Robert David Johnson, *Congress and the Cold War* (New York: Oxford University Press, 2005), 212.

39. Gerald Ford, *A Time to Heal: The Autobiography of Gerald Ford* (New York: Harpers and Row, 1979), 124–25.

40. Suri, "Détente and Its Discontents," 236–38; Dominic Sandbrook, "Salesmanship and Substance: The Influence of Domestic Policy and Watergate," *Nixon in the World: American Foreign Relations, 1968–1977*, ed. Fredrik Logevall and Andrew Preston (New York: Oxford University Press, 2008), 99–100.

41. Letter to Alexandr Solzhenitsyn from Jesse Helms, March 1, 1974, box 2, James L. Buckley Papers, University Archives, St. Augustine's Hall, St. John's University, Jamaica, New York.

42. Text of speech by Aleksandr Solzhenitsyn delivered to the AFL-CIO at Washington D.C., June 30, 1975. Reprinted in Aleksandr Solzhenitsyn, *Détente: Prospects for Democracy and Dictatorship* (New Brunswick, NJ: Transaction Books, 1976), 31–38.

43. Quoted in James Mann, *Rise of the Vulcans: The History of Bush's War Cabinet* (New York: Viking, 2004), 65.

44. William A. Link, *Righteous Warrior: Jesse Helms and the Rise of Modern Conservatism* (New York: St. Martin's Press, 2008), 142–43.

45. William F. Buckley Jr., "The Strangled Cry of Solzhenitsyn," *National Review*, August 29, 1975; Letter to John Duncan from Carol Hummel, August 3, 1975, IT box 104, Commission on Security and Cooperation in Europe 10/1/75–10/7/75 folder, White House Central Files Subject Files (WHCF), GRFL.

46. Jussi Hanhimaki, "They Can Write It in Swahili: Kissinger, the Soviets, and the Helsinki Accords, 1973–1975," *Journal of Transatlantic Studies* I:1 (spring 2003): 37–58.

47. Memorandum from Henry Kissinger to President Ford, folder: Conference on Security and Cooperation in Europe 8/9/74—7/31/75, IT 104 box 13, WHCF, GRFL. For domestic opposition to the Helsinki Accords in the United States, see Michael Cotey Morgan, "The United States and the Making of the Helsinki Final Act," in *Nixon in the World*, 175–76.

48. Letter to President Ford from Victor Alin, August 30, 1975, IT 104 box 14, CSCE 10/8/75–11/28/75 folder WHCF, GRFL.

49. Letter to President Ford from Aloysis A. Masewski, July 24, 1975, IT 104 box 13, Conference on Security and Cooperation in Europe 8/9/74—7/31/75 folder,

WHCF, GRFL; Letter to President Ford from Jonas Talandis, August 7, 1975, IT 104 box 14, CSCE 10/1/75–10/7/75 folder, WHCF GRFL; "Ford's Signing of Helsinki Pact Draws Protest, *Grand Rapids Press*, August 1, 1975, IT 104 box 14, CSCE 9/1/75–9/30/75 folder, WHCF GRFL; Letter to Gerald Ford from Charles Bennett, July 31, 1975, IT 104 box 14, CSCE 10/1/75–10/7/75 folder, WHCF GRFL; Letter to Gerald Ford from Frank Wallace, August 14, 1975, IT 104 box 14, CSCE 10/8/75–11/28/75 folder, WHCF, GRFL.

50. Thomas Borstelmann, *The Cold War and the Color Line: American Race Relations in the Global Arena* (Cambridge, MA: Harvard University Press, 2003), 233–37.

51. Letter to Gerald Ford from Leslie Birchfield, September 29, 1976, box B81, Correspondence—Topics—Kissinger, Henry folder, President Ford Committee papers, GRFL.

52. See Fredrik Logevall, "Bernath Lecture: A Critique of Containment" *Diplomatic History* 28, no. 4 (September 2004): 473–99.

53. Thomas Sugrue and John Skretny, "The White Ethnic Strategy," in *Rightward Bound*, 171–92; Cowie, *Stayin' Alive*, chap. 3; Memorandum for Secretary Kissinger, October 6, 1975, IT box 14, IT 104 CSCE 1129/75 folder, WHCF, GRFL; Letter to John Marsh from Rita Hauser, January 9, 1976, box 17, Notes to Dick Cheney folder, Richard Cheney Files, GRFL.

54. On a scale of 1 to 7, 1 being most amenable to reaching agreements with the Soviet Union and 7 absolutely opposed, Americans ranked themselves at 3.9, Congress at 3.3, and Ford at 2.9. See U.S. National Study November/December 1975, page 42, box 52, U.S. National Study Nov./Dec 1975 (1) folder, Robert Teeter Papers, GRFL.

55. "President Ford: Ten Reasons Why He Should Carry the GOP Banner in November," box 32, Advocates—General folder, Ron Nessen Papers, GRFL; Memorandum for the President from Richard Cheney, October 23, 1975, box 17, Polling folder, Richard Cheney Files, GRFL.

56. Memo dated July 28, 1975, box 8, folder 12, JHH papers.

57. Letter to William Rusher from Dennis Dunn, July 28, 1975, box 5, Washington folder, Citizens for Reagan Papers, Hoover Institution on War, Peace, and Revolution, Stanford University, Stanford, California (hereafter CFR papers).

58. "U.S. Is Criticized in Vietnam's Fall: Reagan and Wallace Offer Views on War to V.F.W., *New York Times*, August 19, 1975.

59. Reagan quoted from Craig Shirley, *Reagan's Revolution: The Untold Story of a Campaign That Started It All* (Nashville, TN: Thomas Nelson, 2005), 92.

60. Letter to John Sears from Mike Kelly, May 29, 1975, box 5, Wisconsin folder, CFR papers.

61. Jules Witcover, *Marathon: The Pursuit of the Presidency, 1972–1976* (New

York: Viking, 1977), 373; Memorandum for Bo Callaway, December 30, 1975, box B2, Marik File, Reagan, Ronald folder, President Ford Committee Records, GRFL.

62. Memorandum for the President from James T. Lynn, November 4, 1975, box 19, Ronald Reagan folder, Richard Cheney Files, GRFL.

63. Stein, *Pivotal Decade*, 145.

64. "Reagan Disparages Own Funds List as 'Some Stuff the Economists Gave Me,'" *Los Angeles Times*, January 28, 1976, box B2, Marik File, Reagan, Ronald folder, President Ford Committee Records, GRFL.

65. "The Economic Scene: The Picture Remains Bright," *New York Times*, February 8, 1976; "Consumer Leads Recover, Retailers Find," *New York Times*, March 22, 1976.

66. Evans-Novak Political Report, March 17, 1976, box 36, Evans-Novak Political Report (1) folder, Ron Nessen Papers, GRFL.

67. Witcover, *Marathon*, 410–11.

68. Memo from David Keene to Governor Reagan, November 20, 1975, box 31, North Carolina folder, CFR papers. For Nixon's success in North Carolina, and Charlotte specifically, in the 1968 campaign, see Matthew D. Lassiter, *The Silent Majority: Suburban Politics in the Sunbelt South* (Princeton, NJ: Princeton University Press, 2005), 138.

69. Letter to Paul Laxalt from Mrs. Armond T. Swisher, August 29, 1975, box 4, North Carolina folder, CFR papers.

70. Link, *Righteous Warrior*, 144–55.

71. Michael Barone, Grant Ujifusa, and Douglas Matthews, *The Almanac of American Politics 1976: The Senators, the Representatives, the Governors—Their Records, States, and Districts* (New York: E.P. Dutton & Co., 1975), 635, 627, 631, 637.

72. *The Right Report*, March 10, 1976, box 32, Campaign—General File folder, Ron Nessen papers, GRFL; Statement by Ronald Reagan, March 4, 1976, box 7, Correspondence—File Copies folder, CFR papers; Letter to Reagan supporter, undated, box 7, Correspondence—File Copies folder, CFR papers; Memorandum for Governor Reagan from David Keene, October 29, 1975, box 4, Florida folder, CFR papers; Notes on yellow legal pad, "Dade—Lou Conde," box 30, Florida (1) folder, CFR papers. Florida's importance to Reagan's candidacy is also emphasized in Link, *Righteous Warrior*, 156; Memorandum from Wayne Valis, March 10, 1976, campaign-general file, box 32, Ron Nessen Papers, GRFL.

73. See polling results in "A Survey of Republican Voters in the State of Illinois for the Citizens of Reagan December 1975," series IV, box 179b, Richard Wirthin Files, Ronald Reagan 1980 Presidential Campaign Files, Ronald Reagan Presidential Library, Simi Valley, California (hereafter RRPL; "A Panel Survey of Republican Voters in New Hampshire, January 1976," box 179c, Richard Wirthin

Files, RRPL. When Republican voters were polled in Illinois, only 2 percent of respondents said that a new direction in foreign affairs was the most important issue; in New Hampshire, that number was 6 percent. Only 7 percent of voters in Illinois claimed foreign policy was the most important issue in the election, compared with 38 percent who said economic issues were their priority. In New Hampshire, the ratio was 41 percent to 13 percent of voters who believed the economy outweighed foreign policy. Taken prior to the economic recovery, these polls partly help explain why Reagan did not emphasize foreign policy until Florida. Furthermore, New Hampshire and Illinois had less of a connection to the military and national defense spending than did later primary states in the South and West.

74. Shirley, *Reagan's Revolution*, 91–92.

75. Excerpt of Remarks by the Hon. Ronald Reagan at the Phillips Exeter Academy, Exeter, New Hampshire, February 10, 1976, R. Reagan Speeches box 21, [2/10/1976, Phillips Exeter Academy, New Hampshire] folder, Series I: Hannaford/California Headquarters, Ronald Reagan 1980 Presidential Campaign Papers, RRPL.

76. Memorandum for the President from Henry Kissinger, November 16, 1971, box 830, Gov. Reagan [Jun 69–Nov 73] folder, National Security Council Names Files, Richard Nixon Presidential Library (RNL), Yorba Linda, California; Michael Schaller, *Ronald Reagan* (New York: Oxford University Press, 2011), 25.

77. Memorandum for Henry Kissinger from Helmut Sonnenfeldt, June 26, 1972, box 830, Gov. Reagan [Jun 69–Nov 73] folder, National Security Council Names Files, RNL; "Overview of U.S.-European Relations," box 830, Gov. Reagan [Jun 69–Nov 73] folder, National Security Council Names Files, RNL.

78. For more on this point, see James Graham Wilson, "How Grand Was Reagan's Strategy, 1976–1984?" *Diplomacy and Statecraft* 18, no. 4 (2007): 773–803.

79. See the past due invoices in box 9, Presidential Campaign 1976 Financial Statements folder, CFR papers.

80. ACU Reagan Project, March 26, 1976, box B8, Hughes Subject File—Reagan Campaign (2) folder, President Ford Committee Records, GRFL; Shirley, *Reagan's Revolution*, 167; "Ford Pictured as Liberal," *Lakeland Ledger*, March 6, 1976; "Reagan Aided by Ads Conservative Groups Paid For," *New York Times*, May 6, 1976.

81. Devin Fergus, *Liberalism, Black Power, and the Making of American Politics, 1965–1980* (Athens: University of Georgia Press, 2009), 221–23.

82. For election results by county in North Carolina, see Department of the Secretary of State, *North Carolina Manual, 1977* (Raleigh: North Carolina Historical Commission, 1977), 723–24. The numbers for Reagan's victories in the three counties where Fort Bragg is located were the following: Cumberland, 1,963–1225;

Harnett, 822–508; and Hoke, 76–43. Reagan lost Moore with a count of 1,587 to 1,286. Reagan therefore won the Fort Bragg area with a total number of 4,448 to 3,062.

83. Department of the Secretary of State, *North Carolina Manual, 1977* (Raleigh: North Carolina Historical Commission, 1977), 723–24.

84. Shirley, *Reagan's Revolution,* 167; Memorandum to Rogers Morton from Bruce Wagner, April 7, 1976, box B4, Hughes Subject File Advertising—Primary Campaign (1) folder, President Ford Committee Records, GRFL; Memorandum to Bruce Wagner from Peter Kaye, April 8, 1976, box B4, Hughes Subject File Advertising—Primary Campaign (1) folder, President Ford Committee Records, GRFL.

85. Memorandum from Peter Hannaford to John Sears, June 18, 1976, box 37, 1976 Campaign—Project "Emissary" [foreign policy strategy] folder, 1980 Presidential Campaign Files, Series I: Hannaford/California Headquarters, Subseries C, General Campaign Files, RRPL.

86. Letter from Barry Goldwater, June 29, 1976, box 9, Barry Goldwater, Letter announcing support for GRF 6/29/76 folder, CFR papers.

87. Capturing Texas: The Most Critical State for Governor Reagan, March 15, 1976, box 31, Texas folder, CFR papers.

88. Texas also received 10 percent of all funds spent on the space program. Barone et al., *The Almanac of American Politics, 1976,* 813.

89. See the comparisons of the excerpts from Reagan's Exeter, New Hampshire, speech and the speeches he gave in Texas on April 15, 1976, Excerpt of Remarks by the Hon. Ronald Reagan at the Phillips Exeter Academy; Excerpts of Remarks by the Hon. Ronald Reagan, Texas events, Thursday, April 15, 1976, box 21, R. Reagan Speeches [4/15/1976, Texas Events] folder, Series I: Hannaford/California Headquarters, Ronald Reagan 1980 Presidential Campaign Papers, RRPL.

90. Memorandum to Roger Morton and Stu Spencer, April 28, 1976, box B8, Hughes Subject File—Reagan Campaign (2) folder, President Ford Committee Records, GRFL; Memorandum from Fred Slight, April 9, 1976, box B8, Hughes Subject File—Reagan Campaign (2) folder, President Ford Committee Records, GRFL.

91. Gilbert Garcia, *Reagan's Comeback: Four Weeks in Texas That Changed American Politics Forever* (San Antonio: Trinity University Press, 2012), 67.

92. Capturing Texas: The Most Critical State for Governor Reagan; "Reagan Attacks Kissinger for His Stand in Rhodesia," *New York Times,* May 1, 1976. Democrats and independents could also vote in the Texas Republican primary, where Reagan's success was partly due to the large presence of "crossover" voters.

93. Letter to Gerald Ford from Bill Boodling, April 29, 1976, box ND 2, ND

1 Aircraft 7/1/75–6/13/76 folder, WHCF, GRFL; "Navy Decision Linked to Texas Primary," *New York Times*, April 20, 1976; Sean P. Cunningham, *Cowboy Conservatism: Texas and the Rise of the Modern Right* (Lexington: University of Kentucky Press, 2010), 170.

94. "President Scores Reagan on Arms," *New York Times*, April 22, 1976; "Reagan's Issues Pursue Ford in Texas," *New York Times*, April 11, 1976.

95. "Ford-Reagan Race Focusing on Arms Issue," *New York Times*, May 11, 1976.

96. "Republicans: Reagan's Startling Texas Landslide," *Time*, May 10, 1976.

97. Letter to President Ford from Lloyd Kinda, box B1, Correspondence—Topics—Kissinger, Henry folder, President Ford Committee Records, GRFL; Letter to President Ford from Paul Woodworth, box B1, Correspondence—Topics—Kissinger, Henry folder, President Ford Committee Records, GRFL; Memorandum to Rogers Morton from Peter Dailey, May 14, 1976, box B4, Hughes Subject File Advertising—Primary Campaign (1) folder, President Ford Committee Records, GRFL.

98. Letter to Gerald Ford from Barry Goldwater, May 7, 1976, box 3, PL (Exec.), 6/1–30/76 folder, White House Central Files Subject File, GRFL.

99. "Reagan Catching Up," *New York Times*, May 5, 1976.

100. "Under Pressure from Reagan, Ford Flip-Flops on Issues," *San Francisco Examiner*, May 10, 1976, box 30, Georgia folder, CFR papers; ". . . Ford on Shaky Ground," *New York Times*, June 10, 1976; Letter from Anne Nixon, April 15, 1975, box 12, folder 11, JHH papers. For the influence of foreign policy in the California primary, see California Poll Tracking, May 24–27, 1976, Series IV, Richard Wirthin files, box 180, RRPL. Foreign policy was ranked the third most important issue by California, with 14 percent of voters saying it was the most important issue, just behind "economic improvement" (18 percent) and "less government control" (16 percent). Reagan was also preferred over Ford by a 33 percent margin to "improve foreign policy," the same amount by which Californians preferred Reagan for his ability to "reduce government control."

101. Letter to Ronald Reagan from William Haggerty, August 16, 1976, box 7, Correspondence Received at the Convention folder, CFR papers; Telegram to Ronald Reagan from Florence Daige, August 14, 1976, box 7, Correspondence Received at the Convention folder, CFR papers; Letter to Nancy Reagan, undated, box 7, Correspondence Received at the Convention folder, CFR papers; Letter to Ronald Reagan from Grace and Lee Wooster, July 7, 1976, box 7, Correspondence, Miscellaneous folder, CFR papers.

102. Letter to Ronald Reagan from Fred Martin, August 19, 1976, box 7, Post Convention Correspondence folder, CFR papers; Telegram to Ronald Reagan

from Reverend Salvator Franco, August 15, 1976, box 7, Correspondence Received at the Convention folder, CFR papers. For Helms's and Ashbrook's reaction to the selection of Schweiker, see Shirley, *Reagan's Revolution*, 275.

103. John Lewis Gaddis, "Rescuing Choice from Circumstance: The Statecraft of Henry Kissinger," in Campbell Craig and Francis L. Loewenheim, *The Diplo-mats: 1939–1979* (Princeton, NJ: Princeton University Press, 1994), 564–92, 587.

104. Letter to Richard Nixon from Ronald Reagan, August 27, 1976, box 1, Post-Presidential Correspondence with Ronald Reagan, RNL.

105. William E. Leuchtenberg, "Jimmy Carter and the Post-New Deal Pres-idency," in *The Carter Presidency: Policy Choices in the Post–New Deal Era*, ed. Gary M. Fink and Hugh Davis Graham (Lawrence: University Press of Kansas, 1998), 7–28.

106. The State of the Union Address Delivered before a Joint Session of Con-gress, January 19, 1978, *Public Papers of the President, Jimmy Carter, 1977–1981*, http://www.presidency.ucsb.edu/ws/index.php?pid=30856#axzz1qpNfEw5d.

107. Jimmy Carter, *Keeping Faith: Memoirs of a President* (Fayetteville: Uni-versity of Arkansas Press, 1995), 148.

108. Washington Report, November 23, 1976, box 18, Media Reaction Reports folder, Committee on the Present Danger Records, Hoover Institution on War, Peace, and Revolution, Stanford University, Stanford, California.

109. Memo to Alonzo McDonald, April 23, 1980, box 107, Memos-Bob Maddox Weekly Reports folder, Office of Anne Wexler Special Assistant to the President, Robert L. Maddox's Subject Files, Jimmy Carter Presidential Library, Atlanta, Georgia (hereafter JCL).

110. For Carter's impressions of the meeting held on January 22, 1980, see Jimmy Carter, *White House Diary* (New York: Farrar, Strauss and Giroux, 2010), 394.

111. "Selected Political Action Committee Activity in 1977–1978 Election Cycle," box 1, Subject file, Campaign Finance folder, Adam Clymer papers, JCL.

112. Eighty percent of Democrats and 86 percent of Republicans favored the United States retaining the canal. See "Confidential Survey Conducted for the Committee of Americans for the Canal Treaties, February 1978," box 11, Statewide Survey in Texas on Attitudes toward the Panama Canal Treaty folder, George D. Moffett papers, JCL.

113. Penn Gardiner, "The Panama Canal Salient," February 15, 1978, *Manches-ter Union Leader*, box 10, Right [Wing—Conspiracy] folder, George D. Moffett papers, JCL.

114. Clymer, *Drawing the Line at the Big Ditch*, 108–14.

115. Clymer, *Drawing the Line at the Big Ditch*, 117.

116. Memorandum to Landon Butler from Stephen R. Aiello, April 8, 1980,

box 49, [Ethnic Votes] Campaign [1980] 2/80–12/80 folder, Carter Presidential Papers—Staff Offices Ethnic Affairs, Aiello, JCL.

117. Memorandum for Anne Wexler from Vicki Mongiardo, June 6, 1979, box 50, Ethnic Leaders—Pennsylvania Area SALT II 6/79 folder, Carter Presidential Papers—Staff Offices Ethnic Affairs, Aiello, JCL.

118. Memorandum for Tim Finchen from Franklin D. Lopez, June 30, 1980, box 48, Carter/Mondale Campaign Memos 3/80–10/80 folder, Carter Presidential Papers Staff Offices—Ethnic Affairs, Aiello, JCL; "General Issues Affecting Ethnics," box 48, Ethnic Issues, Major 7/80 folder, Carter Presidential Papers Staff Offices—Ethnic Affairs, Aiello, JCL.

119. Memorandum from Anne Wexler, June 19, 1980, box 83, Correspondence, 6/80 [2] folder, JCL; Statement by the AFL-CIO Executive Council on Transfer Amendment, RG98-002, box 10, folder 7, Vertical Files, 1882–1990, George M. Meany Archives, Silver Spring, Maryland. For Carter's troubled relationship with labor see Cowie, *Stayin' Alive*, 281–96; Stein, *Pivotal Decade*, 185–90.

120. Jeanne Kirkpatrick, "Dictatorships and Double Standards," *Commentary* 68, no. 5 (November 1979): 34–45.

121. For Carter's shift in defense policy, see Brian Auten, *Carter's Conversion: The Hardening of American Defense Policy* (Columbia: University of Missouri Press, 2008).

122. "Virginia: Leaning toward Reagan," *Telegraph*, October 24, 1980.

123. Memorandum to Anne Wexler from Al From, September 16, 1980, box 7, Campaign 1980 Correspondence Memos Clippings [2] folder, Office of Anne Wexler, Special Assistant to the President, Anne Wexler's Subject files, JCL.

124. Ann Markusen and Joel Yudken, *Dismantling the Cold War Economy* (New York: Basic Books, 1992), 166, 181.

Chapter Five:
War and Peace in the "Age of Inequality"

1. "Reagan Budget Lifts Connecticut Hopes," *New York Times*, March 9, 1981.

2. On the Reagan defense buildup, see Frances Fitzgerald, *Way Out There in the Blue: Reagan, Star Wars, and the End of the Cold War* (New York: Simon and Schuster, 2000); Daniel Wirls, *Buildup: The Politics of Defense in the Reagan Era* (Ithaca, NY: Cornell University Press, 1992).

3. Peter Trubowitz, *Defining the National Interest: Conflict and Change in American Foreign Policy* (Chicago: University of Chicago Press, 1998), 171.

4. Judith Stein, *Pivotal Decade: How the United States Traded Factories for Finance in the Seventies* (New Haven: Yale University Press, 2010), 268. See also,

Thomas Piketty, trans. Arthur Goldhammer, *Capital in the Twenty-First Century* (Cambridge, MA: Belknap Press of Harvard University Press, 2014).

5. Letter to the President from Malcolm Baldridge, September 4, 1981, Defense Budget meeting 09/09/1981 (2), series I, box 2, Richard G. Darman files, subject files, RRPL.

6. David Stockman, *The Triumph of Politics: How the Reagan Revolution Failed* (New York: Harper and Row, 1986), 11.

7. Stockman, *The Triumph of Politics*, 107–9; Fitzgerald, *Way Out There in the Blue*, 159.

8. Stockman, *The Triumph of Politics*, 107; Memorandum for the President from Martin Anderson, September 8, 1981, series I, box 2, Defense Budget Meeting 9/09/1981 folder, Richard G. Darman files, subject file, RRPL; Memorandum to the President from Murray L. Weidenbaum, September 8, 1981, series I, box 2, Defense Budget Meeting 9/09/1981 folder, Richard G. Darman files, subject file, RRPL.

9. Memorandum for the President from Elizabeth Dole, September 8, 1981, series I, box 2, Defense Budget Meeting 9/09/1981 folder, Richard G. Darman files, subject file, RRPL.

10. Briefing Memorandum for the President from Richard G. Darman and Craig L. Fuller, series I, box 2, Defense budget meeting 9/09/1981 (1) folder, Richard G. Darman files, subject file, RRPL.

11. "Reagan Defense Budget Cuts . . . ?," presentation by Casper Weinberger, series I, box 2, Defense budget meeting 9/09/1981 (1) folder, Richard G. Darman files, subject file, RRPL.

12. "Reagan Defense Budget Cuts . . . ?," presentation by Casper Weinberger, series I, box 2, Defense budget meeting 9/09/1981 (1) folder, Richard G. Darman files, subject file, RRPL.

13. Stockman, *The Triumph of Politics*, 297.

14. "Reagan-Congress Rift Seen on Military Spending," *New York Times*, August 4, 1982.

15. "Reagan Military Budget Plan Draws Protests in Congress," *New York Times*, December 19, 1984.

16. See "Board of Directors List," box 18, Lists/Present Danger/Prospective Members/Contributors folder, Committee on the Present Danger Papers, Hoover Institution on War, Peace, and Revolution, Stanford University, Stanford, California (hereafter CPD papers).

17. Letter to Charles Tryoler, April 12, 1983, box 35, CPD papers.

18. NAE/Gallup Poll on Evangelicals Views about the Nuclear Arms Race OA9079, Nuclear Freeze (1 of 16) folder, Morton Blackwell Files, series I, RRPL. In polls, evangelicals supported "pursuing increased nuclear disarmament treaties

with the Soviets" by 72 percent. See Axel Schafer, *Piety and Public Funding: Evangelicals and the State in Modern America* (Philadelphia: University of Pennsylvania Press, 2012), 165.

19. Bradford Martin, *The Other Eighties: A Secret History of America in the Age of Reagan* (New York: Hill and Wang, 2011), 5.

20. On the grassroots, see Martin, *The Other Eighties,* 9–14.

21. Letter to Richard Allen from E. B. Mullen, March 26, 1981, box 65, folder 23, Richard Allen papers, Hoover Institution on War, Peace, and Revolution, Stanford University, Stanford, California.

22. NAE/Gallup Poll on Evangelicals Views about the Nuclear Arms Race, OA9079, Nuclear Freeze (1 of 16) folder, Morton Blackwell Files, series I, RRPL.

23. Harold Johnson, "An Alternative to the Ban-the-Bomb Crowd," *Conservative Digest,* June 1982, OA9076, Coalition for Peace through Security folder, Morton Blackwell files, RRPL.

24. *International Defence Debate Insider,* vol. 1, no. 1, OA9076, Coalition for Peace through Security folder, Morton Blackwell files, RRPL.

25. "Reagan Is Not Welcome Here," OA9076, Coalition for Peace through Security folder, Morton Blackwell files, RRPL; "Reagan's Other Red Carpet," OA9076, Coalition for Peace through Security folder, Morton Blackwell files, RRPL.

26. Peace with Freedom Petition, OA9076, Coalition for Peace through Security folder, Morton Blackwell files, RRPL.

27. Letter from David Rawls to Committee on the Present Danger, November 8, 1982, box 18, Nuclear Freeze folder, CPD papers.

28. "Call for Arms Halt Rejected, but Town Remains Divided," *New York Times,* June 12, 1982.

29. In response to hearing the term "Star Wars applied to SDI," Perle was to have said, "Why not? It's a good movie. Besides, the good guys won." See Fitzgerald, *Way Out There in the Blue,* 39; Memorandum for Robert McFarlane from John Lenczowski, December 20, 1984, box 107, Strategic Defense Initiative 12/19/1984–12/27/1984 folder, Executive Secretariat, National Security Council papers, RRPL.

30. Untitled Handwritten Notes on Speech to Martin Marietta Employees, box 355, Denver SDI 11/24/1987 (6) folder, White House Office of Speechwriting files: Research Office, RRPL.

31. National Security Decision Directive Number 172, "Presenting the Strategic Defense Initiative," June 1985, box 92329, Presenting SDI NSDD folder, William Wright Files, RRPL; "First Reaction: Poll Shows Arms-Control Optimism and Support for Reagan," *New York Times,* October 16, 1986.

32. Strategic Defense Initiative Summary (attached to Memorandum for Robert

C. McFarlane from Ron Lehman, June 11, 1984), box 106, Strategic Defense Initiative 05/16/1984–06/15/1984 folder, Executive Secretariat, NSC Subject File, RRPL.

33. Four components to the corporation included its Astronautics group in Colorado, Electronics and Missiles Group in Orlando, Florida, and its Information Systems Group based in Bethesda. The company's activities in New Orleans dealt with Manned Space Systems. Martin Marietta also was located at Vandenberg Air Force Base, California, and Cape Canaveral. The figures on Martin Marietta are from "General Information," box 355, Denver SDI 11/24/1987 (5) folder, White House Office of Speechwriting: Research Office, 1981–1989, RRPL;

34. This point is made in Joshua B. Freeman, *American Empire: The Rise of a Global Power, the Democratic Revolution at Home, 1945–2000* (New York: Viking, 2012), 127.

35. "Military Issues: 'Fallen Angels,'" *New York Times*, September 15, 1987.

36. Ann Markusen, Peter Hall, Scott Campbell, and Sabina Deitrick, *The Rise of the Gunbelt: The Military Remapping of Industrial America* (New York: Oxford University Press, 1991), 213.

37. "Can Rockwell Thrive without the B-1?," *New York Times*, April 12, 1987.

38. Judith Stein, *Pivotal Decade: How the United States Traded Factories for Finance in the Seventies* (New Haven, CT: Yale University Press, 2009), 268.

39. "Can Rockwell Thrive without the B-1?"

40. Letter to Ronald Reagan from Barber B. Conable Jr. and Jack Kemp, October 5, 1981, box 122, folder 5, Jack Kent papers; "LTV Ends Its Bid for Grumman," *New York Times*, November 17, 1981; "Military Issues: 'Fallen Angels.'"

41. Memorandum for Jay Keyworth from Mike Schwartz, July 31, 1984, box 15, SDI—Strategic Defense Initiative July-December 1984 [07/27/1984–08/16/1984] folder, George Keyworth files, RRPL.

42. "Senate Nominee Pushes 'Star Wars' in Colorado," *New York Times*, October 15, 1986.

43. "Reagan Asserts 'Star Wars' Plan Will Create Jobs and Better Life," *New York Times*, October 31, 1986.

44. Ronald Reagan, "Remarks at a Senate Campaign Rally for Representative Ken Kramer in Colorado Springs, Colorado, October 3 1986," in *Public Papers of the Presidents of the United States: Ronald Reagan, 1981–1989,* http://www.presidency.ucsb.edu/ws/?pid=36370.

45. *Statistics of the Congressional Election of November 4, 1986* (Washington, DC: Government Printing Office, 1987), 7; "1990 Census of Population, Colorado: Social and Economic Characteristics," https://www2.census.gov/library/publications/decennial/1990/cp-2/cp-2-7.pdf.

46. Memorandum for Howard H. Baker Jr. from James Hooley, November

19, 1987, box 355, Denver SDI 11/24/1987 (3) folder, White House Office of Speech-writing, RRPL; Address on SDI/INF Martin Marietta Plant, Denver, Colorado, November 24, 1986, series III, box 30, folder 603, Presidential Speeches, Presidential Handwriting file, RRPL; Drafts of speech to Martin Marietta employees for November 24, 1987, box 355, Denver SDI 11/24/1987 (2) folder, White House Office of Speechwriting, RRPL.

47. Letter to Ronald Reagan from Vin Weber and Jack Kemp, October 7, 1986, folder 5, box 122, Jack Kemp Papers, LOC.

48. James Mann, *The Rebellion of Ronald Reagan: A History of the End of the Cold War* (New York: Penguin, 2009), 291–92.

49. Letter to William Rusher from Herb Berkowitz, August 17, 1982, box 39, folder 3, WRP.

50. The Viguerie Company, OA9077, Conservative Groups (1 of 4) folder, Morton Blackwell files, RRPL.

51. Letter to Ronald Reagan from Don Todd, July 2, 1982, F0003–02, file 086784, WHORM, Subject File, RRPL.

52. Letter to Ronald Reagan from Howard Phillips, et al., August 15, 1982, F0003–02, 095983, WHORM, Subject File, RRPL.

53. Letter to William Rusher from Richard D. Sellers, June 16, 1983, box 148, folder 6, WRP.

54. "Is the Reagan Defense Program Adequate?, box 171, Defense and the Deficit, March 8 1985 folder, Hoover Institution of War, Peace, and Revolution, Stanford University, Stanford, California, CPD papers.

55. Letter to Charls Walker from Richard Perle, July 27, 1984, box 353, first folder, CPD papers. This quote from Perle also appears in Justin Vaïsse, *Neoconservatism: The Biography of a Movement* (Cambridge, MA: Harvard University Press, 2010), 199.

56. Vaïsse, *Neoconservatism*, 199

57. Letter to Morton Blackwell, July 21, 1981, OA9075, American Security Council and Coalition for Peace through Strength folder, Morton Blackwell files, RRPL; Memorandum from Elizabeth Dole, December 10, 1981, American Security Council and Coalition for Peace through Strength, OA9075, American Security Council and Coalition for Peace through Strength folder, Morton Blackwell files, RRPL; Memorandum, "Dr Jonas Savimbi, President of UNITA," OA9075, American Security Council and Coalition for Peace through Strength folder, Morton Blackwell files, RRPL.

58. Presidential Remarks: Budget Even Monday November 30, 1987, box 30, Presidential Handwriting File Series III: Presidential Speeches 11/24/87–2/1/88, RRPL.

59. Michael Schaller, *Ronald Reagan* (New York: Oxford University Press, 2009), 61.

60. Leslie Gelb, "Mr. Bush's Conversion," *New York Times*, September 29, 1991.

61. "Cheney Backs His Budget and His Cuts," *New York Times*, June 13, 1990.

62. "Lobbying Steps Up on Military Buying as Budget Shrinks," *New York Times*, April 9, 1990.

63. "At a Defense Plant, No Peace if Jobs Are Lost," *New York Times*, February 4, 1990.

64. "As Layoffs Loom, Defense Workers Mount a Battle for Jobs," *New York Times*, June 3, 1990.

65. "So Far, St. Louis Handles Arms Cuts," *New York Times*, August 8, 1991.

66. "Peace Starts to Take Toll," *New York Times*, July 23, 1990.

67. "Peace Starts to Take Toll," *New York Times*, July 23, 1990.

68. On Downey and defense spending, see Robert David Johnson, *Congress and the Cold War* (New York: Cambridge University Press, 2005), chap. 7. In conducting interviews with Johnson, Downey admitted to his "hypocrisy" toward defense spending. Like many antimilitarist congressional representatives who came out of the 1970s, Downey still had to confront the reality of the military-industrial complex and the demands it exerted on citizens who depended upon it. See Johnson, *Congress and the Cold War*, 233; "2,500 to Lose Jobs in L.I. Plant as U.S. Ends Jet Contract," *New York Times*, March 14, 1987.

69. Local Military Contractors Cautiously Brace for Peace," *New York Times*, January 3, 1990; "Grumman Will Cut 1,900, and L.I. Will Be Hit Hardest," *New York Times*, April 3, 1991; "Learning to Adapt without Defense," *New York Times*, December 21, 1991.

70. "Learning to Adapt without Defense"; "L.I. Growth Years Over, Looking beyond Defense," *New York Times*, August 13, 1989.

71. "Cuts in Arms Spending: No Help for the Economy," *New York Times*, August 12, 1992.

72. "Defense Spending: Whose Welfare?," *New York Times*, July 17, 1988; "Helping Blacks Get Ahead," *New York Times*, June 26, 1988.

73. Keogh, "Suburbs in Black and White," chap. 3, pp. 9–10.

74. "Defense Spending: Whose Welfare?," *New York Times*, July 17, 1988.

75. "Learning to Adapt without Defense"; "L.I. Growth Years Over, Looking beyond Defense."

76. "Tax Revolt Builds on L.I.," *New York Times*, April 16, 1989; "To Quell Revolt, Halpin Pledges No Tax Increase," *New York Times*, July 2, 1989.

77. *Statistics of the Presidential and Congressional Election of November 3, 1992* (Washington, DC: U.S. Government Printing Office, 1993), 51 and 55, http://clerk

.house.gov/member_info/electionInfo/1992election.pdf; "Lazio Ends Downey's Tenure," *New York Times*, November 4, 1992; "Green and Downey Lose as New York State Delegation Changes Dramatically," *New York Times*, November 4, 1992; "Downey Is Facing His Toughest Challenge," October 11, 1992.

78. "Higher Taxes, Dire Prospects," *New York Times*, February 5, 1989.

79. "Arms Makers Get Aid on Diversifying," *New York Times*, March 6, 1988.

80. "State's Defense Jobs Are Not That Secure," *New York Times*, June 23, 1985.

81. Ann Markusen, "Department of the Peace Dividend," *New York Times*, May 18, 1992.

82. Lisa M. Benton, *The Presidio: From Army Post to National Park* (Boston: Northeastern University Press, 1998), 74.

83. "Long Island's Economy Is Growing at a Gallop," *New York Times*, April 13, 1986.

84. Burton Yale Pines, "Go Ahead, Slash the Military," *New York Times*, March 12, 1990.

85. "Long Island Is an Unlikely Jobs Engine," *Wall Street Journal*, May 16, 2013.

86. "Economy Expected to Absorb Military Spending Cuts," *New York Times*, April 15, 1990. The article noted that companies like General Dynamics in 1990 tried "to sell tanks to Egypt—but with the easing of East-West tensions the overseas market is shrinking."

Conclusion

1. Buzz Bizzinger, *A Prayer for the City* (New York: Random House, 1997), 49–60, 217.

2. Bizzinger, *A Prayer for the City*, 345.

3. "At Oldest Naval Shipyard, Anger and Denial Run Deep as Closing Nears," *New York Times*, March 19, 1995.

4. "Navy Shipyard Closes Down in Philadelphia," *New York Times*, October 2, 1995.

5. Bizzinger, *A Prayer for the City*, 131.

6. Bizzinger, *A Prayer for the City*, 370.

7. Congressional Budget Office, *Defense Spending and the Economy* (Washington, DC: U.S. Government Printing Office, 1983), 59–60.

8. Margaret O' Mara, *Cities of Knowledge: Cold War Science and the Search for the Next Silicon Valley* (Princeton, NJ: Princeton University Press, 2005), 49.

9. "Boeing's Best Union Buster Is South Carolina's Governor Nikki Haley," *Bloomberg*, April 17, 2015; "South Carolina Governor Takes Aim at Union 'Bullies' in Boeing Labor Vote," *Reuters*, April 2, 2015.

10. For more on this point, see Brent Cebul, *The American Way of Growth: Business, Poverty, and Development in the American Century* (Philadelphia: University of Pennsylvania Press, forthcoming).

11. Lily Geismer, *Don't Blame Us: Suburban Liberals and the Transformation of the Democratic Party* (Princeton, NJ: Princeton University Press, 2015).

12. Matthew D. Lassiter, "Political History beyond the Red-Blue Divide," *Journal of American History* 98, no. 3 (December 2011): 760–63.

13. "Naval Shipyard Workers Anxious amid Budget Stalemate," *Detroit News*, March 1, 2013.

14. "With Virginia Shipyard as Backdrop, Obama Warns Again on Cuts," *New York Times*, February 27, 2013.

15. Andrew J. Bacevich, *The New American Militarism: How Americans Are Seduced by War* (New York: Oxford University Press, 2006).

16. George W. Bush, "Statement on Signing the National Defense Authorization Act for Fiscal Year 2002," December 28, 2001, *Public Papers of the Presidents, George W. Bush, 2001–2009*, https://www.presidency.ucsb.edu/documents/statement-signing-the-national-defense-authorization-act-for-fiscal-year-2002.

17. "With Virginia Shipyard as Backdrop, Obama Warns Again on Cuts."

INDEX

administration, 93; and McGovern, 161, 164–65; military spending as an alternative to, 4, 13–14, 16, 21, 25, 65; and the New Deal, 10–11, 16–17, 21, 25–26; and Reagan's policies, 160, 201–2, 206, 221; and Republican Party, 32–33, 39; and Truman's Fair Deal, 29–30; and Vietnam War opposition, 113, 132

Solzhenitsyn, Alexandr, 172–74, 191

Sonnenberg, John, 55–56

Sorensen, Ted, 94–95

S.O.S. (Save Our State) Committee, 223–24

South Carolina, 6–7, 58, 62, 96, 136, 240

Southeast Asia, 105, 112, 130–32, 137–38, 183. *See also* Vietnam War

Southeast Asia Treaty Organization, 36

southern Democrats: and Cold War seminars, 82; and Employment Act (1946), 254n16; land grants given to Pentagon by, 27–28; and McGovern, 163; and racism, 38, 74; and Reagan, 158; and Rhodesia policy, 175–76; Truman's international policies backed by, 38

Southern States Industrial Council (SSIC), 97–98, 100, 109–10, 114, 208

Soviet Union: and ABM, 125–27; Afghanistan invaded by, 13, 196, 200; and AFL-CIO's resistance to defense cuts, 196; and anticommunism, 14, 27, 29–30, 35–37, 48, 82, 84; and Carter, 192–93, 195; decline in the 1980s, 218; diplomatic consultation with, American opinions on, 177, 279n54; and Eastern European immigrants, 195; and Eisenhower's New Look policy, 77; fear of nuclear attack by, 28; and Ford's foreign policy, 177, 189; and Jackson-Vanik Amendment, 172; and Kennedy's foreign policy, 89–97; and Korean War, 65–66; and LTBT, 98; and massive retaliation, 79; New Dealism equated with, 32; and Nixon, 131; and noninterventionist

Right, 67–68; and nuclear arms, 39, 46–47, 91–92, 115, 126, 210–12; and Reagan's 1976 presidential campaign, 189; and Reagan's foreign policy, 218–22; and Reagan's increase in defense budget, 200–201, 204, 206, 208; and SDI, 212, 216–17; space race with, 90; and *Sputnik* launch, 79–80; supersonic plane of, 128; and U.S. air power, 40; and U.S. military spending, 17–18, 28, 64–65, 73, 110, 135, 165. *See also* détente between Soviet Union and United States

space program spending, 186, 282n88

space shuttle program, 166

Sparrow, James, 4, 26

Specter, Arlen, 223

Spock, Benjamin, 119–20

SPS (Students for Peace and Security), 210

Sputnik satellite, 79–80

SST (supersonic transport plane), 128–29, 143, 145–46, 150

Stalin, Joseph, 45, 139

Star Wars. *See* Strategic Defense Initiative

State Department, U.S., 17, 30–31, 36

States Rights Party, 48

Stein, Judith, 202

Stennis, John, 99, 127

Stevenson, Adlai, 63

St. Louis, Missouri, 224, 235

Stockman, David, 205–7

Strategic Arms Limitation Treaty (SALT I), 125, 139, 141, 158, 183

Strategic Arms Limitation Treaty (SALT II), 195

Strategic Defense Initiative (SDI), 2, 16, 201–2, 209, 211–18, 225

Stratford, Connecticut, 1–2

Stratford Army-Engine Plant, 1–2

Students for a Democratic Society (SDS), 120, 122

Students for Peace and Security (SPS), 210

Sturm, Melanie, 210

MICHAEL BRENES is associate director of the Brady-Johnson Program in Grand Strategy and lecturer in history at Yale University. His work has received fellowships and grants from the John Anson Kittredge Fund, the Gerald R. Ford Presidential Foundation, the Harry S. Truman Presidential Library, the Society for Historians of American Foreign Relations, and the City University of New York. His writing has appeared in the *New York Times*, the *Washington Post*, the *New Republic*, the *Nation*, *Foreign Policy*, *Politico*, the *American Prospect*, and the *Chronicle of Higher Education*, among other outlets. He lives in Hamden, Connecticut, with his wife and son.